DNA IN HALAKHAH

OTHER BOOKS BY THE SAME AUTHOR:

Be-Netivot ha-Halakhah, Vols. I–IV

Bioethical Dilemmas: A Jewish Perspective, Vols. I–II

Bircas ha-Chammah

Contemporary Halakhic Problems, Vols. I–VII

J. David Bleich: Where Halakhah and Philosophy Meet

Jewish Bioethics: A Reader (ed. with Fred Rosner)

Jewish Law and Contemporary Issues (with Arthur J. Jacobson)

Judaism and Healing

The Philosophical Quest: Of Philosophy, Ethics, Law and Halakhah

Providence in the Philosophy of Gersonides

Time of Death in Jewish Law

With Perfect Faith: Foundations of Jewish Belief (ed.)

DNA in Halakhah

J. David Bleich

KTAV PUBLISHING HOUSE

DNA IN HALAKHAH

KTAV PUBLISHING HOUSE
527 Empire Blvd
Brooklyn, NY 11225
www.ktav.com
orders@ktav.com
Ph: (718) 972-5449 / Fax: (718) 972-6307

Cover design by Shira Atwood
Typeset in Arno Pro by Raphaël Freeman MISTD, Renana Typesetting

ISBN 978-1-60280-443-2

Printed and bound in the United States of America

לע"נ

אחי היקר

הרב אהרן יצחק זכרונו לברכה

שכל ימיו לן בד' אמות של הלכה

Contents

Preface

This volume has its origin in a semester-long series of *shi'urim* delivered to the students of the *Kollel le-Hora'ah* of the Rabbi Isaac Elchanan Theological Seminary. That material was expanded into a series of four articles that appeared in my "Survey of Recent Halakhic Literature" which is regularly featured in the columns of *Tradition* and is now presented in revised form.

I wish to express my appreciation to my son, Rabbi Dr. Moshe Bleich, for drawing my attention to sources that otherwise would have eluded me and for his many valuable insights; to my son-in-law, Rabbi Benzion Sommerfeld, for his meticulous corrections and penetrating observations; also to Rabbi Dr. Shlomo Zuckier, a member of *Tradition*'s Editorial Committee, for his extremely able editorial assistance; to Rabbi Jeffrey Saks, the editor of *Tradition*, for his encouragement and support; to my dear friend, Rabbi Yitzchak Adlerstein, for his painstaking reading with the eyes of a true *lamdan*, his many corrections and incisive comments; to my esteemed congregant, Mr. Ernest Grunebaum, for noting typographical errors in earlier publications of this material; to Rabbi Moshe Schapiro and Mr. Zvi Erenyi of the Mendel Gottesman Library for their constant helpfulness. I particularly wish to acknowledge the indefatigable efforts of Rabbi Schapiro in making source material available to me during the trying period of the coronavirus pandemic when all libraries were closed.

My appreciation also to Rabbi Joseph Cohen of RIETS and the Technion Medical School for his dedicated, ongoing and extremely valuable assistance over a period of years as well as to my research assistant, Ms. Isabelle Sehati, of the Benjamin N. Cardozo School of Law for making her expertise available at all times and for preparing the index for this volume. Most especially, my thanks to my granddaughter Hadassah Gurwitz whose thorough and meticulous proofreading and thoughtful observations have spared this work from many inadvertent errors; and last, but certainly not least, to my students for their relentless and provocative questioning.

My gratitude also to Rabbi Jonathan Feldman, instructor of Talmud, Yeshivat Frisch, for his graciousness and unsparing efforts in preparing the final manuscript for publication. My appreciation to Moshe Heller and Shira Atwood for their care and concern in shepherding the manuscript through the various stages of publication.

I express my thankfulness to the Almighty for His continued beneficence and mercy in sustaining me in life and granting me the privilege of dwelling in the tents of Torah. Above all, I am grateful to the Almighty for my cherished collaborators – the members of my family. Our prayer to the Almighty is that we continue to be numbered among the *mashkimim le-divrei Torah* and, to paraphrase the words of the *hadran, ke-shem she-'azartanu le-sayyem sefer zeh, ken ta'azrenu le-hatḥil sefarim aḥerim u-le-sayyemam, lilmod u-le-lamed, lishmor ve-la'asot u-le-kayyem.*

Elul 5780

Introduction

The logical positivists of the last century sought to change the nature of philosophy. Their fundamental principle can be captured in a single sentence: The meaning of a proposition is its mode of verification. "Mode of verification" is not simply proof of veracity, nor is it an instrumental means of discovering meaning. For logical positivists, verification and meaning are tautological concepts. Not only is the mode of verification the implied meaning of a proposition but it is the sole meaning of the proposition. To seek more is, intellectually, a fruitless exercise. Unverifiable propositions may be emotive, evocative, inspirational or heuristic, but not subject to analysis by the rational faculty.

Philosophers were suddenly freed from considering, much less resolving, the question of how many angels can dance on the head of a pin. The question has no answer because the question itself is meaningless. The question is meaningless because there is no empirical mode of verification. Metaphysical propositions not amenable to verification may be engaging, aesthetically appealing, enjoyable and, in a manner similar to poetry, perusal of such matters may even be immensely gratifying but, since they can never be resolved, they cannot be the subject of inquiry by the intellectual faculty. Inability to discover the answer to a question is frustrating; dismissal of the question as itself devoid of cognitive meaning is a source of both intellectual and emotional relief. Therein lies the appeal of Logical Positivism.

Halakhic Positivism long predated Logical Positivism. Halakhic Positivism is the notion that the meaning of a proposition is its mode of halakhic verification. Every *ḥakirah*, or theoretical analysis of a halakhic concept or construct, has a *nafka mina*, or concrete normative application, identification of the *nafka mina* may, or may not, make it possible to resolve the *ḥakirah* in favor of one possibility or the other but it certainly crystallizes the issue. Formulation of a *reductio ad absurdum* and demonstration of inconsistency with other already accepted halakhic propositions are modes of disconfirmation.

The doctrine of Halakhic Positivism has never been formally announced but *de facto* it is the matrix that creates a milieu in which students of Halakhah limit their intellectual activities as halakhists to that which is halakhically verifiable. Kabbalistic sources may, at times, declare halakhic imperatives but those imperatives do not establish the veracity of underlying kabbalistic concepts. Rigorous halakhic positivists find extra-halakhic investigations less than intellectually satisfying precisely because they cannot be transposed to the realm of normative practice. Kabbalistic notions may be intriguing in a manner analogous to the way in which poetry is intriguing, engaging in the way metaphysics is engaging, but, ultimately, the concepts are unfathomable. Religious experience, emotionalism, ecstasy and *devekut* may be spiritually valuable but in a manner far different from intellectual cognition.

Science is science because it is the study of the laws of nature, including identification and delineation of the axioms and postulates underlying those laws. The proposition stating that science is the analysis of the laws of the natural universe is a tautology. The predicate merely makes explicit that which is already inherent in the subject. Halakhah is the study of the principles of Halakhah, including its axioms and postulates, and the application of those principles to human life. That, too, is a tautology. But the axioms and postulates of Halakhah are not coextensive with those of science. Indeed, they may, on occasion, be at variance with those of the empirical, and even of the theoretical, sciences.

Science is neither the study nor the reflection of transcendental truth. Euclidean geometry presumes three-dimensional space. We can rationally comprehend the universe only because we perceive it as being three-dimensional. The mode of verification of all manner of propositions is reflected in that world vision. Transcendental truth – whatever that may be – is not only likely to be, but is presumed by mathematicians, physicists and astronomers actually to be, far different from the Euclidean notion of space. Scientists tell us that space is curved and that the universe is really a multi-dimensional sphere. Philosophers of science are quick to point out that we cannot possibly test the validity of our system of scientific knowledge as an entirety. We can test only a single hypothesis at a time while accepting other postulates as the given. Accepting each of those established principles as true, we can determine whether some novel hypothesis is correct or erroneous, i.e., whether it is compatible with the balance of the system or not. The accepted principles are interrelated and interdependent. Once we recognize that any one of the hypotheses accepted as part of the corpus of scientific knowledge may not be true there is no longer a context in relation to which a novel hypothesis can be tested. A single variable can be tested for compatibility with a set of constants but, if everything is variable, there is nothing to test against.

Two simple examples: Water has a uniform boiling point. Establishing the boiling point of water is not at all difficult. But the boiling point varies with atmospheric pressure. The boiling point of water is always uniform, but only if all other variables remain the same. Thus, the boiling point of water can be shown to be a constant at sea level, but as elevation varies, the boiling point of water will also vary. The scientist can only demonstrate that, given all other relevant factors, including scientific propositions accepted as constants, the boiling point of water at sea level is 212° F. Paleontologists can presume to date geological strata but only on the assumption that the testing criteria, e.g., radioactive breakdown or the like, have been constant from time immemorial regardless of climate temperature etc.

It is entirely possible that other universes exist and that entirely different sets of laws of nature are regnant in them. We can say nothing and make no predictions regarding any aspect of any alternative universe without a comprehensive understanding of the laws governing such a universe. Moreover, it is quite obvious that we cannot formulate scientific principles that will enable us to presume to know the laws by which such universes must be governed. We regard talk of four- five- or six-dimensional universes as grist for the mill of science fiction but at the same time the empirical possibility of the existence of universes incomprehensible to our minds cannot be rejected out of hand.

Prior to Kant, it was generally assumed that there exists a universe filled with objects and that human knowledge must accept and conform to those objects; otherwise, what might be thought to be knowledge would be error, misinformation, ignorance or the like. Kant wrought a Copernican revolution in declaring that we have a certain *a priori* knowledge to which objects must conform. It is those *a priori* concepts or categories that we impose upon the objects of the natural universe and only by imposition of such *a priori* concepts upon our perceptions does knowledge become possible. It is not our knowledge that is created by, and which conforms to, the objective reality of the universe; rather it is the universe that is apprehended through the intermediacy of, and which must conform to, those *a priori* categories. Space and time are the primary categories of such knowledge. Little wonder, then, that the Sages, *Ḥagigah* 11b, admonish us not to ask what is above or what is below the universe. A Kantian would remark that never was a truer admonition uttered. Space and time are not ontological entities; space and time are concepts that we impose upon the universe. Where there is no universe, there is no space and there is no time.

One may certainly inquire whether Halakhah does, or does not, take cognizance of any particular proposition of scientific understanding and whether or not any particular halakhic provision is rooted in, or coextensive with, empirically established propositions. By and large, the answer is in the affirmative but there are instances in which halakhic postulates and empirical reality are not one and the same.

Halakhah construes a series of posts connected with wire or string that is attached upon them as a wall and declares that, on *Shabbat*, one may carry within the area circumscribed by that wall. Halakhah does not prescribe that such a wall protect us against the elements. Some may choose to call such a wall a legal fiction or even a myth but terming it a "meta"-wall would dispel the befuddlement. Terming that construct a "halakhic wall" would be the most accurate nomenclature. The wall is a halakhic "construct" in more than one sense of that term and its meaning as a "wall" lies in its halakhic purpose and halakhic mode of verification. The empirical wall and the halakhic wall share a common meaning in part, but not *in toto*.

Similarly, presence or absence of residual blood in a piece of meat is not halakhically determined by a laboratory test or by chemical analysis. The chemist will provide a precise definition of blood using terms and criteria appropriate to blood chemistry. The halakhist expresses the halakhic definition of blood as that which is extracted from meat by salt within a specific period of time; all else is *ẓir* or "meat juice." The definition of blood as the halakhic mode of verification of its presence constitutes a tautology.

Scripture does not admonish "Thou shalt not kill." The commandment is "Thou shalt not murder." What constitutes murder? Murder is that which the Oral Law defines as murder, certainly not self-defense or Torah-mandated punishment or even biblically commanded warfare. To say that murder is what the Oral Law defines as murder is a tautology.

The Torah prohibits not only forbidden foods but the "taste" of forbidden foods as well. What is the threshold level of "taste"? *De gustibus non disputandum est.* Matters of taste cannot be disputed because the phenomenon of taste is not uniformly perceived. Halakhah has its own objective criteria that do serve to define taste; perhaps "meta"-taste is a more accurate appellation. To learn the halakhic definition of taste, I must consult *Shulḥan Arukh, Yoreh De'ah,* not a chemist. Such concepts are "meta"-physical, not in the sense of being other-worldly or unperceivable by sensory organs but because they are "*meta*," i.e., "beyond," the customary denotation of such terms.

The "truths" of Halakhah and the "truths" of the created world are not necessarily one and the same. But that does not imply that the truths of Halakhah are entirely transcendental. Halakhah governs man and Halakhah reigns in this world. Accordingly, it should not be surprising that Halakhah must be interpreted and applied by the human intellect. That recognition is inherent in the meaning of the biblical passage "It is not in Heaven" (Deuteronomy 30:12). Resolution of ambiguity, doubt and novel application of received principles are the province of the human intellect.

Rambam records the doctrine that the Torah will not be altered, either in its entirety or in part, as one of the Thirteen Principles of Faith. A remarkable corollary to the principle of the immutability of the Torah is the principle that, following the revelation at Sinai, no further Heavenly clarification of doubt or resolution of ambiguity is possible. Clarification and elucidation are themselves forms of change. The divine nature of the Torah renders it immutable and hence the Torah does not admit of amendment or modification. Since there can be no new revelation, a prophet who claims the ability to resolve disputed legal points by virtue of his prophetic power stands convicted by his own mouth of being a false prophet.

Once revealed, the Torah does not remain in the Heavenly domain. Although Torah itself is immutable, the Sages teach that interpretation of its myriad laws and regulations is within the province of human intellect. Torah is divine but "*lo ba-shamayim hi* – it is not in Heaven" (Deuteronomy 30:12); it is to be interpreted and applied by man. Man is charged with interpretation of the text, resolution of doubt and application of the laws of the Torah to novel situations. The Gemara, *Bava Meẓi'a* 59b, offers a dramatic illustration of the principle of *lo ba-shamayim hi* in a narrative concerning a dispute between R. Eliezer and the Sages regarding a point of ritual law. R. Eliezer refused to be overridden by the view of the majority and went to great lengths in invoking miracles and Heavenly signs in support of his own position. He called upon a carob tree to uproot itself and move a distance of one hundred cubits, a stream to reverse its course, the walls of the house of study to collapse – only to be steadied by R. Joshua in mid-fall – and, finally, to summon a Heavenly voice to declare that the Halakhah is in accordance with R. Eliezer. R. Eliezer had sufficient power to change the course of nature, to work miracles and even to summon a Heavenly voice in support of his position but the Sages, quite correctly, failed to be impressed. Interpretation of Halakhah was entrusted by God to man and, accordingly, human intellect must proceed in its own dispassionate way, uninfluenced and unprejudiced by supernatural phenomena. The Gemara teaches unambiguously that the Law was designed to be understood, interpreted and transmitted by man. Accordingly, man's understanding of the Torah must prevail. Man's interpretation is not only inherent in the content of revelation but is the one which God himself wills to prevail.

Why, then, were miracles performed in support of R. Eliezer's opinion, a view that must be disregarded by normative Halakhah? Why did the Heavenly voice proclaim, "The Halakhah is in accordance with R. Eliezer" when it is precisely the opposite that is the case? *Tosafot, ad locum,* and *Yevamot* 14a, explain that the Heavenly voice was a manifestation of the esteem in which R. Eliezer was held and a sign of respect for his scholarship. Those phenomena demonstrated that, although he had been vanquished by the majority, in no way did that diminish his stature or mitigate R. Eliezer's standing in the eyes of Heaven.

R. Nissim Ga'on, cited by *Shitah Mekubbeẓet, Bava Meẓi'a* 59b, declares that the miracles were in the nature of a test designed to determine whether the Sages would remain faithful to the dogmatic teachings of the Torah regarding canons of halakhic decision-making despite powerful motivation to do otherwise. The Sages, in effect, were being challenged to ignore the Heavenly voice. Placed in a historical context, the miracles and the Heavenly voice may well have been a divine response to the test posed by the advent of Christianity in which the notion of a superseding revelation was a foundational heresy.

It seems to this writer that the miracles and the Heavenly voice served a most fundamental purpose. Miracles belong to the realm of the divine. The miracles performed in support of R. Eliezer demonstrated that, insofar as transcendental principles are concerned, R. Eliezer was entirely correct. But transcendental principles do not necessarily govern human life. The Heavenly voice was, in effect, proof, in the Elizabethan sense of the term, of the Torah's declaration "It is not in Heaven." The Heavenly voice may have been a test of the fidelity of the Sages but it was certainly a test of the ambit of the dictum "It is not in Heaven." The Heavenly voice was designed to prove the full extent of the applicability of that principle. It served to demonstrate that the Torah is not in Heaven even when a Heavenly voice rules in favor of R. Eliezer. The Heavenly voice that proclaimed "The Halakhah is in accordance with R. Eliezer" was designed to establish precisely the opposite, *viz.*, that, despite the Heavenly voice, the Halakhah remains in accordance with the majority. Human truth is not transcendental truth. Man is commanded to use, and to rely upon, human intellect even when human intellect is, from the divine perspective, all too fallible. The Heavenly voice was designed to underscore the principle that one must employ human intellectual prowess and follow its dictates even when, from the divine perspective, the truth as humanly determined is not in conformity with transcendental truth. The miracles and the Heavenly voice demonstrated most dramatically that human intellectual perceptions and transcendental truth are not always uniform. The proclamation "The Law is in accordance with R. Eliezer" is a statement of transcendental truth. It was designed to emphasize to the Sages and their successors that there may be a stark difference between the truth discerned by human intellect and truth announced by Heaven and – even more strikingly – that man is commanded to ignore the latter as irrelevant to the determination of Halakhah.

There are other instances in which the Torah does not demand, and may even negate, what to the human mind is absolute truth. The Torah demands acceptance of the credentials of a person who has fulfilled the prescribed criteria for recognition as a prophet although, in actuality, he may well be a false prophet.[1] Rambam tells us in no less than three places in his *Mishneh Torah* that the Torah demands acceptance of the testimony of two qualified witnesses even though

1 See Rambam, *Hilkhot Yesodei ha-Torah* 7:7.

perjury can never be entirely excluded.[2] The other side of the coin is that if Moses and Aaron appear together before a *bet din* their testimony will be dismissed – with an explanation, but not with an apology. They will be dismissed because the Torah prescribes that two brothers cannot jointly testify with regard to any matter, no matter how credible their testimony and no matter how impeccable their credentials. No apology will be offered because, in dismissing their testimony, the *bet din* is not questioning the probity of Moses and Aaron; the *bet din* is declaring that, under the circumstances, truth is not the determinant factor.

No evidence is infallible. Witnesses can commit perjury; every *rov* admits of a *mi'ut*; a *ḥazakah* is no more than a legal presumption. The issue with regard to DNA is not scientific reliability, albeit if DNA evidence is not scientifically reliable there cannot be a halakhic conversation. The issue is solely whether DNA testing fits into one of the halakhic categories of acceptable evidence for any or for all purposes; the issue is whether DNA fits into one or none of the defined categories of halakhic truth.

The issue is not science versus Halakhah. The truths of science and the truths of Halakhah are not necessarily coextensive. But discerning the truths of science *qua* science does serve to fulfill a decidedly halakhic function. Rambam, *Hilkhot Yesodei ha-Torah* 2:2, defines the commandment "And you shall love the Lord, your God" (Deuteronomy 6:5) as demanding examination and comprehension of the wondrous nature of the created universe. Rambam adds that both that commandment as well as the commandment "The Lord, your God, shall you fear" (Deuteronomy 6:13) are fulfilled by "reflecting upon His wondrous and great works and creation." In his *Teshuvot Pe'er ha-Dor,* no. 53, Rambam admonishes, "Scrutinize His works for from that you will recognize He Who declared and the world came into being".[3] In his *Sefer ha-Mizvot, mizvot aseh,* no. 3, Rambam develops

---

2 See Rambam, *Hilkhot Yesodei ha-Torah* 7:7 and 8:2 as well as *Hilkhot Sanhedrin* 24:1.

3 Cf., *Sifrei,* Deuteronomy 6:6.

that concept at great length and describes intellectual appreciation of God's "commandments, utterances and works" as giving rise to the love of God that is incumbent upon us. In *Hilkhot Yesodei ha-Torah* 4:12, Rambam declares that increased understanding of the nature of created entities carries in its wake enhanced love of God.

Every Englishman has his pub. The dons of Cambridge are wont to frequent an establishment known as the Eagle. Rumor has it that its portals are closed to persons of merely normal intelligence. Christopher Hitchens reports that, on February 28, 1953, Sir Francis Crick dashed out of his laboratory in Cambridge, rushed into the Eagle and announced to all and sundry that he and his colleague, James Watson, had found "the secret of life."[4] The discovery of the structure of DNA would lead to a Nobel Prize for Watson and Crick in 1962.

Both the logical positivist and the halakhic positivist would react to Francis Crick's exclamation by declaring it to be void of cognitive meaning. The logical positivist will deconstruct the proposition. What is known is not a secret. Every newly-formulated proposition is a revelation of that which was heretofore unknown. The structure of DNA is simply one of the now known aspects of life. If "the secret of life" means the mechanism by which life was created, there is nothing in the description of DNA that lends itself to verification. Verification could occur only by harnessing DNA to create life *de novo*. Not only the halakhic positivist, but every knowledgeable Jew, recognizes that both *ma'aseh merkavah*, the mystery of the divine domain, and *ma'aseh berehshit*, the mystery of creation, are beyond human ken.

Nevertheless, both the logical positivist and the halakhic positivist understand the nature of Crick's exclamation. "We have found the secret of life" is not a cognitive statement of fact but is a highly emotive response to a unique and profoundly moving experience. The halakhic positivist would say that such a response is the halakhic fulfillment of the divine commandment "And you shall love the Lord, your God."

All of mankind is descended from Adam, the primordial man. Coins struck from a single die are indistinguishable from one another. Yet, no

4 See Christopher Hitchens, *Arguably* (New York, 2011), p. 140.

two human countenances are identical. Phenotype is determined by genotype. But, if all genotypes are inherited from a common ancestor, all genotypes should be identical. Ninety-nine and nine-tenths percent of all DNA is the same in every human being. Human diversity stems from the minuscule one-tenth of one percent of microscopic DNA that varies from person to person. That diversity arises from mutations that occur in cells produced by the reproductive organs – mutations that occur with extreme frequency. The minuscule deoxyribonucleic acid is arranged in the shape of a double helix. Chromosomal crossover at points of contact yield structures different from those of either parent, yet considerably similar to each parent. Segments of homologous chromosomes break and reconnect with segments of the matching chromosome. Genetic material is exchanged and results in recombinant chromosomes. The new combinations of genes are different from either parent and yield genetic diversity. One can but marvel upon seeing diagrammatic reproductions of that phenomenon. How awesome and wondrous must have been observation under a microscope of the result of such actual occurrences. To perceive that phenomenon is not to discover the secret of life but to apprehend the awesome and majestic nature of God's creation. For a thinking person to know that is to be filled with love and awe of the Deity.

The paradox is truly wondrous. Uniformity of species, yet idiosyncratic DNA that accounts for the uniqueness of every particular member of the human community. The paradox lies in the DNA. To understand DNA is to understand the paradox. To understand the paradox is to marvel at the Creator and His handiwork. To marvel at the Creator is to fulfill the halakhic injunction "And you shall know the Lord, your God."

God is One, but His truth is multi-faceted: "For My word is... like a hammer that shatters a rock" (Jeremiah 23:29). As the Gemara, *Shabbat* 88b, remarks, just as a hammer splinters a rock into myriad fragments so too is the divine word divisible into "seventy" truths. Let us, then, examine the evidentiary value of DNA analysis through the prism of Halakhah. That endeavor is not science but an exercise in the noblest of all endeavors – *talmud Torah*!

"... For man stamps many coins with a single seal and all are like one another. But the Holy One, blessed be He, stamps every man with the seal of Adam and not a single one is identical to his fellow...."

SANHEDRIN 38a

Chapter One

DNA Evidence in Halakhah

I. THE NATURE OF DNA EVIDENCE

Deoxyribonucleic acid (DNA) testing is most often associated with attempts to identify criminal perpetrators or to exonerate persons accused of a crime. Identification by means of DNA is particularly useful in placing a suspect at the scene of a crime. Except for identical twins, no two persons are known to possess identical DNA. In 1984, scientists developed a means of isolating DNA in a sample provided by a crime suspect or victim and comparing it with a sample recovered from a crime scene or from clothing worn by the suspect. Although the presence of DNA does not in itself conclusively prove the guilt of a suspect, it is often a crucial factor in establishing guilt by means of circumstantial evidence.

DNA evidence is, logically speaking, most compelling in establishing paternity since a shared DNA profile constitutes extremely strong statistical evidence of a paternal-filial relationship. In paternity cases, a partial overlap of some DNA structures in different individuals is evidence that the persons compared had at least one common progenitor and hence are related.

Establishing a reliable DNA match is fraught with difficulty. One earlier commonly employed method in DNA testing is termed DNA fingerprinting or DNA profiling. The method involves a technique known as restriction fragment length polymorphism (RFLP) analysis in which long strands of DNA are extracted from body tissue and broken into fragments. Those fragments vary in length from person to person. If two samples contain fragments of different lengths they cannot have a common source. In order to reduce the likelihood that two people might each have a fragment of common length, a number of different fragments that have been discovered to be subject to a great degree of variability are measured. Those fragments are known as variable number tandem repeats (VNTRS). VNTRS of different lengths are presumed to have come from different individuals, Much as is the case with regard to fingerprints, VNTRS of equal length located at a similar position on a chromosome indicates that the two samples came from the same individual.[1] RFLP of a minimum of six VNTRS yields profiles that are believed to be unique to each person. Acceptance of RFLP analysis relies upon adequate standards and controls necessary to assure reliability of the test, diligence and skill in determining that the DNA profiles do indeed match as well as the veracity of assumptions concerning the unique nature of DNA profiles.[2]

A second method of DNA testing involves a technique known as polymerase chain reaction (PCR). An area of DNA in which there are

---

1 It has been suggested that the introduction of a chemical, ethidium bromide, during the measuring process causes unpredictable shifts in position and thus calls the reliability of this test into question. See Committee on DNA Technology in Forensic Science, "National Research Council, 1992 DNA Technology," *Forensic Science*, VII (1992), pp. 57–58 and 68 (hereinafter *NRC Report*) and Paul Hagerman, *Loading Variability and the Use of Ethidium Bromide: Implications of the Reliability of the FBI's Methodology for DNA Typing*, cited in *United States* v. *Yee*, 129 F.R.D. 629 (N.D. Ohio 1990).

2 The difficulties involved in distinguishing matching and non-matching DNA was a matter of concern in *People* v. *Castro*, 545 N.Y.S.2d 985 (N.Y. Sup. Ct. 1989). For a report of disagreement among experts see *People v. Keene*, 591 N.Y.S.2d 733 (N.Y. Sup. Ct. 1992). For a list of reviews of the controversy surrounding the reliability of DNA evidence see William C. Thompson, "Evaluating the Admissibility of New Genetic Identification Tests: Lessons from the 'DNA War,'" *Journal of Criminal Law and Criminology*, vol. 84, no. 1 (Spring, 1993), p. 22, note 3.

variations from person to person is selected and the DNA strands are caused to replicate themselves multiple times. Enhanced samples are then typed by use of genetic probes engineered to detect specific forms or alleles of a given gene. Those probes are termed "allele specific gene oligonucleotide probes." If two samples have the same type they may have a common source; if they do not have the same type they cannot have a common source. This method may be susceptible to error caused by inadvertent contamination of samples and also because some alleles may be amplified to a greater extent than others. There is also evidence that particular combinations of alleles are far more common in some demographic groups than in others. If so, the statistical chance of a match in a specific group is far greater.[3]

Next Generation Sequencing (NGS), also known as Massively Parallel Sequencing, is the newest available technique. This technique allows for simultaneous sequencing of thousands of overlapping locations in the DNA. Massive amounts of data can be generated and reassembled in order to recognize overlapping sequential fragments. That is possible because NGS compares sets of DNA variations that do not tend to cross over because they are extremely close and pass without recombination and also because NGS compares single nucleotide polymorphisms that are not part of a gene but are present between genes.

The first method involves a process in which a DNA profile appears as a pattern of black bands on an X-ray plate known as an autoradiogram or autorad. The bands indicate the relative lengths of the DNA fragments being compared. Using a complex process, the fragments are arranged according to size and bound to a nylon membrane and

3 This description of DNA testing is largely based upon Thompson, "Evaluating the Admissibility of New Genetic Identification Tests," pp. 26–30 and 33–42. For extensive citations regarding the dispute surrounding the reliability of DNA evidence and its admissibility in judicial proceedings see pp. 22–23, notes 3–5. For a comprehensive discussion of the reliability of DNA evidence see William C. Thompson and Simon Ford, "DNA Typing: Acceptance and Weight of the New Genetic Identification Tests," *Virginia Law Review*, vol. 75, no. 1 (February, 1989), pp. 45–108.

then X-rayed. The positions of the bands correspond to the positions of the VNTR fragments. Different lengths indicate that the samples come from different individuals. Matching is difficult because bands may be obscured, spurious dark spots may easily be mistaken for bands and the print may be faint or blurred. Even when computer-assisted imaging is employed, determination is often the product of subjective judgment on the part of laboratory technicians.[4] Moreover, the number and position of bands in a single person's DNA may change slightly depending on the quality of the biological sample and the testing conditions.[5] Thus, DNA prints of the same person may not always be identical. Laboratories have developed quantitative matching rules that specify how closely bands in two DNA prints must align in order to be regarded a match.[6] Hence, as might be anticipated, experts have differed with regard to whether a particular test has or has not reliably established a match. That issue figured significantly in two prominent court cases, *People* v. *Castro*[7] and *People* v. *Keene*.[8]

Matching DNA samples can indicate the likelihood that they come from a single individual only if the probability that two persons do not share a single DNA profile can be determined. It is presumed that the possibility of two people having an identical DNA profile of

---

4 For a report of a person wrongfully convicted of rape as a result of error on the part of a technician see Matthew Shaer, "The False Promise of DNA Testing," *The Atlantic*, June, 2016, https://www.theatlantic.com/magazine/archive/2016/06/a-reasonable-doubt/480747/. See also Erin Murphy, *Inside the Cell: The Dark Side of DNA* (New York, 2015). Cf., Barry Scheck and Peter Neufeld, *Actual Innocence: When Justice Goes Wrong and How to Make It Right* (New York, 2003).

5 See William C. Thompson and Simon Ford, "The Meaning of a Match: Sources of Ambiguity in the Interpretation of DNA Prints," *Forensic DNA Technology*, ed. Mark Farley and James Harrington (Chelsea, Michigan, 1991), pp. 73–95 and William M. Shields, "Forensic DNA Typing as Evidence in Criminal Proceedings: Some Problems and Potential Solutions," *Proceedings of the Third International Symposium on Human Identification* (1992), pp. 1–50.

6 See *NRC Report*, pp. 51–73.

7 545 N.Y.S.2d 985 (N.Y. Sup. Ct. 1989).

8 591 N.Y.S.2d 733 (N.Y. Sup. Ct. 1992).

a single allele is remote while the probability that they might share identical profiles of multiple alleles is infinitesimally small. Thus a match is declared only if a sufficient number of profiles are found to be identical. Generally, four or six alleles are matched in determining identification. If the position and length of multiple DNA profiles found in two samples match they are deemed to have belonged to a single person. Since any single set of matching DNA segments may well have come from different sources, it is only in the aggregate of matching different segments that the possibility of a second source can be eliminated.

Determining the statistical probability that the samples may have come from different persons begins with determining the frequency of each band in a database containing DNA profiles of a large number of individuals. For comparison of DNA profiles of members of various racial or ethnic groups to be meaningful, the database must assure that it is representative of the entire population. The major concern is that the frequency of alleles may vary among different ethnic groups. For example, the frequency of particular alleles may be higher among certain central African black tribes than among coastal African tribes. The percentage of blacks in the database may be disproportionately greater for a particular black group with the result that the likelihood of a match with a member of a different subgroup effectively excluded from the database may be much higher.

A second concern is that the statistical analysis depends upon combining the frequency of occurrences of different alleles. Thus, for example, if one allele is present in 10% of the population there is a 10% chance that two identical samples come from two unrelated individuals. That would present a very weak statistical indicator. If another allele is present in the same sample and it also occurs in 10% percent of the population, the presence of the second allele by itself is no stronger evidence than the presence of the first. But, if both are present, the likelihood that both did not come from the same person is $1/10 \times 1/10$ or $1/100$ – a far lower statistical probability that the match is a random coincidental occurrence rather than coming from a single source. However, that is true only if it assumed that the alleles are statistically independent, i.e., a particular person having a particular allele is in no way affected by the presence or absence of the other allele. If, however, 50% of those having the first allele also have the second allele, the presence of the second allele in 50% of the database adds much less to the likelihood that the two samples have a common source.[9] The fact that 50% of those having the first allele also have the second allele means that 50% of the linkage is not a random occurrence. It is only the independent occurrence of the second allele that is of statistical importance. Thus, the random likelihood that the samples have a common source is increased from $1/10 \times 1/10$ or $1/100$ to $1/10 \times 1/2$ or to $1/20$. Put somewhat differently: If the two probabilities are independent, the random likelihood that the samples have a common source is $1/10 \times 1/10$, or 1%. If the two probabilities are dependent on one another as above, where 50% of those having one allele have the other, the random likelihood that the samples have a common source is $1/10 \times 1/2$, or 5%. Whether or not the alleles in the DNA profile are in fact statistically independent is crucial and such independence must be established with every allele included in the profile.

It must be remembered that alleles occur in pairs, one allele inherited from the father and one from the mother. Together they constitute a genotype. Those alleles usually have different frequencies. The frequency of any pair of alleles is the frequency of one allele multiplied by the frequency of the other allele and then multiplied by two since each allele may come from a different parent. But determination of the genotype frequency is valid only if allele frequencies are not interdependent. If, however, the two alleles are common in a particular subgroup and members of that subgroup engage in endogamous mating, i.e., people in the subgroup tend to mate with each other, the allele frequency will be higher than in the general population, making

9 Large differences have been shown to exist among groups of American Indians. See J.R. Kidd *et al.*, "Studies of Three Amerindian Populations Using Nuclear DNA Polymorphisms," *Human Biology*, vol. 63, no. 6 (December, 1991), pp. 775–794.

it more likely that the samples containing the different alleles come from different individuals.[10]

NGS methods are potentially more reliable for determining genetic heterogeneity. However, the tremendously higher numbers of haplotypes, i.e., sets of DNA variations, or polymorphisms, that tend to be inherited together, that are examined results in a corresponding increase in the absolute numbers of potential error.[11] The error rate of conventional NGS is approximately 1%. A number of methods for error correction have been developed that may reduce the error rates to as low as 0.1% in optimal scenarios.[12]

DNA testing involves comparing various haplotypes. In order to sharply decrease the statistical probability that they came from different individuals, multiple haplotypes are compared. The more haplotypes compared, the less likely it is that two individuals share all of those haplotypes. This again assumes that there is no interdependence between separate haplotypes. If such a linkage exists, the presence of multiple haplotypes becomes less significant. At present, scant information is available with regard to such interdependence.

Using older methods of DNA analysis, identical DNA profiles have been found in at least one study. The comparison of Karitian Indians of Brazil found an over twenty percent match in four or more probes. In at least one case there was a six-probe match. In addition, a six-probe

10 By way of analogy, ten percent of Europeans have blond hair, ten percent have blue eyes and ten percent have fair skin. Multiplying those frequencies would mean that only 1 in 1,000 Europeans have blond hair, blue eyes, and fair skin. The actual frequency, particularly among Scandinavians, is much higher. That is so because there is a definite linkage, probably because of endogamous marriage, in the genetic factors responsible for those traits. See *NRC Report*, p. 76.

11 See Jesse J. Salk, Michael W. Schmitt and Lawrence A. Loeb, "Enhancing the Accuracy of Next-Generation Sequencing for Detecting Rare and Subclonal Mutations," *Nature Reviews Genetics*, vol. 19, no. 5 (May, 2018), p. 3.

12 *Ibid.*, pp. 3–35.

match was discovered between one Karitian Indian and a member of a different group, a Maya Indian.[13]

Nor is DNA testing used to disprove the existence of a blood relationship infallible. Some individuals, known as chimeras, may have two or more types of genetically distinct DNA. One of those lines of DNA may be passed on to progeny to the exclusion of others. Comparison of the DNA of a child with a parent's cells containing DNA that has not been passed on will lead to the erroneous conclusion that no filial relationship exists.[14]

The first natural human chimera was reported in 1953. A British woman was found to have both Type O and Type A blood. It was later shown that she had acquired some blood cells in utero from a fraternal twin.[15] Cell transfer between dizygotic twins in utero[16] and from mother to fetus[17] is not uncommon. That phenomenon is known as fetal cell microchimerism or FMC. Similar cell transfers may also

---

13 See Laurence Mueller, "The Use of DNA Typing in Forensic Science," *Accountability in Research*, vol. 3, no. 1 (November, 1993), pp. 55–57. Obviously, use of additional probes or later-developed NGS methods might have yielded a different result.

14 There are other naturally occurring phenomena that may render DNA results less than absolute. It has long been known that DNA mutations occur during germline meiotic cell division with the result that the child's DNA cannot be identified with the DNA of either parent. A possible unfortunate effect may be a dominant genetic disorder in a child born to two normal parents. It is recognized that the same phenomenon can occur in mitotic cell division in a parent. The outcome is mosaicism, defined as the presence of different cell populations with distinct genotypes within one individual. See Ian M. Campbell, Bo Yuan *et al.*, "Parental Somatic Mosaicism Is Underrecognized and Influences Recurrence Risk of Genomic Disorders," *American Journal of Human Genetics*, vol. 95, no. 2 (August 7, 2014), pp. 173–182.

15 See I. Dunsford, C.C. Bowley, Ann M. Hutchison *et al.*, "A Human Blood-Group Chimera," *British Medical Journal*, vol. 2, no. 4827 (July 11, 1953), p. 81.

16 Gavin S. Dawe, Xiao Wei Tan, and Zhi-Cheng Xiao, "Cell Migration from Baby to Mother," *Cell Adhesion & Migration*, vol. 1, no. 1 (January–March, 2007), p. 20.

17 *Ibid.*, p. 20.

occur during transplantation of organs[18] or transfusion of blood.[19] Much less common, but having more far-reaching consequences, is cell transfer that occurs through fertilization of two ova by two spermatozoa followed by fusion of the zygotes. That phenomenon is known as tetragametic chimerism and is described colloquially as a "vanishing twin."[20]

There are a number of celebrated cases in which DNA testing thought to exclude a maternal relationship was shown to be quite fallible. Karen Keegan, a mother of three children, suffered from renal failure and required a kidney transplant. She underwent histocompatibility testing in order to determine donor suitability. The DNA results indicated that Karen could not be the genetic mother of two of her sons because her sons had a haplotype that originated from someone other than their presumed parents. Further testing showed that Karen's brother carried the same haplotype as those two sons. Other tissue samples were then removed from Karen's thyroid gland, mouth and hair. Those samples revealed that Karen had one type of DNA in some tissues and another type of DNA in other tissues. The latter type of DNA included the haplotype that was found in her two sons. Researchers concluded that the variant DNA was the result of tetragametic chimerism, i.e., that Karen had fused with a hitherto

18 Thomas E. Starzl and Anthony J. Demetris, "Transplantation Tolerance, Microchimerism, and the Two-Way Paradigm," *Theoretical Medicine and Bioethics*, vol. 19, no. 5 (September, 1998), pp. 441–455.

19 Margot S. Kruskall, Tzong-Hae Lee, Susan F. Assmann *et al.*, "Survival of Transfused Donor White Blood Cells in HIV-Infected Recipients," *Blood*, vol. 98, no. 2 (July 15, 2001), pp. 272–279.

20 W. R. Mayr, V. Pausch, and W. Schnedl, "Human Chimaera Detectable Only by Investigation of Her Progeny," *Nature*, vol. 277, no. 5693 (January, 1979), pp. 210–211; W. R. Mayr, "Human Chimerism," *Revue Française de Transfusion et Immuno-hématologie*, vol. 24, no. 1 (1981), pp. 19–26; and Neng Yu, Margot S. Kruskall, Juan J. Yunis *et al.*, "Disputed Maternity Leading to Identification of Tetragametic Chimerism," *New England Journal of Medicine*, vol. 346, no. 20 (May 16, 2002), pp. 1545–1552.

unknown fraternal embryo while gestating in her mother's womb and had retained the variant DNA of that embryo.[21]

In 2003, a second remarkably similar incident occurred. Lydia Fairchild, a mother of two children, applied to receive funds through a welfare program. The State of Washington demanded a blood test to verify parentage. The result of Lydia's blood test showed that it was impossible for Lydia to be the mother of her putative children. She was denied assistance and prosecution for welfare fraud was commenced. Lydia attempted to rebut the DNA findings by producing her children's birth certificates as well as verification from her obstetrician who was present at both births. During the course of legal proceedings, she again became pregnant. The Court ordered an officer to accompany Lydia during labor and to remain with her until delivery of her third child and then to serve as a witness to immediate post-natal DNA testing. The DNA tests of the baby and Lydia, performed immediately after birth, showed that it was impossible for Lydia to be the biological mother of the child. Lydia was then accused of having acted as a surrogate for another woman. Fortunately, her attorney read of the earlier case of Karen Keegan and insisted upon further testing. Subsequent blood results[22] demonstrated that Lydia was a chimera.[23]

A third incident involved Tyler Hamilton, an American cyclist who won the 2004 gold medal in the Athens Olympics. In 2005, the United States Anti-Doping Agency found Hamilton guilty of homologous blood doping, i.e., an illicit method of boosting an athlete's

21 See Claire Ainsworth, "The Stranger Within," *New Scientist*, vol. 180, no. 2421 (November 15, 2003), pp. 34–37 and Robert Russell Granzen, "The Human Chimera: Legal Problems Arising from Individuals with Multiple Types of DNA," *Law School Student Scholarship*, Paper 485 (May 2, 2014), pp. 13–15.

22 For a survey of various types of human chimeras and testing methods to determine their existence see Robert E. Wenk, "A Review of the Biology and Classification of Human Chimeras," *Transfusion*, vol. 58, no. 8 (August 2018), pp. 2054–2067.

23 See Granzen, "The Human Chimera," pp. 13–15 and "She's Her Own Twin," ABC News Network (August 15, 2006), https://abcnews.go.com/Primetime/shes-twin/story?id=2315693.

red blood cell supply in advance of competition, and rescinded the gold medal that had been awarded. Red blood cells serve as a source of oxygen and, accordingly, increasing the number of red blood cells in the athlete's blood gives the athlete additional oxygen to combat fatigue. Hamilton claimed that the positive test result was not due to a homologous blood transfer but reflected the presence of blood of a "vanishing twin" in his body and that he was, in fact, a tetragametic chimera. Unfortunately for Hamilton, his defense failed to convince the authorities and the agency's finding was upheld.[24]

Thus, DNA testing constitutes far less than infallible proof. Unsurprisingly, there have been numerous challenges in United States courts to admissibility to DNA evidence. Most jurisdictions have applied the Frye doctrine, first established in *Frye* v. *United States,*[25] that allows scientific evidence to be presented to a jury if the court determines that it has gained "general acceptance in the particular field in which it belongs."[26] The Frye standard was abrogated insofar as federal courts are concerned by a decision of the U.S. Supreme Court in *Daubert* v. *Merrell Dow Pharmaceuticals, Inc.*[27] The Supreme Court ruled that expert testimony is governed by the more expansive federal rule of evidence that states:

> If scientific, technical or other specialized knowledge will assist the trier of fact to understand the evidence or determine a fact at issue, a witness qualified as an expert by knowledge, skill, experience, training, or education may testify thereto in the form of an opinion or otherwise.[28]

Without identifying any factor as controlling, the Court enumerated a number of considerations that must be weighed, including whether the theory or technique has been tested, subjected to peer

24 Granzen, "The Human Chimera," pp. 15–17.
25 293 F. 1013 (D.C. Cir. 1923).
26 *Ibid.*, p. 1014.
27 509 U.S. 579 (1993).
28 Fed. R. Evid. 72.

review and publication, its estimated rate of error and, probably most significantly, its acceptance in the relevant scientific community.

Consequently, courts have differed with regard to admissibility of DNA evidence both because of questionable procedures and safeguards employed by various laboratories and because of applicable legal standards.[29] For obvious reasons, DNA evidence is more likely to assist in exonerating a suspect than in convicting a defendant.

II. CIRCUMSTANTIAL EVIDENCE IN HALAKHAH

1. Two Types of Circumstantial Evidence

Judaism's two-witness rule requiring the testimony of two unimpeached witnesses is not based upon the presumption that eyewitnesses are infallible. That is made abundantly clear by Rambam in *Hilkhot Yesodei ha-Torah* 7:7. Rambam spells out the criteria that must be met by a person seeking credibility as a prophet. Upon listing the relevant criteria, Rambam adds that it is not beyond the sphere of the possible that a charlatan might establish himself as a prophet but, despite that possibility, a person who has satisfied those criteria must be accepted as such because "thus have we been commanded." Almost gratuitously, Rambam adds a parallel comment to the effect that we are commanded to obey the prophet "just as we have been commanded to determine the verdict on the basis of two qualified witnesses even though it is possible that they testified falsely...." Similarly, in *Hilkhot Yesodei ha-Torah* 8:2, Rambam writes, "...[with regard to] every prophet who shall arise after Moses, our teacher, we do not believe in him because of signs alone...but because of the commandment Moses commanded in the Torah...just as he commanded us to deliver the verdict on the basis of two witnesses even though we do not know whether they testify truthfully or falsely...." Rambam reiterates that point in *Hilkhot Sanhedrin* 24:1: "...for when [two witnesses] come before the judge he shall judge on the basis of

29 See Thompson, "Evaluating the Admissibility of New Genetic Identification Tests," pp. 42–51.

their testimony even though he does not know whether they testified truthfully or falsely."[30]

The object of the criminal law system established by the Torah is not necessarily to convict and punish every perpetrator. As reported by the Mishnah, *Makkot* 7a, the requirements for conviction are so rigorous that execution was a rarity. But there must be provision for punishment, if only to serve as a deterrent or to express a pedagogical message. The divine Lawgiver, declares Rambam, in His wisdom, ordained the two-witness rule with full realization that undiscoverable perjury is a distinct possibility. At the same time He excluded other types of evidence despite their compelling nature.

Western societies recognize that certainty in criminal prosecutions is virtually impossible. Consequently, they have adopted a "beyond a reasonable doubt" standard. What is "reasonable doubt"? Whatever doubt a juror perceives to be reasonable. Doubt almost always exists; the sole issue is the "reasonableness" of such doubt. What one person finds reasonable another finds absurd. What one finds so remote as to defy credulity another finds to be within at least the outer limits of reasonableness. At the risk of being branded a sophist, one may argue that any and all doubts are reasonable; otherwise, the reservation could not be truthfully articulated as a doubt. The very act of formulating, articulating and meaningfully expressing the psychological phenomenon of doubt demonstrates its existence. Doubt expressed by a rational being and cognitively communicated must be reasonable. The same doubt attends upon eyewitness testimony as well but the divine Legislator chose to impose the two-witness standard upon us.

Circumstantial evidence, by its very nature, is subject to doubt. The prosecutor has the burden of convincing the trier of fact that the likelihood of any alternative explanation is so remote that it need not be "reasonably" considered. Epistemologists recognize that there are

30 See also *Teshuvot Ḥatam Sofer, Even ha-Ezer* II, no. 131, s.v. *ve-i ba'it eima*. Cf., R. Shimon Yehudah ha-Kohen Shkop, *Sha'arei Yosher, sha'ar* 6 chap. 7; R. Elchanan Wasserman, *Kovez̩ He'arot*, no. 33, secs. 3–5; as well as *Netivot ha-Mishpat* 81:7.

varying degrees of certainty. Propositions of logic are regarded as certain, but only because the human mind is incapable of fathoming otherwise. Parallel lines do not ever converge but only because the human mind is incapable of picturing lines that are both parallel and convergent. Indeed, some philosophers would argue that the proposition "Parallel lines do not converge" is nothing more than a tautology, a matter of semantic notation, that tells us something about linguistic expression but nothing about the universe. The human mind is incapable of conjuring a geometric object endowed with both the properties of a circle and the properties of a square. It is simply impossible to conceive of an object that both exists and does not exist at the same time.

Similarly, deductive logic is forced upon all rational beings. Aristotelian logic dictates, not the empirical truth of certain arguments, but the incontrovertibility of certain argument forms. "All men are mortal. Socrates is a man. Therefore Socrates is mortal." One simply cannot affirm the truth of both the major and minor premises and deny the conclusion that some men are mortal. Perhaps not all men are mortal. Perhaps Socrates is the name of a cat. But a person who accepts the original premises as stated and refuses to acknowledge that Socrates is mortal is either a liar or mentally deficient, i.e., "irrational." The human mind is constrained, or "programmed," to think, i.e., to reason, in a certain way and is denied the freedom to do otherwise.

Other than tautologies, propositions outside of deductive logic and mathematics are accepted with greater or lesser degree of certainty depending upon antecedent experience, compatibility with earlier gleaned information, credibility of the speaker, etc. But those propositions always admit of an element of doubt, however remote. To declare otherwise is to be "unreasonable" in the technical, if not in the colloquial, sense of the term.

Deductive reasoning is valid as a matter of necessity in the sense of rational compulsion; inductive reasoning is always subject to a measure of doubt, even if the doubt is *de minimis*, and can never be regarded as absolutely certain. Empirical generalities are the building blocks of science. Laymen come to think of some scientific principles as immutable, but philosophers of science correctly recognize such principles as nothing more than working hypotheses subject to disconfirmation at any time by the appearance of even a single contradictory phenomenon. Discovery of the law of gravity can be categorized by a fictional narrative: One may conjecture that Sir Isaac Newton had occasion to observe apples falling from a tree. In the course of that and similar observations he recognized an unvarying pattern: Apples, when separated from the tree, did not rise to the sky but fell to the ground. One may surmise that he would have made the identical observation with regard to oranges, peaches, pears and coconuts. Indeed, other people did make the same observations but it was Newton who first realized that there is a common element manifest in each of those phenomena. It occurred to him that he was not observing haphazard phenomena but that all bodies possessing mass are attracted by the earth's gravitational field. Thus was born the law of gravity, applicable to all bodies possessing mass.

We have come to accept the phenomenon of gravity as an immutable law of nature. It may be the case that matter is endowed with a "mysterious" force called gravity and that defiance of the law of gravity requires a miracle. However, our formulation of the law of gravity is the product of mere empirical generalization. We have observed uniform behavior on numerous occasions and have yet to observe a single instance of contradictory behavior. Those experiences have led us to conclude that what we have observed is not a series of discrete, independent coincidences but the mandated effect of a causal principle. A single disconfirming event would force us either to reject the law of gravity as false or to reformulate the rule by modifying it to account for an otherwise aberrant phenomenon.

There is controversy among philosophers with regard to the propositions of mathematics. Is "two plus two equals four" an immutable rule akin to a postulate of Euclidian geometry or is it merely an empirical generalization? No scientist would dismiss evidence contradicting the law of gravity out of hand; no philosopher would give credence to an eyewitness account of parallel lines that actually converge. Consider a report of the synthesis of a new element accompanied by an announcement that the molecules of the new element behave in a peculiar way. When two molecules of that element are added to two other molecules of the same element the result is five molecules of the same element. If submitted to a jury of philosophers, the jury would have to decide whether the report is unworthy of investigation or whether time, effort and societal resources should be invested in analyzing the novel phenomenon that carries the potential of being harnessed and used for the betterment of the human condition and for the welfare of society. The votes of the various members of the panel would reflect their respective views regarding the nature of mathematics.

Halakhah does accept laws of nature as immutable, barring miracles. And it does accept mathematics as akin to application of the rules of logic. But, when confronted with circumstantial evidence, it is more than skeptical. However, one must exercise caution in defining the notion of circumstantial evidence subject to such skepticism. *Tosafot, Shevu'ot* 34a, s.v. *de-i*, regard some forms of circumstantial evidence as admissible even in criminal cases.[31] The Gemara, *Sanhedrin* 37b and *Shevu'ot* 34a, states:

> R. Simon ben Shetaḥ said:
>
> "May I not see the consolation of Zion if I did not see a man running after his fellow into a ruin and I ran after him and found him with a sword in his hand, blood dripping and the victim in death throes. I said to him, "Wicked one! Who killed this man, I or you? But what can I do since your blood is not given into my hand for the Torah said, 'by the mouth of two witnesses or three witnesses shall he who is to die be put to death.'"

That report would appear to bar all forms of circumstantial evidence. Indeed, that is the position of Me'iri, *Shevu'ot* 34a, and *Yad*

31 This also appears to be the opinion of Rambam, *Hilkhot Ḥovel u-Mazik* 5:5. Cf., however, R. Jacob Pester, *Ha-Pardes,* Kislev 5730, p. 17, reprinted in his *Birkat Ya'akov*, no. 14.

Ramah, Sanhedrin 37b.[32] Nevertheless, *Tosafot, Shevu'ot* 34a, s.v. *de-i*, distinguish between different forms of circumstantial evidence and regard one type of circumstantial evidence as sufficient even in capital cases. For example, if witnesses testify that only two people were in a confined space without possibility of unobserved entry or egress and one is found to have sustained a mortal wound that could not possibly have been self-inflicted, his sole companion may be judged guilty of causing the victim's death despite the absence of eyewitness testimony to the actual act of homicide.[33]

Tosafot, in effect, draw an epistemological distinction between two types of circumstantial evidence. Circumstantial evidence involves circumstances in which a trier of fact apprised of the known facts draws certain conclusions. Given a single mauling camel among a group of docile camels and a carcass in their midst, a reasonable person would certainly conclude that responsibility lies with the aggressive camel. The certainty of that conclusion may be open to question but it

---

32 See also R. Joseph Colon, *Teshuvot Maharik*, no. 129.

33 The testimony of two eyewitnesses is the normative standard of evidence with regard to criminal matters. Nevertheless, the Gemara, *Bava Batra* 93a, *Sanhedrin* 37b and *Shevu'ot* 34a, records a controversy between Rav Aḥa and the Sages in a situation involving a group of camels. One camel was observed kicking its legs and subsequently another camel was found mauled to death. R. Aḥa accepts such circumstantial evidence as sufficient to hold the aggressive camel's owner liable in tort. *Tosafot, Shevu'ot* 34a, s.v. *de-i*, maintain that R. Aḥa would recognize the admissibility of comparable evidence in criminal prosecutions as well. Other early-day authorities regard R. Aḥa's view as limited to financial matters. In any event, many halakhic decisors rule in accordance with the majoritarian view of the Sages.

Teshuvot Maharik, no. 129, rules that circumstantial evidence even of the nature of the anecdote related by R. Simon ben Shetaḥ is not admissible even in monetary matters. *Maharik* maintains that the sages who disputed R. Aḥa's position reject the view of R. Simon ben Shetaḥ as well. See also *Avnei Nezer, Even ha-Ezer*, no. 119. See, *inter alia*, *Netivot ha-Mishpat* 15:2. However, Rambam, *Hilkhot Sanhedrin* 21:1 and 21:9 and *Shulḥan Arukh, Ḥoshen Mishpat* 15:5, rule that a *bet din* may issue a decision on the basis of their subjective evaluation of the evidence. See also *Teshuvot Ge'onei Batra'i*, no. 54; R. Jonathan Eybeschutz, *Tumim* 90:14; and R. Elchanan Wasserman, *Kovez̩ Shi'urim*, II, no. 38.

is reached on the basis of an *umdena*, i.e., an assessment of contextual circumstances. Certainly, some circumstances may be more compelling than others. At times, a conclusion may be accepted because it is regarded as true beyond reasonable doubt, at times because the evidence is clear and compelling and at times because the conclusion is regarded as more likely than not. There is certainly no way to draw clear and precise boundaries between the three standards of proof. The result is a slippery slope. In the words of Rambam, *Sefer ha-Mizvot, mizvot lo ta'aseh,* no. 290:

> A judge is commanded not to determine matters on the basis of strong inclination even if it approaches [absolute] truth.... For of matters in the realm of possibility there are some that are highly probable, some that are highly improbable and some intermediate between the two. The realm of the possible is extremely broad. If the Torah would have allowed determination of guilt in capital cases on the basis of the highest degree of probability that might exist... we would breach the barrier [by accepting evidence] a bit distant [from that degree of certainty] and [then] also by accepting evidence exceedingly distant until the barriers are [entirely] breached and people put to death on the basis of scanty assessment according to the judge's surmise and thinking. Therefore, the exalted One closed the door and declared that punishment not be determined unless witnesses testify that they know with certainty, without doubt and without any assessment at all.

Circumstantial evidence of such nature, i.e., based upon *umdena*, can, at the very most, establish conclusions in a manner approaching certainty but never with absolute certainty.

Other situations may present facts that would lead to inescapable deductive conclusions. A victim is found in a cave with a knife wound in his back. The only other person in the cave is holding a knife dripping with blood. A knife wound cannot occur spontaneously. If the wound could not be self-inflicted, and it has been established that no other person was present and that it would have been impossible for any other perpetrator to enter or exit the space, the lethal wound could not possibly have been caused other than at the hands of the individual whose presence in the confined space has been established. Given the laws of natural science that govern both man and matter, no other conclusion is possible.[34]

In those circumstances, culpability has been established not only beyond reasonable doubt but also beyond all cogent doubt. The identity of the murderer is known with the same degree of logical certainty as is attendant upon the conclusion of an Aristotelian syllogism. The facts are amenable to one interpretation and to one interpretation only. The conclusion is undeniably compelled by canons of logic and hence is known to be valid with absolute certainty. Indeed, circumstantial evidence of that nature is not simply the equivalent of, but superior to, eyewitness testimony. Eyewitness testimony is not infallible; deductions based upon known rules of nature are compelling barring some form of miraculous intervention, the possibility of which is not a factor in legal determinations.[35]

---

34 Deductive inferences are integral to testimony of witnesses and conclusions of a *bet din*. The point formulated by *Tosafot* – and disputed by *Yad Ramah* and Me'iri – is that accepted laws of nature established by empirical science can also serve as premises to which deductive reasoning may be applied.

That appears to be the basis for the distinction between "*mayim she-yesh la-hem sof*" – an enclosed body of water and "*mayim she-ein la-hem sof*" – an unenclosed body of water. Generally speaking, a person who enters a vast body of water and does not return has perished by drowning. If the opposite shore cannot be seen, there remains a possibility that the person emerged on the other side and survived; it is only a *rov* who do not survive. If the opposite side can be seen and the person has not surfaced his demise is deemed a certainty. But that fact can be deduced only by recognizing laws of nature governing human physical prowess and survival. That, too, is a form of circumstantial evidence based upon deductive inference from laws of nature.

35 Indeed, the Gemara, *Rosh ha-Shanah* 25b and *Bekhorot* 20b, declares that testimony of witnesses to phenomena inconsistent with the dictates of the laws of nature are to be dismissed as false. For a more immediate application see R. Zevi Ashkenazi, *Teshuvot Ḥakham Ẓevi*, no. 77, who declares that he would dismiss testimony of witnesses to the absence of a heart in a chicken as contrary to the laws of nature and the rejoinder of R. Jonathan Eybeschutz, *Kereti u-Peleti* 40:4, to the effect that, although this is the case with regard to

Rabbinical courts have not administered statutory capital punishment or forty stripes since forty years prior to the destruction of the Second Temple.[36] Consequently, the admissibility of circumstantial evidence in criminal cases is not an issue of immediate concern. Nevertheless, reliability of circumstantial evidence in general, and of DNA evidence in particular, is of importance in a wide variety of matters:

1. Burial in a Jewish cemetery.
2. Substantiation of a claim to burial in a reserved grave.
3. Observance of mourning rituals.
4. Identification of body parts for burial in a single grave.
5. Establishing a paternal-filial relationship for the purpose of the obligation of honoring a parent.
6. Proof of paternity in order to exempt a widow from levirate obligations.
7. Rebuttal of a father's presumptive credibility in disclaiming a paternal relationship.
8. Confirmation or negation of paternity for purposes of custody and/or child support.
9. Determination of the status of a child as a *mamzer.*
10. Establishing eligibility of a daughter of an unwed mother to marry a *kohen* in situations in which such a marriage is not permitted because of doubtful paternity.
11. Evidence of death of a spouse in order to establish capacity to enter into a new marriage.
12. Establishing identity in instances of possible inadvertent exchange of infants.
13. Establishment or denial of a right of inheritance.
14. Establishing status as the son of a *kohen* or a levite for purposes of religious law.

---

the vast majority of chickens, such testimony is plausible because the particular chicken may have had a malformed or unrecognizable organ that performed the functions of the heart.

36 See *Sanhedrin* 41a.

15. Determination of paternity for the purpose of marrying a woman pregnant with another person's child or a woman within the twenty-four month period following birth of such child. Many authorities forbid marriage even if the prospective husband acknowledges paternity. However, when there is acceptable proof of paternity, the father is permitted to marry the woman in question.
16. Establishing a filial relationship with a woman of known Jewish ancestry for purposes of eligibility to marry a Jew.
17. Establishing a person's identity as a Jew on the basis of the so-called "Jewish gene" for purposes of privileges and benefits arising from religious law or the Israeli Law of Return.
18. Status as a *kohen* on the basis of the presence or absence of the so-called "*kohen* gene." Presence of the gene is significant only for establishing entitlement to ritual privileges and honors due a *kohen*. However, the effect of absence of the gene, if dispositive, would eliminate the restrictions to which a *kohen* is subject such as coming in contact with the body of a deceased person or marrying a divorcee.

2. Fingerprint Evidence

Modern science and technology have introduced a number of novel forms of evidence that, because of their scientific nature, are regarded as highly reliable and certainly more credible than the testimony of eyewitnesses. Those forms of evidence include: fingerprints, blood types, and DNA. Of those, reliance upon fingerprint evidence for matters of Halakhah, despite its scientific basis, is particularly problematic.

Deductive inferences are based upon laws of nature. Those laws are presumed to regulate natural occurrences by means of principles and forces that are regular, orderly and inviolate. It is regularity of sequential occurrence that causes observers to formulate hypotheses that account for such regularity and which then may be used to predict future occurrences. The human mind regards regularity of occurrence as evidence of an underlying law of nature. The cause is inferred from its effect. The direction and velocity of falling objects leads to postulation of the law of gravity to explain that phenomenon; the attraction of iron filings by, and their adaptation to, the shape of certain metals leads to postulating the existence of a magnetic field. In the absence of contradictory explanations of such phenomena, we regard these hypotheses as proven precisely because regularity of occurrence gives rise to the assumption that there is an identifiable cause responsible for that regularity. We reify the cause by giving it a name even when the causal force or principle cannot be perceived directly. Perception of regularity in the operation of nature is the meta-hypothesis that makes all scientific hypotheses possible.

The widespread acceptance of fingerprint evidence lies in the fact that, despite phenomenally large databases, no two prints have ever been found to be identical. If it were to be assumed with certainty that nature dictates assignment of unique fingerprints to each individual it might be conclusively determined that fingerprints found on any object must be ascribed to the individual whose fingers match those prints. The crucial point is that uniformity of occurrence is either the product of causal connection or mere happenstance. When the statistical probability of identical random occurrence is beyond credulity, the only alternative is the presence of a causal connection. Such an invariable causal connection leads to recognition of a law of nature that is manifested in such events. The identified law of nature, assuming it is veridical, is readily apprehended by the intellect and, once established, is accepted as a guarantee of future reiteration. The guarantee is not the cumulative effect of statistical improbability of past events having been random, but the underlying "law" which unifies the observed phenomena in a causal manner thereby negating mere coincidence. Thus, the law acquires predicative reliability.

Fingerprint evidence is not of such nature. To be sure, millions of individuals have been fingerprinted; no two individuals have been found to have the same fingerprint. Ergo, 1) there is some principle of nature that precludes such a result; 2) the phenomenon, incredible as it may seem to be, is a colossal coincidence; or 3) the Creator, for reasons best known to Himself, has decided to stamp each of His creatures with individuality in the form of a unique set of fingerprints. Science has failed to discern any natural rule that would mandate that each person be endowed with a unique set of fingerprints. Hence, past experience has no reliable predictive value. By way of example, in tossing a coin, the chances in each toss that it will result in heads is 50% and the chance that it will result in tails is 50%. If one sets out to perform ten tosses the statistical probability that all ten tosses will result in heads is extremely remote. The probability that all ten tosses will result in heads is ½10, or one in 1024 to be precise. Given those odds, a prudent person will refuse to wager that the coin will land on heads ten times in succession. But, if nine already completed tosses have already resulted in heads, the chance that the tenth toss will also result in heads is no different from the probability that the first toss would result in heads. In each individual instance the probability is one out of two. Of course, if the coin is weighted in a particular manner, the probability of tossing a head may approach or equal 100%. That is tantamount to saying that the result is not random but attributable to some "law" or causal factor. The problem is formulating a hypothesis, i.e., identifying a law, that explains the observed phenomena.

Science has yet to discover a rational explanation for the idiosyncratic nature of fingerprints. We may suspect that such an undiscerned cause is present but the phenomenon, at least at present, is not ascribable to any physical or biological factor. The presence of a contradictory occurrence invalidates a hypothesis, but absence of a contradictory phenomenon proves nothing. The remarkably high incidence of unique fingerprints marked by the absence of even a single matching set may lead us to assume that there is some law in our universe governing fingerprints that we have not perceived. But absent apprehension of such a principle, the possibility of wildly improbable random occurrences cannot rationally be excluded. Hence the claim that matching fingerprints "proves" anything regarding the source of such fingerprints is invalid.[37] At best, it represents an educated guess, but not a proof.

The difference between random, temporally sequential occurrences and manifestation of an inherent law of nature is the presence

37 See *infra*, p. 28, note 1.

of an underlying force or principle that endows physical events with causality. When the human intellect succeeds in positing a rational explanation that establishes causal connections between empirical phenomena we rely upon that principle as a prescriptive, and hence predictive, law of nature.[38] If we are unable to explain the temporal sequences in a manner reflecting an underlying rule of nature we cannot but consider them to be discrete phenomena that occur haphazardly and hence of no logically predictive value.

The classic example of the latter lies in the belief held by some tribes in Africa to the effect that the reappearance of the sun following a solar eclipse is dependent upon their beating of tom toms. Each time there is an eclipse of the sun, they beat the tom-toms and, lo and behold, the sun reappears. They are convinced that there is a causal connection between those events such that if they were to withhold the beating of tom-toms the sun would not reappear. The result would be catastrophic; hence, their reluctance to refrain from beating the tom-toms.

Neither they nor the scientific community can elucidate a causal connection between the beating of tom toms and the reappearance of the sun. An ascription of such a connection between those phenomena is a classic example of the logical fallacy *post hoc ergo propter hoc*, or "after this, therefore because of this." The difference between a logical fallacy and a veridical manifestation of causality lies in identification of an inherent, identifiable causal law. The practical difference is

---

38 For purposes of this discussion there is no need to explore Ramban's position asserting that there are no laws of nature but that what we perceive as natural causality is merely the manifestation of discreet "miraculous" acts of the Deity. Ramban uses the term "*nes nistar*," or "hidden miracle," to describe such phenomena precisely because the human intellect (erroneously) perceives them as immutable cause and effect occurrences. According to Ramban, overt miracles were performed in order to cause us to reflect and recognize that natural phenomena are also miraculous. See Ramban, *Commentary on the Bible*, Exodus 13:17. It seems correct to say that, for Ramban, the halakhic system is predicated upon how the world appears to man rather than upon ontological reality.

predictability and reliability. When a causal factor is present the law will dictate future events and make them absolutely predictable. When there is no law we may marvel at the regularity but must fully recognize that there is no inherent logical reason that past phenomena should have predictive value for future events. Science has not been capable of formulating a theory to explain the existence of a law dictating idiosyncratic individual fingerprints. In the absence of a scientific explanation we cannot affirm with any degree of certainty that the fingerprints of two individuals cannot be identical. The assumption that they can never be identical is logically fallacious.[39]

---

39 Cf., R. Chaim David Regensberg, *Mishmeret Ḥayyim*, no. 37, who accepts fingerprint evidence as admitting of no exception and hence infallible to the point of asserting that testimony to the contrary must be dismissed as perjury. See *supra*, p. 19, note 35. See the response of R. Jacob Pester, *Ha-Pardes*, Tammuz 5729 and Kislev 5730. For further discussion of fingerprint evidence see R. Shlomoh Fisher, *No'am*, II (5719), 211–222, and sources cited by Prof. Nahum Rakover, *Oẓar ha-Mishpat* (Jerusalem, 5735), p. 252; R. Joshua Aaronberg, *Teshuvot Dvar Yehoshu'a*, III, *Even ha-Ezer*, no. 4 and R. Gad Navon, *Dine Yisra'el*, VII (5737), 129–144.

Implicit reliance upon fingerprint evidence fails to take notice of bias and error of judgment in comparing prints. A celebrated case of that nature involved identification of the Madrid Bomber who detonated ten bombs on trains in Madrid in 2004. A latent fingerprint was found on the bag of detonators and matched with that of an American attorney whose fingerprints had been entered into the automated fingerprint identification system. Three FBI analysts confirmed the identification and the attorney was subsequently held in custody for two weeks. The attorney had never been to Spain and did not possess a US passport. He was, however, a Muslim and had earlier defended a known terrorist. The real bomber was later identified and apprehended by Spanish police. See Sarah V. Stevenage and Alice Bennett, "A Biased Opinion: Demonstration of Cognitive Bias on a Fingerprint Matching Task Through Knowledge of DNA Test Results," *Forensic Science International*, vol. 276 (July, 2017), pp. 93–106.

Chapter Two

Paternity and Child Support

I. HALAKHIC PRESUMPTIONS

There are a number of basic halakhic principles employed in determining paternity. The most fundamental is the principle that in cases involving a married couple the lawfully wedded husband is presumed to be the father of any child born during the marriage provided that the husband had access to the wife within a twelve-month period preceding birth of the child. The wife's ascription of pregnancy to an adulterous relationship is not given credence. That principle is quite similar to the common law rule that no person has standing to challenge the paternity of a child so long as the father was present "within the five seas of England" during the requisite period of time. That rule has been modified in many jurisdictions to allow for rebuttal on the basis of incompatible blood types and the like. In those jurisdictions the principle retains a *prima facie* validity as a rebuttable presumption of law.

The common law rule was based on considerations of public policy rather than upon factual considerations. The law refused to hear challenges to presumed paternity because of a policy designed to preserve the marital relationship and to quell allegations of adultery which, whether or not based on fact, would have the certain effect of damaging marital tranquility, sullying reputations, defamation of character, public embarrassment and humiliation as well as social ostracism. Additionally, the policy was designed to preserve orderly disposition of estates by applying anticipated principles of inheritance. Were allegations of bastardy to be entertained, ultimate disposition of an estate would be subject to an element of uncertainty both during and after the lifetime of the decedent. Accordingly, even a factually correct allegation of bastardy was to be dismissed as a matter of law. Suppression of evidence of bastardy made it far less likely for the allegation to be made in a public forum and thus nipped social and legal problems at their point of inception.

The Jewish law principle is based on a general empirical presumption rather than upon policy considerations. The halakhic principle is the majoritarian rule of *rov*. That general rule is employed to determine questions of status. Given the existence of two distinct sets, a major set and a minor set, when doubt arises with regard to the status of a particular person or entity, the person or entity whose status is in doubt is assigned to the major set. Thus, for example, although some animals are *treifot*, the majority of all animals are not *treifot*. Consequently, if a question arises with regard to the status of a particular animal, the animal is presumed to belong to the major set of animals that are not *treifot*.

A child of a married woman sired by a man other than her husband is a *mamzer*. Status of a *mamzer* is dependent upon determination of identity of the participants in the conjugal act leading to conception. Based upon opportunity of access, the husband is in a position to engage in conjugal acts more frequently than a paramour. Since the husband's acts are presumed to be more frequent and regular than those of other sexual partners, conception of the child is deemed to have resulted from one of the major set of conjugal acts.[1] Accordingly,

1 The talmudic formulation is "*Rov be'ilot aḥar ha-ba'al* – the majority of conjugal acts – stem from the husband" (*Sotah* 27a). R. Pinchas ha-Levi Horowitz, *Panim Yafot, Parashat Aḥarei Mot,* s.v. *ervat aḥotekha,* observes that since we find no statement in early-day compendia limiting the rule to demonstrable frequency of access, the rule seems to apply even if the couple were known to have secluded themselves only once. *Panim Yafot* interprets the *rov,* not as

the husband is halakhically regarded as the father of any child born to his wife. That, however, is only a *prima facie* assumption, subject to rebuttal.

A countervailing consideration is the biblical principle of *yakkir* that arises from Deuteronomy 21:17, "... rather, he shall recognize the first-born to give him a double portion...."[2] At the very minimum, that halakhic rule accords the husband authority to disclaim paternity of a child otherwise presumed to be his by declaring a younger child to be the firstborn and thereby establishing the status of the older child as a *mamzer*. Thus, the effective rule is presumption of a paternal-filial relationship with regard to progeny born to a lawfully wedded wife unless disclaimed by the putative father. Neither the principle of *rov* nor the rule of *yakkir* pertains in the case of a child born to an unwed mother when there is otherwise no presumption of paternity.

Many authorities significantly limit the ambit of *yakkir*:

1. *Ba'al Halakhot Gedolot* limits the credibility of the father to the circumstances explicitly spelled out in Deuteronomy 22:15–17, i.e., the father does not directly deny paternity but recognizes a

---

a reference to frequency of access, and hence frequency of intercourse, but a somewhat different notion to the effect that the majority of sexually active women are impregnated by their husbands. In effect, *Panim Yafot* interprets "*rov be'ilot*" as "*rov be'ulot*."

2 For a discussion of the nature of the father's credibility see sources cited in *Encyclopediah Talmudit*, XXIV (Jerusalem, 5760), 503–504 as well as R. Joseph Rosen, *Ẓofnat Pa'aneaḥ*, *Hilkhot Issurei Bi'ah* 15:12 and R. Naftali Trop, *Ḥiddushei ha-Granat*, *Ketubot*, no. 37. *Bet Shmu'el*, *Even ha-Ezer* 6:26 and 7:15; *Shev Shem'ateta*, *shem'ata* 2, chap. 20; and *Avnei Milu'im* 6:5 maintain that the rule of *yakkir* applies even if the husband has no personal knowledge but relies upon his wife's account. The Jerusalem *bet din*, *Piskei Din*: *Dinei Mamonot u-Birurei Yuḥasin*, VIII, 382, expressed doubt with regard to whether such credibility extends to a husband whose knowledge is based upon DNA analysis. *Bet Me'ir*, *Even ha-Ezer* 6:13; *Teshuvot Bet Shlomoh*, *Even ha-Ezer*, no. 74; *Teshuvot Ḥavaẓelet ha-Sharon*, no. 20; and R. Eleazar Menachem Shach, *Avi Ezri*, *Hilkhot Yibum* 3:4, disagree with the fundamental position and rule that the husband's credibility is limited to allegations based upon his own knowledge.

younger son as his firstborn thereby implicitly denying that the older child is his.

2. *Ri'az*, following *Sefer ha-Makhri'a*, no. 64, cited by *Shiltei Gibborim*, *Kiddushin* 78b, limits the credibility of the father to situations in which the father acknowledges paternity but asserts that the child is a *mamzer* for reasons other than having been born of an adulterous relationship, e.g., the issue of a consanguineous union. This is also the position of *Yam shel Shlomoh*, *Kiddushin*, 4:15.[3]
3. *Tosafot Rid*, *Kiddushin* 74a and *Bava Batra* 128b, maintains that the husband's assertion is given credence only if it is not contradicted by his wife.
4. Many authorities maintain that the husband's credibility is limited to an allegation that his wife was forcibly raped but that he has no credibility to claim the child is the issue of consensual adultery. In the latter case, his declaration is regarded by those authorities as suspect. Since a willful adulteress may not consort with her husband, the husband's statement is suspect because he may be motivated by a desire for divorce.[4]
5. *Teshuvot Shivat Ẓion*, no. 6, asserts that Rambam maintains that the father's credibility is limited to an assertion regarding a fetus but that he lacks credibility once the child has been born and has acquired a *ḥezkat kashrut*, i.e., an attendant presumption of legitimacy. R. Akiva Eger, *Ḥoshen Mishpat* 277:7 and *Teshuvot R. Akiva Eger*, no. 128, s.v. *od* and *hashmattot*, nos. 110 and 115; as well as *Teshuvot Ḥatam Sofer*, *Even ha-Ezer*, I, no. 76, s.v. *ve-hineh*, express an opposing view to the effect that the father has no credibility with regard to a fetus.[5]

---

3 Citing this controversy the Jerusalem *bet din* ruled that the usual situation in which a husband disclaims paternity creates a situation of halakhic doubt with the result that the child is a *safek mamzer*. See *Piskei Din shel Bet ha-Din le-Dinei Mamonot u-le-Birur Yahadut*, IV, 324.

4 See *Tevushot Ḥavaẓelet ha-Sharon*, *Even ha-Ezer*, no. 10; *Teshuvot Mishkan Aryeh Kiryat Arba*, no. 17; *Teshuvot Maharsham*, IV, no. 26; *Teshuvot Imrei Yosher*, II, no. 114; and *Piskei Din Rabbaniyim*, V, 104. Cf., the contradictory opinion of *Avi Ezri*, *Hilkhot Naḥalot* 14:6.

5 See also R. Chaim Halberstam, *Divrei Ḥayyim*, *Hilkhot Naḥalot*, no. 4;

6. *Teshuvot Ḥatam Sofer, Even ha-Ezer,* I, no. 13, observes that the strength of the father's testimony cannot be stronger than the testimony of eyewitnesses. Thus, since witnesses must testify solely on the basis of actual knowledge, but not on the basis of conjecture or circumstantial evidence, the father must similarly testify on the basis of knowledge rather than on the basis of an unsubstantiated surmise or circumstantial evidence.
7. Similarly, asserting that the father's credibility can be no greater than the credibility of two witnesses, *Ḥatam Sofer, Even ha-Ezer,* I, no. 76, s.v. *u-bar min dein,* followed by *Teshuvot Binyan Olam,* no. 6, sec. 11, maintains that the father has no credibility in situations in which it is in the father's self-interest to deny paternity. That view is contradicted by *Tashbaẓ,* II, no. 90, and *Teshuvot Rivash,* no. 41, who extend that credibility to the father even when his assertion is in the context of a denial of an obligation of child support.[6]

R. Naphtali Zevi Judah Berlin, *Teshuvot Meshiv Davar,* III, no. 8; R. Joseph Rosen, *Mikhtavei Torah,* no. 187; and R. Baruch ha-Levi Epstein, *Mekor Barukh,* I, no. 40. Cf., R. David Friedman, *Yad David,* chap. 9, sec. 79, note 5.

Regarding the father's credibility during the first forty days of gestation see R. Shalom Mordecai Schwadron, *Teshuvot Maharsham,* IV, no. 26; R. Judah Tabak, *Erekh Shai, Even ha-Ezer,* no. 6; *Mekor Barukh,* I, no. 40; as well as R. Chaim Samuel Lopian and R. Eleazar Menachem Shach, *Sefer Sakotah le-Roshi,* ed. R. Issachar Kalman Bergman (5763), II, 62–65.

Perishah, Ḥoshen Mishpat 277:15, cites earlier authorities who maintain that the father has no credibility until seven days after birth. See also *Encyclopediah Talmudit,* XXIV (Jerusalem, 5760), 500, note 28.

6 It is likely that the issue is contingent upon the rationale underlying disqualification of an interested party. The disqualification of an interested party is predicated upon either 1) being regarded as a quasi-litigant who is disqualified, not because of lack of credibility, but because a person is his own closest relative or 2) his truthfulness is suspect. If a self-interested party is regarded as a quasi-litigant, the father, who is accorded credibility even though he is a "relative," should have credibility even in cases of self-interest; if an interested party is disqualified because of lack of credibility (unlike a relative who is disqualified simply on statutory grounds), it should follow that a father who has a personal interest should be disqualified. See *Piskei Din Rabbaniyim,* V, 349.

8. *Tosafot R. Akiva Eger, Yevamot* 2:26, expresses doubt with regard to whether the rule of *yakkir* extends to transgressors who are disqualified from offering testimony as witnesses.[7]
9. *Tosafot ha-Rosh, Kiddushin* 74a; Ritva, *Bava Batra* 127b; and *Nimmukei Yosef, Bava Batra* 127b, maintain that the father has no credibility if his statement incriminates him with regard to a willful transgression, e.g., the father declares that his son is a *ḥallal,* or a disqualified *kohen,* because the child was born of his union with a divorcée.[8]
10. Apart from the question of *mamzerut, Keẓot ha-Ḥoshen* 277:2, cites *Tosafot* and Rashbam who limit the father's credibility to situations in which the child is already presumed to be his son. This is also the position of *Tashbaẓ,* II, no. 19. Even though Ramban and Rosh disagree as does *Teshuvot Rivash,* no. 41, *Keẓot* rules in accordance with *Tosafot* and Rashbam.

II. INCOMPATIBLE BLOOD TYPES AND HLAS

1. Blood Test Evidence

Blood typing can serve to disprove paternity by applying principles of Mendelian genetics. Human beings are endowed with three basic blood types, A, B, and O, each of which indicates the presence of a different antigen on the surface of red blood cells. Every person

---

7 *Keẓot ha-Ḥoshen* 46:13 maintains that a person disqualified because of a transgression of religious law is not disqualified because of lack of probity but because of statutory disqualification rooted in the passage "You shall not put your hand with a wicked man to be a false witness" (Exodus 23:1). If so, the father would have credibility even if he is a transgressor. However, *Netivot ha-Mishpat* 46:17, asserts that all transgressors are suspected of a predilection for offering false testimony. According to *Netivot,* a father who is a transgressor would not have the credibility of *yakkir.* Consequently, a father found to have been a transgressor with regard to financial matters who is disqualified for reason of lack of credibility would be disqualified according to all authorities.

8 For both exceptions to the rule and conflicting authorities, see *Encyclopediah Talmudit,* XXIV, 512–513.

inherits two alleles, one from each parent, that become encoded on a single chromosome. The A allele and the B allele are codominant whereas the O allele is recessive. A person whose blood type is O must inherit two O alleles, otherwise the A or B allele would be dominant. A person whose blood type is A may have either two A alleles or one A allele and one O allele. In the latter case, the O allele is not expressed since the A allele is dominant. Similarly, if a person has type B blood he has either two B alleles or one B allele and one O allele. Since A and B alleles are codominant, a person may have type AB blood as a result of inheriting an A allele from one parent and a B from the other parent.

It is thus readily evident that a male whose blood type is AB could not be the father of a child with type O blood since all of his children would inherit either an A or a B allele from him. Even if the child inherited an O allele from the mother the child could not have type O blood because A and B are dominant. Identification of inherited blood antigens such as the Rh factor makes it possible further to exclude the possibility of paternity on the basis of applicable Mendelian principles.

Introduction in the 1970s of testing for human leukocyte antigens, or HLAs, added a further distinguishing factor that makes it possible to exclude with 80% effectiveness individual men as the father of a specific child. The genes responsible for HLA are responsible for antigen presentation to T cells. The HLA system is highly polymorphic, with well over 3,000 different alleles having been identified thus far. Analysis of HLA alleles is essentially a form of DNA testing and carries with it a remarkably high statistical probability. Unlike evidence based upon comparison of blood types, HLA testing can be used both to confirm and to disprove paternity.[9] The halakhic perspective regarding DNA evidence will be discussed in a later section.

The earliest reference in rabbinic sources to recognition of scientific,

9 James Robinson *et al.*, "IMGT/HLA and IMGT/MHC: Sequence Databases for the Study of Major Histocompatibility Complex," *Nucleic Acids Research*, vol. 31, no. 1 (January, 2003), pp. 311–314 and T.M. Williams, "Human Leuko-

or pseudoscientific, blood test evidence is found in *Sefer Ḥasidim* (Jerusalem, 5717), no. 232, in the report of an anecdote involving R. Sa'adia Ga'on. Leaving his pregnant wife at home, a person of significant means is reported to have journeyed to a distant land together with his servant. With the passage of time the master died leaving an extensive estate. The slave seized the master's estate claiming, "I am his son." A son born in the interim appeared and asserted that he was the rightful heir. The king charged R. Sa'adia with adjudicating the dispute. R Sa'adia directed each of the litigants to let blood into separate bowls. R. Sa'adia took a bone from the deceased and placed it in the slave's bowl of blood. The bone failed to absorb blood. R. Sa'adia then took the same bone and placed it in the son's bowl where it did absorb blood.[10] Thereupon, R. Sa'adia awarded the estate to the son whose blood was absorbed by the father's bone.[11]

The modern day parallel would be blood typing. Blood typing cannot establish a paternal relationship but incompatible blood types do conclusively establish the absence of a paternal relationship. Acceptance of evidence in the form of incompatible blood types in order to avoid the husband's obligation of child support has long been a subject of controversy.

The reported decision of R. Sa'adia Ga'on is widely cited as precedent for relying upon incompatibility of blood types. Nevertheless, the anecdote should not be regarded as either precedent or paradigm.[12]

---

cyte Antigen Gene Polymorphism and the Histocompatibility Laboratory," *Journal of Molecular Diagnosis*, vol. 3, no. 3 (August, 2001), pp. 98–104.

10 R. Sa'adia's test is problematic in that it involved use of a corpse for human benefit. For a discussion of whether mere visual observation is a forbidden form of benefit, see *Contemporary Halakhic Problems*, VI (Jersey City, NJ, 2012), 399–406. See also *Ḥazon Ish, Yoreh De'ah*, no. 208:7 and R. Joseph Shalom Eliashiv, *Kovez̧ Teshuvot*, I, no. 125. Unless it is assumed that all bloodletting is therapeutic, there would have been an additional problem with regard to "wounding" involved in obtaining a blood sample. See R. Moshe Feinstein, *Iggerot Mosheh, Ḥoshen Mishpat*, I, no. 103.

11 See *Teshuvot ha-Rosh, klal 78*, chap. 3. See also *Teshuvot ha-Rosh, klal 68*, chap. 23 and R. Simon ben Z̧emaḥ Duran, *Tashbaz̧*, I, no. 80.

12 R. Eliezer Waldenberg, *Z̧iz̧ Eli'ezer*, XIII, no. 104, sec. 3, comments that R.

R. Sa'adia was not sitting as a judge in a rabbinic court. He was delegated by a non-Jewish monarch to employ his sagacity in adjudicating a controversy in an *ultra vires* manner, perhaps even with the consent of the litigants. *Eliyahu Rabbah, Oraḥ Ḥayyim* 568:15, points to a comparable incident recorded in *Bava Batra* 58a reporting that a certain individual directed that his estate be given to one of his ten sons but did not specify which son. His wife declared that her husband was the biological father of only one of her sons, whom she identified. R. Bena'ah directed each of the claimants to strike the father's grave until the father would appear and reveal which of them is actually his son.

One of the sons refused to participate in that indecorous procedure and declined to ignominiously strike his father's grave. R. Bena'ah declared that son to be the sole heir and awarded him the entire estate.[13] *Eliyahu Rabbah* queries, if R. Sa'adia's test is available, why did R. Bena'ah not employ it to resolve the issue?[14]

2. Blood Type Evidence in Decisions of *Batei Din*

Acceptance of incompatibility of blood types as a means of disproving paternity and of DNA evidence for confirming or disproving paternity rest to a large extent upon common issues. Primary sources are a number of decrees of Rabbinical District Courts in Israel. The earlier cases include a discussion of the Haifa *bet din* authored by Rabbi Yisra'el Dov Rosenthal, dated 24 Ḥeshvan 5717, *Piskei Din Rabbaniyim*, II, 112–124 and a decision of the Tel Aviv *bet din* authored by Rabbi M. Schlesinger, dated 3 Av 5725, *Piskei Din Rabbaniyim*, V, 342–352. Both

---

Sa'adia's test cannot be employed in our day for two reasons: 1) it is not mentioned in the Gemara or in any halakhic work; and 2) we have no knowledge of the manner in which the test was carried out.

13 See Rashba, *ad locum*, who comments that, in the context presented, a *bet din* would have had total discretion in assigning the estate because none of the parties was in possession of the estate. See also *infra*, pp. 127–128.

14 Cf., *Reshash, ad locum*. In response it may be argued that R. Bena'ah did not have the halakhic option of disinterring the body for a postmortem analysis to support a claim of an heir. See *Bava Batra* 154a. Cf., R. Menasheh Klein, *Mishneh Halakhot*, IV, no. 164.

decisions address negation of paternity on the basis of incompatibility of blood types. DNA evidence is discussed in a decision of the *bet din* of Ashdod issued some twenty years later, on 19 Sivan 5742, authored by R. Shlomoh Deichovsky, *Piskei Din Rabbaniyim*, XIII, 51–68, and reprinted in *Sefer Assia*, V, 163–178.[15] Subsequent opinions by R. David Levanon and R. Yigal Lerer appear in *Shurat ha-Din*, V, 66–90 and *Shurat ha-Din*, IX, 44–93 respectively. A decision of R. Zevi Yehudah Ben-Ya'akov is published in his collected *piskei din*, *Mishpatekha le-Ya'akov*, V 136–137. The issue is also addressed in a number of decisions of the Jerusalem *bet din*, *Piskei Din shel Bet ha-Din le-Dinei Mamonot u-le-Birur Yahadut*, and published in its collected decisions, vol. II, 259–268; III, 323–325; IV, 319–320; V, 187–195 and 241–250; VI, 193–197, 217–228 and 245–249; and VIII, 379–383.[16]

The first authority to address the issue of halakhic reliability of blood tests was R. Ben-Zion Uziel. *Sha'arei Uzi'el*, II, *sha'ar* 40, 1:18, who dismisses the reliability of blood tests showing incompatibility between father and son in the context of litigation involving child

15 Additional unpublished decisions of the *Batei Din Rabbaniyim* include: Rabbinical District Court of Netanya, No. 29336/2, 20 Sivan 5771; Rabbinical District Court of Petach Tikvah, No. 870160/1, 28 Iyar 5772; Rabbinical District Court of Haifa, No. 954915–1, 20 Elul 5773; Rabbinical District Court of Haifa, No. 569557/8, 12 Adar 5775; Rabbinical District Court of Haifa, No. 565897/3, 25 Kislev 5777; Rabbinical Supreme Court of Appeals, No. 927675/4, 4 Kislev 5777; and Rabbinical Supreme Court of Appeals, No. 1060062/1, 29 Tevet 5779.

16 R. Shlomoh Aviner, *Assia*, No. 67–68, vol. 17, no. 3–4 (Shevat 5761), pp. 99–100, presents a valuable prècis of the various halakhic positions in conjunction with a discussion of whether one is required to disclose negative results of a paternity test. Overviews of the topic, both from the scientific and halakhic vantage points, are presented by Prof. Dov Frimer, *Shenaton ha-Mishpat ha-Ivri*, V (5738), 219–242 and Assia, No. 35, vol. 9, no. 3 (Shevat 5743), reprinted in *Sefer Assia*, V (5746), 185–209 as well as by Rabbi Mordecai Halpern *et al.*, *Teḥumin*, IV (5743), 431–450, reprinted in *Torah u-Madda*, X (Sivan 5744), 6–27. An English version of Professor Frimer's article, "Establishing Paternity by Means of Blood Type Testing in Jewish Law and Israeli Legislation," *ASSIA – Jewish Medical Ethics*, vol. 1, no. 2 (May, 1989), pp. 20–35.

support.[17] Rabbi Uziel and R. Ovadiah Yosef, *Yabi'a Omer, Even ha-Ezer,* no. 18, rely upon a variant reading of *Niddah* 31a that declares:

> There are three parties in [the conception of] man: the Holy One, blessed be He, the father and the mother. The father provides the white which develops bones, tendons, nails and the brain in its head, the mother the red which develops skin, hair, and the black [iris] of the eye and the Holy One, blessed be He, bestows the spirit, the soul upon him.

She'iltot de-Rav Aḥai Ga'on, Parashat Yitro, She'ilta 56 includes blood among the contributions of the mother[18] as does R. Elijah of Vilna in a gloss on *Niddah* 31a and in his *Bi'ur ha-Gra, Yoreh De'ah* 263:4. That declaration of the Sages apparently contradicts the scientific assumption that at least some portion of the blood can be traced to the father.[19]

Ostensibly, the halakhic applicability of that statement is the subject of controversy between *Shulḥan Arukh* and Rema, *Yoreh De'ah* 263:2. Death of two brothers subsequent to circumcision is presumptive evidence of hemophilia and since hemophilia is hereditary in nature those deaths preclude the circumcision of a third child who may be similarly afflicted. *Shulḥan Arukh* adds a clause indicating

---

17 *Sha'arei Uzi'el* is cited and relied upon in the decision published in *Piskei Din Rabbaniyim,* II, 123.

18 See also *Tosafot, Zevaḥim* 69b, s.v. *kal va-ḥomer.*

19 See *Piskei Din Rabbaniyim,* II, 124; Jerusalem *bet din, Piskei Din shel Bet ha-Din le-Dinei Mamonot u-le-Birur Yahadut,* VI, 195; *Teshuvot Dvar Yehoshu'a,* II, no. 13 and III, *Even ha-Ezer,* no. 5, secs. 2–4; *Mishneh Halakhot,* IV, no. 164; *Teshuvot Ẓiẓ Eli'ezer,* XIII, no. 104; R. Ovadiah Yosef, *Yabi'a Omer, Even ha-Ezer,* no. 13; and R. Israel Veltz, *Teshuvot Divrei Yisra'el, Even ha-Ezer,* no. 8. However, R. Shlomoh Zalman Auerbach is cited by Dr. Abraham S. Abraham, *Lev Avraham,* II, 17, and *idem, Nishmat Avraham,* III (Jerusalem, 5738), *Even ha-Ezer* 4:13, sec. 1, as dismissing that conclusion. R. Auerbach apparently regarded that statement as aggadic in nature and apparently also regarded the statement as limited to blood plasma but not necessarily inclusive of cells responsible for blood types. See also *Koveẓ Torah u-Madda,* X, no. 744, and *Shenaton ha-Mishpat ha-Ivri,* V, 219 and *Sefer Assia,* V, 195.

that the rule applies even if children are born to different mothers. Rema comments that some authorities disagree and limit the rule to the death of maternal siblings. *Taz, Yoreh De'ah* 263:1, and *Bi'ur ha-Gra, Yoreh De'ah* 263:4, explain that the controversy is rooted in the halakhic applicability of the statement in *Niddah* indicating that the blood of a child is derived from the father.[20] The authors of several decisions of Israeli rabbinical courts regard halakhic reliability of scientific evidence to be the subject of controversy between Rambam, *Guide of the Perplexed*, Part III, chap. 14, followed by R. Simon ben Ẓemaḥ Duran, *Teshuvot Tashbaẓ*, I, nos. 163–165, and R. Isaac ben Sheshet, *Teshuvot Rivash*, no. 447.[21] Rambam writes, "for the science of mathematics was deficient in their time; they did not speak with regard to mathematics on the basis of a tradition received from the prophets regarding such matters. Rather, [they spoke of such matters] because they were the wise men of those generations or on the basis of what they heard from the wise men of those generations."[22] Rivash, however, declares that scientists cannot be relied upon when they contradict the Sages of the Talmud.[23]

In point of fact, there is no clear evidence that such a controversy exists. Rivash, addressing pronouncements that are clearly halakhic in nature but which seem to be contradicted by scientific knowledge, firmly asserts that halakhic directives are not subject to change on the basis of scientific findings. Rambam clearly addresses matters of

---

20 See R. Moshe Sofer, *Teshuvot Ḥatam Sofer, Even ha-Ezer*, I, no. 136, who suggests a different basis for the ruling of *Shulḥan Arukh*.

21 See *Piskei Din Rabbaniyim*, II, 193; V, and XII, 57. See also *Teshuvot ha-Rashba*, I, no. 98 and *Teshuvot Rashbash*, no. 513.

22 See also R. Menachem Kasher, *Torah Shelemah, Bereshit* 1:21, secs. 150–151; R. Abraham Price, *Mishnat Avraham, Sefer Ḥasidim*, I, no. 291; *Mishmeret Ḥayyim*, no. 37; and R. Ephraim Fishel Weinberger, *Yad Efrayim*, no. 7, See *Yad Efrayim*, no. 7, sec. 8, who unconvincingly endeavors to show that there is a talmudic dispute with regard to this point.

23 See also R. Joseph Karo, *Teshuvot Avkat Rokhel*, no. 210; R. Joseph Rosen, *Mefa'aneaḥ Ẓefunot, ma'amar* 7, chap. 7:2; R. Abraham I. Kook, *Da'at Kohen*, nos. 79, 94, and 140–142; *idem, Ezrat Kohen*, no. 104; *Teshuvot Mishneh Halakhot*, V, no. 214; as well as sources cited in *Sefer Assia*, V, 193, note 55.

pure science exclusively in stating that the Sages had no *masorah* with regard to science. They clearly had a *masorah* with regard to Halakhah. Rambam does not at all address apparent conflicts between Halakhah and science.[24]

Rivash states, "We rely upon our Sages of blessed memory...for they received the truth and elucidation of the commandments one from the mouth of another back to Moses our teacher, peace be upon him." Rivash further criticizes the Greek and Muslim scholars "who spoke only on the basis of their conjecture or on the basis of some experiment without paying attention to the many doubts that may arise from that experiment."

Rivash does add a further comment to the effect that the scholars of antiquity disagreed with the Sages regarding many matters surrounding "the mystery of the creation." Rivash includes among them the statement of *Niddah* concerning the respective contribution of each parent whereas the scholars of antiquity maintained that material cause of the fetus comes from the mother while the function "of the seed of the father is to transform the seed of the wife," as is the function of rennet to milk. Rivash, however, stops short of asserting that non-halakhic statements of that nature are part of that received *masorah*.[25]

The statement of the Gemara, *Niddah* 31a, to the effect that blood is contributed to the fetus by the mother, was first adduced in conjunction with blood typing by R. Ben-Zion Uziel, *Sha'arei Uzi'el*, chap.1, sec. 18. Rabbi Uziel peremptorily dismisses the evidentiary value of

24 See J. David Bleich, "Scientific Hypotheses and Halakhic Inerrancy," *Contemporary Halakhic Problems*, VII (Jerusalem, 2016), 73–100. Cf., Rabbi Moshe Meiselman's book-length study of this issue, *Torah, Chazal and Science* (Jerusalem, 2013).

25 See *Teḥumin*, IV, 433. Many latter-day authorities state that scientists have credibility with regard to general scientific findings. See *Teshuvot Ḥatam Sofer, Yoreh De'ah*, nos. 158 and 175; *Pitḥei Teshuvah, Yoreh De'ah* 187:30 as well as sources cited by R. Yitzchak Ya'akov Weiss, *Teshuvot Minḥat Yiẓḥak*, I, no. 125, sec. 6 and no. 127, sec. 2 as well as by *Sedei Ḥemed, ma'arekhet tet, klal* 5. Cf., *Teshuvot Shem Aryeh, Even ha-Ezer*, no. 112.

blood tests in establishing paternity as being contradictory to the teaching of the Sages. Rabbi Uziel's opinion is cited in an early case brought before the Rabbinical District Court of Haifa.[26] The purpose of the proceedings in that case is somewhat unclear. The case involved three petitioners: a married couple and a third person who claimed to be the father of the child born to the wife during her marriage. Both husband and wife requested a divorce. Both the wife and the third party claimed that the latter was the child's biological father. All three joined in a petition for a declaratory judgment confirming their claim that the third party was the biological father of the child. The husband had no reason to presume that he was not the father of the child, but claimed to rely upon his wife's narrative. There seems to have been no dispute between the parties. The third party certainly recognized that if his claim to paternity were to be recognized he could be held liable for child support. The husband does not appear to have demanded custody or to have expressed a desire to avoid child support. Of course, the implication of their common position was that the child is a *mamzer*.[27] There is no indication of why the

---

26 This rejection of scientific evidence is also endorsed by R. Ovadiah Yosef in a decision of the Supreme Rabbinical Court of Appeals, dated 19 Tevet 5747 and published in Rabbi Yosef's *Teshuvot Yabi'a Omer,* x, *Even ha-Ezer,* no. 13 and in a responsum published in R. Shalom Messas, *Shemesh u-Magen,* III, *Even ha-Ezer,* no. 18. See also the letter of Rabbi Ovadiah Yosef published in *Piskei Din shel Bet ha-Din le-Dinei Mamonot u-le-Birur Yahadut,* V, 194; *Or Torah* (Tammuz 5757), pp. 779–780; as well as *Sefer Zikaron le-ha-Ga'on Rav Shiloh Refael* (Jerusalem, 5758), pp. 496–497. *Ẓiẓ Eli'ezer,* XIII, no. 104, similarly declares that results of "scientific tests" are not to be accepted when they contradict "the trusted tradition of the Sages." See also R. Israel Veltz, *Teshuvot Divrei Yisra'el, Even ha-Ezer,* no. 8; R. Joshua Aaronberg, *Dvar Yehoshu'a,* III, *Even ha-Ezer,* no. 5, secs. 2–4; and R. Shlomoh Aviner, *Assia,* No. 67–68, vol. 17, no. 3–4 (Shevat 5761), pp. 99–100; Menasheh Klein, *Mishneh Halakhot,* III, no. 143 and IV nos. 163–164; *Shemesh u-Magen,* III, *Even ha-Ezer,* no. 17; R. Moshe Sternbuch, *Teshuvot ve-Hanhagot,* I, no. 896; *Piskei Din Rabbanayim,* II, 123–124; and R. Abraham Akiva Rodner, *No'am,* IV (5761), 59.

27 That, however, need not necessarily be the case. The wife's paramour may have been a non-Jew; if so, the child would not be a *mamzer.* See *Even ha-Ezer* 4:29. See *Mishmeret Ḥayyim,* no. 301 and *infra,* p. 44, note 38.

parties petitioned for a declaratory judgment determining paternity of the child. Of course, an issue did exist with regard to amending the child's birth certificate to register proper paternal identity. That issue, however, is not mentioned nor is it at all clear that the *bet din's* finding would cause the Ministry of Health to amend the birth certificate.

The Haifa *bet din* did not find the scientific foundation of blood typing to be contradicted by the Gemara. Astonishingly, citing *Tur Shulḥan Arukh, Even ha-Ezer* 136, the *bet din* suggested that the hematological disorder responsible for fatality as a result of circumcision might be the result of improper conjugation of the blood caused by "weakness of the blood vessels."[28] Furthermore, they opined that the Gemara's statement is limited to blood plasma but does not necessarily extend to cells or genes that may well be contributed by the father.[29] Nevertheless, the primary finding of the *bet din* was that legal ramifications of paternity cannot be adjudicated "on the basis of scientific principles that change from period to period."[30] Much later, in a concurring opinion to a decision of the Rabbinical Supreme Court of Appeals, No. 927675/4, 4 Kislev 5777, R. Eliyahu Heishrik declared that a *bet din* would have no choice but to ignore the results of a DNA test that contradicted the already accepted testimony of witnesses.[31]

Other authorities adopted a diametrically opposite position. In a letter reproduced in *Assia*, V, 196–197, dated 2 Sivan 5714, R. Isaac ha-Levi Herzog declares in quite forceful language that science has conclusively established the reliability of blood test evidence and that it should be accepted as dispositive by rabbinical courts.[32] R. Chaim

---

28 See also *Piskei Din Rabbaniyim*, V, 350–352. Cf., *Sefer Assia*, V, 194.

29 *Nishmat Avraham*, III, *Even ha-Ezer* 4:13, sec. 1, observes that the Gemara may be referring to red blood cells whereas HLA testing includes white blood cells which may not be part of the "red" material contributed by the mother.

30 The Haifa *bet din* rejected a claim of denial of paternity on the basis of the principle of *yakkir* because it was based upon unsubstantiated conjecture and conclusions rather than upon actual knowledge. See *Teshuvot Ḥatam Sofer, Even ha-Ezer*, I, no. 13.

31 See *infra*, pp. 152–155.

32 See also *Yad Efrayim*, no. 7, p. 91.

David Regensberg, *Mishmeret Ḥayyim,* no. 37, accepts blood test results as incontrovertible proof that the husband could not be the father of the child whose paternity is in dispute.[33] R. Abraham Price, *Sefer Ḥasidim,* I, *Mishnat Avraham,* no. 291, is similarly prepared to accept well-grounded evidence as conclusive.[34]

R. Ovadiah Hedaya, *Yaskil Avdi,* V, *Even ha-Ezer,* no. 13, cites an earlier unpublished decision of the Rabbinical Supreme Court of Appeals, dated 5 Iyar 5714, directing the parties to undergo blood tests. The *bet din* indicated that if the tests conclusively established an absence of paternity it would exempt the husband from child support.[35]

Later, a more nuanced position was espoused by the Rabbinical District Court of Tel Aviv, *Piskei Din Rabbaniyim,* V, 350–351, in an opinion dated 3 Av 5572. That case involved a husband's contention that he should not be held liable for child support on the grounds that he was not the child's father. The Tel Aviv *bet din* failed to find that science has conclusively established that a child can acquire a blood type solely by inheriting it from a parent. The *bet din* regarded any presumption to that effect to be a statistical probability based solely

---

33 See *supra,* p. 25, note 39.

34 R. Shlomoh Zalman Auerbach is cited in Dr. Abraham S. Abraham, *Nishmat Avraham,* III, *Even ha-Ezer* 4:35, sec. 6, as having stated:

> However if this test becomes [The Hebrew is ambiguous and might be rendered as "becomes" or as "is."] widely known and accepted in the entire world as true and certain on the basis of many clear-cut experiments, it is logical that it may be relied upon also for purposes of Halakhah.

Particularly in light of Rabbi Auerbach's earlier announced view that such evidence cannot be accepted with certainty, as cited by *Nishmat Avraham, Even ha-Ezer* 4:13, sec. 1, and *Sefer Assia,* V, 195, note 61, it is not clear to this writer that those criteria have been met. See *infra,* note 57. Cf., R. Mordecai Halpern, *Assia,* No. 67–68, vol. 17, no. 3–4 (Shevat 5761), p. 101.

35 There is nothing in Rabbi Hedaya's discussion indicating that the blood test findings would be recognized by the *bet din* as conclusive proof. As recognized by the Tel Aviv *bet din,* blood type incompatibility may establish only doubt with regard to paternity in order to counter a claim for child support. Cf., *Sefer Assia,* V, 197 and R. Shlomoh Aviner, *Assia,* No. 67–68, vol. 17, no. 3–4, (Shevat 5761) p. 100. For a discussion regarding whether the husband can compel testing of the child see *infra,* section VI.

upon the fact that no one has ever been found to possess a blood type different from both parents. As such, all that can be concluded is that in the majority of cases such a phenomenon does not occur.[36] Ordinarily, a *rov*, i.e., a majority of that nature would be dispositive.[37] However, presumption of paternity is also based on a *rov*, *viz.*, so long as a husband has access, the majority of the wife's conjugal acts are with her husband as partner. As indicated, a disclaimer of paternity on the basis of incompatible blood types is supported only by application of the principle of *rov*. But, when the child is born to a married woman there exists a contradictory *rov* that serves to identify the husband as the father. In effect, the two principles of *rov* cancel one another. In a petition for child support, the burden of proof is on the plaintiff. If the results of a blood test are not regarded as disproving paternity with certainty, those results can serve only as countervailing evidence against the presumption of the husband's paternity. But, since child support can be demanded of the husband only if the plaintiff's burden of proof is substantiated with certainty, there can be no such award in the face of blood types shown to be incompatible.

In a matter not involving child support, the Jerusalem *bet din*, *Piskei Din le-Birur Yahadut*, III, 324, cited a gloss of R. Akiva Eger, *Yevamot* 4:20, sec. 46, ruling that in a matter involving conflicting *rovs* a *ḥazakah* in the form of behavior and comportment is decisive. Accordingly, in cases in which the child has been publicly regarded as the issue of a married couple, the child is not to be considered a *safek mamzer*. R. Elchanan Wasserman, *Koveẓ Shi'urim, Bava Batra*, sec. 81, demonstrates that the question of whether *ḥazakah* is dispositive in a case of contradictory *rovs* is a controversy among early-day authorities. In light of the controversy a *bet din* could not hold the father liable for child support even in such circumstances.

---

36 See also *Piskei Din shel ha-Bet Din le-Dinei Mamonot u-le-Birur Yahadut*, V, 191–195 and 248–250 and VIII, 382–383; *Bet Hora'ah* of R. Samuel Woszner, *Teḥumin*, XXI (5761), 121–123; *Divrei Mishpat*, VI, 132. Cf., R. David Levanon, *Shurat ha-Din*, V, 69 and *Piskei Din shel Batei ha-Din ha-Rabbaniyim*, No. 927654/4, 4 Kislev 5777.

37 Cf., however, *infra*, p. 220, note 87.

A finding that the *rov* established by the presence of incompatible blood types is contradicted by an antithetical *rov* in the form of *rov be'ilot* would have been sufficient to nonsuit a plaintiff claiming child support on the grounds that the question of paternity remains unsettled. The Tel Aviv *bet din,* however, found additional grounds auguring against the father's denial of paternity. *Tosafot, Ḥullin* 11b, s.v. *kegon,* points to the fact that the mother enjoys a *ḥezkat ẓadeket,* i.e., a presumption that she is a "righteous" woman who would not engage in an adulterous act. In light of the presence of contradictory expressions of *rov,* neither *rov* is dispositive. The *bet din* concluded that the mother's *ḥezkat ẓadeket* should govern and lead to a conclusion confirming the husband's paternity. The *bet din* added what it regarded to be a somewhat novel finding to the effect that, in a situation in which the mother's comportment has compromised her *ḥezkat ẓadeket,* incompatibility of blood types would render the child a doubtful *mamzer.*

However, the Tel Aviv *bet din* was not at all sanguine with regard to application of the mother's *ḥezkat ẓadeket* as the deciding criterion. *Maharsha, Ḥullin* 11b, comments that later in its discussion the Gemara establishes that the possibility of forcible rape can never be excluded. If so, the mother's *ḥezkat ẓadeket* cannot lead to exclusion of the possibility of a conception resulting from rape. Consequently, the mother's *ḥezkat ẓadeket* could not dispel doubt resulting from a conflict between a *rov* based upon incompatible blood types and the *rov* of *rov be'ilot.*

Despite the *bet din*'s conclusion regarding doubtful paternity, the *bet din,* while recognizing that child support cannot be awarded against the husband in instances of doubt, refused to issue a decision regarding the doubtful legitimacy of the child and stated that "because blood testing is a novel matter and has as yet not been clarified and is not found in [the writings of] decisors" the *bet din* would not make a final determination with regard to the child's legitimacy.[38] The clear

38 The Tel Aviv *bet din* declined to extend credibility to the father on the basis of *yakkir* because of the positions of *Ri'az, Ba'al Halakhot Gedolot, Tosafot*

implication is that if DNA evidence suffices to generate a doubt a *bet din* would be forced to declare the child to be a doubtful *mamzer*. As will be shown subsequently, some later scholars concluded that such a determination would be unwarranted.[39]

III. DNA EVIDENCE IN ESTABLISHING PATERNITY

Putting aside the statement of the Gemara declaring that the mother is the source of the fetus' blood, a much stronger case could be made for acceptance of incompatibility of blood types as an absolute proof of non-paternity than can be made for acceptance of DNA evidence. The empirical evidence indicating that a child's blood type is inherited from one of its parents leads to formulation of a scientific hypothesis explaining why that must be the case. Assuming that no disconfirming instance of a father and child having incompatible blood types has ever been detected, there would be strong reason to accept the principle, not simply as a *rov*, but as an absolute rational principle establishing that such incompatibility can never exist.[40] If so, that hypothesis would represent a scientifically demonstrated immutable law of nature that has predictive validity. In contradistinction, DNA evidence indicating that two DNA prints belong to the same person because no two individuals share identical DNA[41] is no more than an

---

Rid and the authorities who maintain that self-interest in seeking to avoid child support disqualifies the father's testimony as cited *supra*, note 27 and accompanying text. The *bet din* also discussed the likelihood that the father might be a non-Jew, particularly in a city in which a majority of males are non-Jews, in which case the child is not a *mamzer*. See *Piskei Din Rabbaniyim*, v, 248–289. See also *supra*, p. 40, note 27.

39 See *infra*, section v, pp. 68–71.

40 Although there are no reported cases in the scientific literature it would appear to be the case that the father might be a chimera having two separate blood types. See *supra*, p. 8, note 15, for a report of a British woman having both type O and type A blood.

41 Surprisingly, this is essentially correct even with regard to identical twins. Formerly, differences between identical twins could be discovered only on the basis of cumbersome whole-genome sequencing which revealed differences

empirical generalization from which no exception has been found but with regard to which science has not succeeded in formulating an explanation for why that must be so. Consequently, the absence of any two individuals possessing identical DNA must be regarded as a remarkable coincidence rather than the result of an immutable law of nature. Much as is the case with regard to fingerprints, there is no basis for declaring the strength of DNA evidence to be greater than that of a *rov*.

If one assumes that the statistical probability that two people have identical DNA prints is so remote that it may be ignored and that two such prints can be precisely matched, DNA analysis can effectively verify that the two prints have a single source. DNA evidence demonstrating a parental relationship – or any other familial relationship – is another matter entirely. Parents and children demonstratively do not have identical DNA prints. Although DNA analysis can be employed to establish parentage with an extremely high probability the underlying rationale is complex. The fundamental premise of the DNA verification of parentage paradigm is that all heritable information passed from

---

in a very limited number of Single Nucleotide Polymorphisms (SNPs). See J. Weber-Lehmann *et al.*, "Finding the Needle in the Haystack: Differentiating Identical Twins in Paternity Testing and Forensics by Ultra-Deep Next Generation Sequencing," *Forensic Science International: Genetics*, vol. 9 (March, 2014), pp. 42–46. Later a process was developed involving the study of DNA fragments modified with sodium bisulfite and subjected to methylation. The results show different DNA methylation patterns. See Jose Javier Marqueta-Gracia *et al.*, "Differentially Methylated CpG Regions Analyzed by PCR-High Resolution Melting for Monozygotic Twin Pair Discrimination," *Forensic Science International: Genetics*, vol. 37 (November, 2018), pp. 1–9. More recent studies show that MicroRNAs (miRNAs) can be sued to discriminate between identical twins. MicroRNAs are non-coding RNA molecules that exist in a variety of eukaryotic cells that serve to regulate gene expression. See Chen Fang *et al.*, "MicroRNA Profile Analysis for Discrimination of Monozygotic Twins Using Massively Paralleled Sequencing and Real-Time PCR," *Forensic Science International: Genetics*, vol. 38 (January, 2019), pp. 23–31 and Chao Xiao *et al.*, "Differences of MicroRNA Expression Profiles Between Monozygotic Twins' Blood Samples," *Forensic Science International: Genetics*, vol. 41 (July, 2019), pp. 152–158.

parents to offspring is contained within a complex molecule called deoxyribonucleic acid. The DNA paradigm is made up of a set of concepts which describe the structure of DNA and the way in which it functions as a repository of genetic information.

The structure of DNA is similar to a long, twisted ladder. The sides of the ladder, which are composed of phosphate and sugar molecules, are linked by "rungs" consisting of pairs of molecules called "bases." The order of the four bases along the DNA ladder, known as the DNA sequence, constitutes a genetic code. This code carries the information required for producing the many proteins which make up the human body. Most sections of the DNA ladder vary little from one individual to another within a given species. Certain sections, however, are variable or polymorphic, meaning they may take different forms in different individuals. These polymorphic sections are the basis of DNA typing. A sequence of bases which is responsible for producing a particular protein is called a gene. Some genes are polymorphic, i.e., they have two or more different versions called alleles. For example, the genes responsible for producing proteins and antigens in the blood are polymorphic; consequently, they produce a number of distinct blood types in the human population.

The DNA ladder can be disassembled in various ways. The long chain of DNA molecules can be broken into shorter fragments. Also, the two sides of the DNA ladder can "unzip" into two single strands of DNA. A single, unzipped strand of DNA is attracted to other single strands. Two strands which can pair up together according to the base-pair rule are called "complementary strands." Such strands will gravitate toward each other and "zip" together to create a double-stranded molecule in a process called "hybridization."

The DNA molecule consists of two strands wrapped around one another forming a double helix. Within the backbone formed by this double helix are the small, molecular groups or bases that link one strand to the other. There are four such nucleotides, generally referred to by their initials A, T, G and C. The bases are paired according to the "base-pair rule." Due to electrical forces mutually attracting A to T and G to C, the A on one strand only pairs with T on the other and the G bonds only to C. A molecule of DNA is extremely long and may have millions of pairs of bases. The two complementary strands will gravitate toward each other and zip together to create a double-stranded molecule in a process called hybridization.

One writer has suggested that it may be helpful to think of the bases as four colors, azure, tangerine, green and cyan, strung on a necklace in a particular order. A molecule of DNA is like two necklaces wrapped together, with the azure bead from one always touching the tangerine on the other and a green bead always matched on a cyan. In order to obtain a second double necklace with beads in the same order as the original it is necessary always to pull the strands of the two necklaces apart and to give each strand to a separate craftsman. The two craftsmen can then take the two single stranded necklaces and fashion a new strand with complementary colored beads. The result will be two double stranded necklaces whose beads are in the same order as in the original duplex necklace.

Each cell divides into two cells in this fashion, reproducing the original chromosomes within a human. Humans have 23 pairs of chromosomes. At conception each parent contributes a single specialized cell that has only 23 chromosomes rather than the full complement of 23 pairs of chromosomes. At fertilization these two cells – the ovum and the sperm – combine to form a cell with the full complement of 46 chromosomes – one set of 23 contributed by the father and the other set of 23 contributed by the mother. This single cell divides to form two cells with equivalent sets of chromosomes.

DNA analysis involves examination and comparison of fragments of DNA within a chromosome. Bases within each chromosome are frequently arranged in a particular repetitive sequence. Each repeated sequence contains between eleven and sixty bases. The points of sequence of base pairs within a chromosome vary from individual to individual. Those polymorphisms are inherited. Since variations in the DNA at any given site are inherited, if a child possess a variation that the mother lacks, the variation must have been contributed by the father. If the husband lacks the variation he cannot be the father; if he possesses that variation he is a possible father. DNA testing involves examining DNA acquired from a mother, a child and the putative father. The DNA is sequenced, i.e., the order of all base pairs are determined.

It is relatively easy to disprove paternity on the basis of DNA analysis. A positive determination of paternity depends upon a sufficient number of sequences matching those of the father. Many people might share any particular sequence of base pairs but the greater the number of matches of sequenced base pairs the less likely it becomes that some individual shares each of those sequences. The statistical probability that some other man is the father becomes infinitesimally small.[42]

Moreover, in addition to the considerations noted earlier,[43] there are a number of objective factors that may affect the results of DNA analyses, rendering them less than foolproof. One such factor is the possible occurrence of unequal crossing-over during spermatogonial or oogonial miosis. If this takes place close to, or at the site where, restriction enzyme cleavage would normally occur it will lead to the appearance of a banding pattern in the child's DNA profile different from that expected on the basis of analogy of parental DNA. The frequency of unequal crossing-over has been determined through surveys of families where parentage is not in dispute. Those studies show that an average of one offspring fragment in three hundred cannot be detected in either parent. This circumstance could lead to the erroneous conclusion that the biological parents are not related to the child.[44]

---

42 For comprehensive discussions of DNA testing in determining parentage see Harry D. Krause, "Scientific Evidence and the Ascertainment of Paternity," *Family Law Quarterly*, vol. 5, no. 2 (June, 1971), pp. 252–281; Thompson and Ford, "DNA Typing: Acceptance and Weight of the New Genetic Identification Tests," pp. 45–108; D.H. Kaye, "Presumptions, Probability and Paternity," *Jurimetrics*, vol. 30, no. 3 (Spring, 1990), pp. 323–349; and D.H. Kaye, "DNA Paternity Probabilities," *Family Law Quarterly*, vol. 24, no. 3 (Fall, 1990), pp. 279–304.

43 See *supra*, pp. 3–6.

44 See A.J. Jeffreys, "Highly Variable Minisatellites and DNA Fingerprints," *Biochemical Society Transactions*, vol. 15, no. 3 (June, 1987), pp. 309–317.

A second problem can arise from occurrence of mutation in gamete-forming cells if a mutation occurs in a restriction-enzyme cleavage site on a chromosome. It will result in a unique DNA fragment in an offspring's profile and thereby confuse parental determination.

A third factor that can produce an ambiguous situation is the formation of a zygote in uniparental disomy, i.e., both members of a particular numbered chromosome pair are derived from one parent. In the first such verified case, which did not involve disputed parentage, the child inherited two identical copies of chromosome seven from her mother. Both mutations and uniparental disomy have a relatively rare rate of occurrence. But the fact that they can and do occur bolsters the conclusion that DNA testing can only establish a *rov* with regard to parentage.[45]

IV. DNA IN THE DECISIONS OF *BATEI DIN*

If the position formulated by the Tel Aviv *bet din* to the effect that, as a matter of Halakhah, blood type evidence cannot disprove paternity with certainty but serves only to establish doubt, the same is certainly true with regard to DNA evidence as well. In both cases the observed phenomena lead to an empirical generalization in the nature of a *rov* but cannot result in absolute certainty. Although, generally, *rov* would be sufficient to resolve matters of paternity, in the case of a married woman it is contradicted by *rov be'ilot* with the result that the status of the child remains a matter of doubt. The countervailing argument that hematological evidence must be disregarded because the Sages declared that blood comes solely from the mother does not have a counterpart with regard to DNA. Accordingly, the many scholars who reject out of hand incompatible blood types as a factor in disproving paternity would have no reason to adopt a similar stance with regard to DNA evidence.

As shown earlier, *Tosafot* recognize circumstantial evidence as

45 See Louis Levine and Lawrence Kobilinsky, "DNA Typing and Parentage," *BioScience*, vol. 39, no. 9 (October, 1989), pp. 588–589.

definitive when such evidence is based on deductive inference from established laws of nature. A law of nature is a hypothesis that serves to explain the causal nature and hence the regularity of occurrence of particular phenomena. At least at this juncture of scientific development, a scientific hypothesis explaining the presumption that no two people can have identical fingerprints is simply not available. As is the case with fingerprint evidence, DNA proof begins with the assumption that every person's genotype is unique. But unlike fingerprints, there is good reason to assume that uniqueness is not coincidental. Unlike fingerprints that, insofar as we know, are not influenced by genetic factors, each individual DNA genotype is inherited. Those genotypes are passed on randomly much as tossing a coin randomly results in a head or a tail.

DNA proof is not predicated upon the notion that two identical samples cannot possibly come from two different individuals but rather that the likelihood that such is the case is infinitesimally small. Statistical probability is invoked, not to show that no other person's DNA can match an identified person's, but to show the high degree of statistical improbability that two individuals share repeated multiple random occurrences of multiple DNA. The issue is acceptance of statistical improbability of a common source, an improbability whose nature is readily grasped.

If the position formulated by the Tel Aviv *bet din* to the effect that, as a matter of Halakhah, blood test evidence cannot disconfirm paternity with certainty but serves only to establish doubt is accepted, the same would be true with regard to DNA evidence as well. In both cases the observed phenomena lead to an empirical generalization in the nature of a *rov* but cannot result in absolute certainty. Although, generally, *rov* would be sufficient to resolve matters of paternity, in the case of a married woman the *rov* established by DNA evidence is contradicted by *rov be'ilot* with the result that the status of the child remains a matter of doubt. The countervailing argument that the Sages declared that blood comes solely from the mother and hence paternal-filial blood type incompatibility is of no halakhic consequence does not have a counterpart with regard to DNA. Accordingly, the many scholars who reject hematological evidence out of hand would have no reason to adopt a similar stance with regard to DNA evidence.

Were it possible to test for every single sequence present in every chromosome and a one hundred percent match was found, parental identity would be established on the basis of deductive inference predicated upon on the rational principles of genetics. Ostensibly, such proof would be in the nature of deductive inference accepted by *Tosafot, Shevu'ot* 34a. Nevertheless, there would still remain the highly unlikely possibility that there might be another male whose DNA profile is identical to that of the putative father and that it is that individual who is, in fact, the biological father.[46] However, such a person would, in terms of genetics, be an identical biological twin. The possibility is not as far-fetched as it may seem. DNA analysis cannot exclude the existence of an actual identical twin who may have been separated at birth and whose existence is unknown.

Beginning with the *bet din* of Ashdod, *Piskei Din Rabbaniyim*, XIII, 51–68, the decisions of the various *batei din* that address admissibility of DNA evidence regard such evidence only as establishing a *rov*[47] and recognize, as did the Tel Aviv *bet din* with regard to hematological evidence, that it is contradicted by *rov be'ilot*. If so, since one *rov* is contradicted by another *rov*, the result should be an unresolved doubt.[48] The implications of establishing doubtful paternity are that a claim to child support must be denied but the status of the child, if born to a married woman, is that of a *safek mamzer*, or *mamzer*

---

46 It is this writer's impression that it is this quality of DNA evidence that R. Shlomoh Zalman Auerbach envisioned in the statement attributed to him cited *supra*, p. 42, note 34.

47 See also R. Ben-Zion Uziel, *Mishpetei Uziel*, II, 40:1, sec. 18; R. Eliezer Waldenberg, *Ẓiẓ Eli'ezer*, XIII, no. 104; R. Joshua Aaronberg, *Teshuvot Dvar Yehoshu'a*, III, *Even ha-Ezer*, no. 5; *Koveẓ Torah u-Madda*, X, no. 744; *Piskei Din le-Birur Yahadut*, IV, 319–320; and R. Mordecai Eliyahu, *Ginekologiyah, Genetikah, Poriyut ve-Yeludim le-Or ha-Halakhah*, ed. Joel Catane (Jerusalem, 5760), II, 110 ff.

48 The Jerusalem *bet din*, *Piskei Din shel Bet Din le-Birur Yahadut*, III, 125, maintains that *rov be'ilot* constitutes a "super *rov*" tantamount to certainty and hence is superior to the *rov* established by DNA analysis.

doubtful. However, the authors of those decisions advance a number of considerations in arguing that *rov be'ilot* should be discounted when contradicted by the *rov* inherent in DNA evidence. Those considerations would also serve to establish that the *rov* established by incompatibility of blood types should prevail against *rov be'ilot.*

1. DNA as Superior to *Rov Be'ilot*

A) THE AFFIRMATIVE VIEW

The Jerusalem *Bet Din le-Birur Yahadut,* III, 365, cites R. Chaim Shmuelevitz, *Sha'arei Ḥayyim, Kiddushin,* no. 27, who maintains that some forms of *rov* are of sufficient weight to establish particular facts with halakhic certainty. If so, that type of *rov* might be compelling even in financial matters. That is so, not because of the unique nature of the *rov,* but because they are the *sine qua non* of halakhic institutions they support in the sense that they serve as antecedent premises making the declared halakhic rules feasible. For example, there could not be capital punishment for homicide unless the victim is determined not to be a *treifah.* Thus, there could be no punishment other than upon reliance of the attendant *rov* that the majority of people are not *treifot.*

The biblical statute imposing capital punishment for the crime of homicide is possible only because the Torah mandates reliance upon that *rov.* In establishing culpability for murder, that *rov* has the halakhic effect of establishing the status of the victim with certainty. Similarly, the biblical provision of punishment for striking a father presumes halakhic recognition of a paternal relationship. Antecedent establishment of a paternal-filial relationship must be predicated upon *rov be'ilot.* If so, the biblical provision for punishment of a child who strikes his father has endowed that *rov* with certainty for halakhic purposes. Accordingly, maintains *Sha'arei Ḥayyim,* since the *rov* of *rov be'ilot* is endowed with certainty, it acquires a privileged status and prevails over other forms of *rov.*[49]

---

49 Cf., *Teshuvot R. Akiva Eger,* no. 107. See also *Piskei Din Rabbaniyim,* III, 320 and VIII, 382.

In a later decision the *Bet Din le-Birur Yahadut*, VI, 217–228, the *bet din* addressed the case of a man who claimed to be the father of a child conceived by a married woman. The putative father submitted DNA evidence supporting his allegation. Without providing a detailed analysis, the Jerusalem *bet din* invoked the principle of *rov be'ilot* in permitting the son to marry a woman of legitimate birth and reports that R. Ovadiah Yosef endorsed their decision.

Unlike the *batei din* of Tel Aviv and Ashdod that had earlier accepted scientific evidence as establishing only a *rov* rather than as being absolutely dispositive, Rabbi David Levanon, *Shurat ha-Din*, V, 58–69, in his discussion of child support, does not dwell upon the consideration that the evidentiary value of *rov* is canceled by an antagonistic *rov* based upon the husband's frequency of access, *viz.*, *rov be'ilot aḥar ha-ba'al*. Instead, he endeavors to show that the nature of the *rov* presented by DNA typing is either tantamount to the testimony of two witnesses or is of no value whatsoever at least insofar as financial claims are concerned, thereby avoiding a discussion of *rov be'ilot* in conjunction with that matter.

Rabbi Levanon's position is that, although DNA evidence can be regarded only as proof in the nature of *rov*, nevertheless, the statistical probability of identical DNA being present in unrelated people is so extremely remote that it constitutes a *mi'uta de-mi'uta* or a "minority of a minority," i.e., a miniscule minority. He further opines that a *rov* admitting of only infinitesimal exceptions is more compelling than a conventional *rov* and, since it constitutes a "super *rov*," it should be acceptable proof even in situations in which a conventional *rov* is not sufficient.

Nevertheless, Rabbi Levanon concedes that acceptance of a super *rov* for purposes of substantiating a financial claim is a matter of controversy among early-day authorities. The Gemara, *Gittin* 2b, declares that court scribes are presumed to be proficient in their knowledge of regulations pertaining to drafting a *get*. *Tosafot*, *loc. cit.*, s.v. *stam*, indicate that the exceptions are a *mi'uta de-mi'uta*.[50] *Pnei Yehoshu'a*

---

50 However, the Gemara, *Ḥullin* 11b, argues that the principle of *rov* is derived

infers that Rashi, *ad loc.*, disagrees and assumes that a super *rov* is no different from an ordinary *rov* and cannot be employed as satisfying a plaintiff's burden of proof in financial matters. Therefore, according to *Pnei Yehoshu'a*, Rashi found it necessary to interpret the Gemara as declaring that all scribes are proficient in the requisite regulations.

B) THE NEGATIVE VIEW

Rabbi Deichovsky advances a contradictory position in asserting that the *rov* established by DNA analysis is superior to *rov be'ilot*. Ramban, *Milḥamot ha-Shem, Kiddushin* 50b, distinguishes between a *rov* that is empirical in nature and a *rov* born of human conduct. The former reflects a natural state of affairs and is not subject to variation whereas the latter is dependent upon human action and is subject to an individual's determination to comport himself in accordance with the majority. Many authorities maintain that an empirical or natural *rov* prevails over a volitional *rov*.[51] If so, the empirical *rov* of DNA evidence would prevail over *rov be'ilot*.

There is, however, some evidence that *rov be'ilot* establishes a presumption greater than that established by other forms of *rov* for yet another reason. *Shulḥan Arukh, Even ha-Ezer* 4:14, rules that a child is not deemed to be a *mamzer* unless the husband lacked access to his wife for a full twelve months prior to the birth of the child. That is so despite the fact that the majority of women give birth upon culmination of nine months of gestation. In that situation as well, antagonistic principles of *rov* are present, *viz.*, *rov be'ilot* versus the majority of pregnancies that are no longer than nine months in duration. Ostensibly, the result should be that, if the husband lacked

from license to eat meat of an animal that has been properly slaughtered even though it is possible that the animal had a preexisting perforation of the esophagus. Failure to take that contingency into consideration shows that it is possible to rely upon a *rov*. The Gemara does not object that the possibility that the slaughterer's incision was superimposed upon an existing perforation is so slight that the presumption that there is no such perforation constitutes a super *rov* and hence we may deduce only that a super *rov* may be relied upon.

51 See *Shev Shem'ateta, shem'ata* 4, chap. 6.

access for longer than the nine months of normal pregnancy, the child should have the status of a doubtful *mamzer.* Since the child is regarded as being entirely without stigma, it must be the case that *rov be'ilot* prevails over other forms of *rov.* Why is that so?

The Gemara, *Ḥullin* 11a, seeks a scriptural basis substantiating the probative value of the principle of *rov.* The Gemara points to the various commandments involving a paternal relationship. Since there cannot be direct eyewitness testimony establishing such a relationship, the Gemara deduces that a paternal-filial relationship must be regarded as having been established on the basis of *rov be'ilot.*

R. Elijah of Vilna, *Bi'ur ha-Gra, Even ha-Ezer* 4:57, challenges the cogency of that inference. Might it not be the case that all commandments predicated upon establishment of paternal identity are limited to situations in which the paternal relationship is acknowledged by the father? As earlier noted, quite independent of the principle of *rov,* Halakhah recognizes a husband's prerogative to confirm or to disavow paternity. Granting the husband capacity to disavow paternity implies that there exists a presumption of paternity that will prevail unless paternity is disavowed. That presumption must arise from the principle of *rov be'ilot.* If so, argues *Bi'ur ha-Gra,* the principle of *rov* could readily be inferred from the rule of *yakkir* and further scriptural support is redundant.

As discussed earlier,[52] there is a fundamental controversy with regard to the ambit of the principle of *yakkir.* There is controversy among early-day authorities whether it applies when there is no prior presumption of paternity, as is usually the case when the parents have not been living as a couple. Rashbam and *Tosafot, Bava Batra* 134b, maintain that such credibility is extended only in the context of an established filial relationship, *viz.,* the child is known and accepted by the public at large as the child of a certain individual on the basis of behavior and comportment. Rambam, *Hilkhot Naḥalot* 2:14, and Rosh, *Bava Batra* 8:39, maintain that a person has such credibility even if there is no previous basis for assuming the existence of a

52 See *supra,* pp. 29–32.

paternal-filial relationship. *Keẓot ha-Ḥoshen* 277:2 rules in accordance with Rambam and *Tosafot.*

Citing R. Moshe Sokolovsky, *Imrei Mosheh,* no. 11, Rabbi Lerer asserts that even according to Rambam a person has no authority to declare a total stranger to be his bastard son. Rather, he has such credibility only when the paternal relationship has been antecedently established. He understands *Tashbaẓ,* II, no. 19, as stating that, according to Rambam, a person is accorded credibility to declare a younger child to be his first-born only for purposes of primogeniture but not for the purpose of rendering an older child a *mamzer.*

Bi'ur ha-Gra concludes that a husband has no independent authority to acknowledge paternity. The father's credibility is predicated entirely upon *rov be'ilot.* Thus, it is the father's authority that itself proves the principle of *rov.* Accordingly, it has been asserted that if DNA evidence is to be entertained as presumptively establishing its conclusions on the basis of *rov,* it follows that, when DNA tests contradict the father's acknowledgement of paternity, the father should not have credibility to declare the child to be a *mamzer* certain. Rather, the two antagonistic principles, *viz.,* the *rov* of DNA versus *rov be'ilot* should give rise to an unresolved doubt with the result that the status of the child would be that of a doubtful *mamzer.*[53]

In a situation in which the husband disclaims paternity (generally because he wants to avoid child support) but DNA evidence contradicts his assertion and shows a paternal-filial relationship, the halakhic resolution is somewhat different. If the matter involved simply one *rov* contradicted by another *rov* the child would be a doubtful *mamzer* in that situation as well.

However, if the husband disclaims paternity, the principle of *yakkir* confers credibility upon the husband in declaring his wife's child to be a *mamzer* certain despite the seemingly contradictory evidence of *rov be'ilot.* The situation appears to be paradoxical. The husband's credibility is anchored in the principle of *rov be'ilot* yet, in declaring

53 Cf., however, *infra,* section V, pp. 68–71.

the child to be a *mamzer*, the husband is denying the very *rov* upon which his credibility is predicated.

Rabbi Levanon contends that there is no paradox because there is no absolute contradiction between the husband's disclaimer and that which is established by the *rov*. *Rov*, by its nature, recognizes both an existing major class and an existing minor class. *Rov* assigns doubtful instances to the major class. Even when challenged by the husband, the *rov* remains correct with regard to the majority of situations. The husband's claim is only that he knows with certainty that this particular child is an exception to the rule of *rov* by virtue of being a member of the minor class. Thus the husband's assertion is entirely consistent with *rov be'ilot* being an accurate depiction of the majority of cases.

Accordingly, contends Rabbi Levanon, since the Torah extends credibility to a husband to declare that a particular child is not a member of the major class, i.e., the class of children sired by the husband, *mutatis mutandis*, the husband has the same standing to declare that the child is similarly not a member of another class defined by the principle of *rov*, *viz.*, the class of children who inherit DNA from a parent, but is a member of the minor class comprised of children who do not inherit DNA from a parent. Hence, even in the face of contradictory evidence, the child is to be regarded as a *mamzer* certain on the basis of the father's testimony. That conclusion is congruent with the assertion that, for purposes of Halakhah, DNA evidence is not regarded as reflecting an immutable principle and hence is not assigned absolute probative value, but is accepted as being true in at least the majority of instances and thereby establishing presumptive proof on the basis of *rov*.

That conclusion is subject to objection on two grounds. The Torah assigns credibility to the husband to contradict the particular *rov* of *rov be'ilot* by virtue of his claim to personal knowledge identifying an exception to that rule. But what evidence is there that it also assigns similar recognition to the husband's testimony in contradicting any other *rov*? Moreover, when a husband disclaims paternity, he contradicts the single *rov* of *rov be'ilot* and is granted credibility to do so but it does not necessarily follow that the husband is also accorded credibility when his declaration contradicts two separate *rovs*, *viz.*, *rov be'ilot* substantiated by a second *rov* based upon DNA evidence.

Rabbi Levanon, *Shurat ha-Din*, v, 58–69 and in a minority opinion of the Supreme Rabbincal Court of Appeals in a matter involving inheritance of an estate, No. 927654/4, 4 Kislev 5777, accepts DNA evidence as demonstrating that a paternal relationship does not exist in the majority of cases in which DNA of the presumed father does not match that of the child. Rabbi Levanon accepts a finding that a conclusion based on the evidence of *rov* is sufficient to negate a claim to child support, to share in the putative father's estate, for entitlement to the privileges of priesthood and to rebut a contention that a claim to filial identity would serve to negate any levirate obligations that might devolve upon the putative father's widow. Rabbi Levanon also concludes that, in the case of an unwed mother, if there is a match between a *mamzer* or a consanguineous relative and that of the child, the *rov* established by DNA evidence is sufficient to establish paternity and hence the child is to be declared a *mamzer vadai*, i.e., a *mamzer* certain, or an unequivocal *mamzer*, rather than a doubtful *mamzer*.[54]

2. DNA as *Umdena de-Mukhaḥ* or *Anan Sahadei*

Rabbi Levanon and Rabbi Yigal Lerer both assert that the concept of *rov* as invoked with regard to the idiosyncratic nature of DNA is different from other types of *rov* and consequently can be invoked to substantiate a monetary claim. The Gemara, *Bava Batra* 93a, states that Rav Aḥa's presumption that it is the aggressive camel that is responsible for the death of its companion is based upon a *ḥazakah*, i.e., an *umdena* or presumption in the nature of a common sense conclusion. Such a conclusion, although not a matter of certainty, rises to the level of a conviction similar in nature to the notion of "we are

54 Rabbi Levanon fails to address the possibility that the father may have been a non-Jew in which case the progeny are not *mamzerim*. Hence, in a locale in which a majority of males are non-Jews the child would not necessarily be a *mamzer*. Cf., *Mishmeret Ḥayyim*, no. 37, *supra*, p. 44, note 38 and *infra*, section v, pp. 68–71.

witnesses."[55] That standard is roughly equivalent to certainty "beyond a reasonable doubt."

Rabbi Lerer, *Shurat ha-Din*, IX, cites *Teshuvot Ḥatam Sofer, Even ha-Ezer*, I, no. 101, who states that the Sages disagreed with R. Aḥa because they did not accept the circumstantial evidence of a "kicking camel" as sufficiently compelling to generate an *umdena de-mukhaḥ* (self-evident *umdena*). Accordingly, they regarded such evidence as no stronger than a conventional *rov*. However, *Shulḥan Arukh, Ḥoshen Mishpat* 15:4, rules that "a proficient judge who is singular in his generation" may adjudicate on the basis of an *umdena de-mukhaḥ*. DNA evidence is certainly in the category of an *umdena de-mukhaḥ*.[56]

Rabbi Levanon further argues that the Sages who disagreed with Rav Aḥa and refused to assess tort damages against the owner of the kicking camel disagreed only because there are countless other camels in the world who might be responsible for the death of one of the camels. Thus, according to the majoritarian opinion of the Sages, there is a "majority" that contradicts the *ḥazakah*, i.e., our intuitive assessment, and generates halakhic doubt.

Consequently, argues Rabbi Levanon, were other camels to have been physically barred from coming into contact with the mauled camel, even the Sages would agree that responsibility must be assigned to the aggressive camel despite the lack of absolute proof. The Sages disagree with Rav Aḥa only because of a *rov* contradicting our intuitive presumption.

Tosafot, Shevu'ot 34a, s.v. *de-i*, rule that, according to Rav Aḥa, comparable circumstantial evidence is sufficient for conviction even in capital cases. If so, if the Sages disagree only because of a contradictory *rov*, when such a contradictory *rov* is not present they would concede

---

55 See *Teshuvot Maharik*, no. 129, who explains that the concept of *umdena* applies only to matters of intent but is not applicable in establishing matters that are practical in nature. Cf., *Kovez̧ Shi'urim*, II, no. 38.

56 Cf., *Ginat Veradim*, *klal* 5, chap. 1, who declares that a *bet din* cannot find for the plaintiff other than upon "an assessment recorded in the Talmud or upon an exceedingly compelling *umdena* (*umdena de-mukhaḥ tefei*)." DNA evidence certainly meets even that higher threshold.

that an *umdena* of such nature is sufficient for conviction in capital cases as well. However, as noted earlier, Me'iri and *Yad Ramah* disagree in maintaining that even conclusive and irrefutable circumstantial evidence is not admissible. Wherein lies the controversy?[57]

The controversy certainly centers upon the question of whether eyewitness testimony is a *sine qua non* in criminal cases because the Torah has decreed that even absolute certainty is insufficient in the absence of eyewitness testimony. A comparable situation exists in which two persons witness a criminal act but do not see each other, *viz., edut meyuḥedet.* There can be no question of the truth of the witnesses' testimony but the requirement for eyewitnesses includes a requirement that the witnesses witness each other in addition to witnessing the act. In civil matters there is no such requirement because "knowledge" in the nature of certainty is sufficient.[58]

Rabbi Levanon asserts that a *rov* in the nature of *rov be'ilot* is also more than a *rov* – it actually constitutes an *umdena* or *anan sahadei.* Indeed, the Palestinian Talmud, *Kiddushin* 4:8, describes a husband's paternity as established on the basis of *ḥazakah* rather than on the basis of *rov be'ilot.* Rambam, *Hilkhot Issurei Bi'ah* 1:20, follows the Palestinian Talmud in stating that all consanguineous relationships are established on the basis of *ḥazakah* "even though there is no absolute proof." R. Chaim of Volozhin, *Teshuvot Ḥut ha-Meshulash,* no. 5, comments that the *ḥazakah* depicted by the Palestinian Talmud is identical to the *rov be'ilot* of the Babylonian Talmud. The Palestinian Talmud is simply stating that a *rov* of that nature rises to the level of *umdena* or an *anan sahadei* and hence is categorized as a *ḥazakah.*[59]

---

57 For a possible analysis of the controversy see the thesis advanced by R. Chaim Shmuelevitz, *Sha'arei Ḥayyim, Kiddushin,* no. 37, discussed *infra,* pp. 259–260.

58 Thus, in civil matters two witnesses need not even testify to a single act. If one witness testifies to a loan extended one day and the second testifies to the same amount of money loaned on another day, they constitute two witnesses to a single obligation. Each one has "knowledge" of a loan. Together they satisfy the two-witness rule with regard to knowledge of at least a single loan.

59 Rabbi Deichovsky takes note of the contradiction between the Babylonian Talmud's establishment of a paternal relationship on the basis of *rov be'ilot* and

A similar *ḥazakah* is the *ḥazakah* that a person does not pay a debt before it is due. That *ḥazakah* is also born of an awareness that the vast majority of people comport themselves in that manner and thereby creates a presumption with regard to human conduct.[60]

The term "*ḥazakah*" is used in such contexts in the sense of "common knowledge." Such common knowledge is born of our awareness of the nature of the marital relationship, *viz.*, that a husband enjoys frequency of access, coupled with the presumption posited by the Gemara, *Yevamot* 35a, that a woman who engages in an extramarital liaison takes measures to assure that she not become pregnant. Those factors establish with near certainty the "common knowledge" that the husband is the father of all children born to his wife. Although a *rov* cannot be invoked in support of a monetary claim, a *ḥazakah* is dispositive in such matters. In the absence of contrary evidence, such a *ḥazakah* leaves no room for doubt and hence can be relied upon even in support of a monetary claim. Consistent with that thesis, Rabbi Levanon explains that DNA evidence (and logically, fingerprint evidence as well) constitutes a "super *rov*" that rises to the level of *anan sahadei* and hence is acceptable for all purposes.

Rabbi Levanon suggests that the underlying concept is the subject of a controversy between the *Keẓot ha-Ḥoshen* 46:8 and *Netivot ha-Mishpat* 46:8. A found object must be restored to its rightful owner if the latter can identify it by means of a *siman*, i.e., a distinctive mark or feature, the presence of which would not be known to others. *Tosafot, Ḥullin* 96a, s.v. *planya*, comment that evidence in the form of a *siman* is of no avail in an attempt to compel a person to disgorge an object if the person in possession claims that the object in dispute was not a lost object that he happened to find but that he is the original rightful owner. *Keẓot* observes that, although eyewitnesses are competent to identify a defendant on the basis of direct observation of his countenance, they cannot do so by means of a *siman*, i.e., by

---

the Palestinian Talmud's invocation of the concept of *ḥazakah* establishing the same position and asserts that the latter term is used simply to indicate that the *rov* arises from conventional behavior. Cf., p. 256, note 20.

60 See *Bi'ur ha-Gra, Ḥoshen Mishpat* 78:17.

identification of a particular birthmark or other individual feature, no matter how distinct. Similarly, argues *Keẓot,* no *siman* is sufficient in itself to establish a claim of ownership in a suit against a person in possession; a *siman* is sufficient only when the person in possession acknowledges that the object was found, i.e., that his possession is legally meaningless insofar as a claim of title is concerned.

Netivot disagrees and points to the fact that a promissory note is actionable against the obligee on the basis of the assumption that the person bearing that name is the debtor named in the instrument. There is no need for the witnesses on the note to offer testimony confirming the identity of the named debtor on the basis of physical recognition. In the absence of known existence of another person bearing the same name, identification by means of a given name and a patronym constitutes a *siman muvhak.* A *siman muvhak,* rules *Netivot,* although not acceptable as evidence in penal proceedings, is sufficient to support a monetary claim. *Tosafot's* comment to the contrary, asserts *Netivot,* must be understood as limited to an ordinary *siman.* The distinction lies in the fact that in criminal matters there is a statutory requirement for eyewitness testimony whereas knowledge regarded as certain, however it is acquired, is sufficient in adjudicating financial disputes.

Rabbi Levanon regards DNA evidence to be in the nature of a *siman muvhak* and hence, according to *Netivot,* acceptable for matters such as substantiating a claim for child support. Nevertheless, Rabbi Levanon acknowledges that, in light of the contradictory position of *Keẓot,* a *bet din* could not award child support on the basis of such evidence.

3. Multiple Applications of *Rov*

The general rule in a civil case is that a plaintiff cannot secure an award on the basis of *rov.* Thus, for example, absent contextual evidence, a person who purchases a bull that proves to be aggressive cannot invalidate the sale on the grounds that such an animal is not suitable for farm work even though the majority of purchasers seek to acquire animals for that purpose rather than for slaughter.[61] *Hafla'ah, Ketubot*

61 See *Bava Batra* 92b.

15b, points to a seeming inconsistency in the application of *rov*. The father of a young woman unjustly accused by her husband of committing adultery subsequent to *eirusin*, i.e., the preliminary marriage ceremony, but before consummation, is fined one hundred silver coins payable to the father.[62] The existence of a paternal relationship, and hence the father's monetary claim, can be established only on the basis of *rov*. Similarly, the owner of an ox that has been gored is entitled to compensation for the animal's full value despite the fact that, were it possible to demonstrate that the animal is a *treifah*, its value would be far less. That provision is based upon the fact that the majority of animals are not born with a congenital anomaly nor have suffered a trauma that would render the animal a *treifah*, whose meat is forbidden.

Hafla'ah responds by formulating the thesis that *rov* can not be applied only when invoked specifically for purposes of exacting financial compensation. However, when ancillary religious issues are also in question, *rov* may be invoked for all purposes.[63] The reasoning is that acceptance as evidence for purpose of religious law is acknowledgement of an empirical fact; logic then dictates that the same fact be recognized in civil matters as well. Establishing that an animal is not a *treifah* is necessary for religious matters far removed from the question of the animal's market value; consequently, its market value for purposes of tort recovery is that of a healthy animal. Establishment of paternity is significant for a host of non-monetary purposes. Consequently, paternity is recognized as having been established for financial matters as well.

---

62 See Deuteronomy 22:13–16.

63 See also *Teshuvot R. Akiva Eger, mahadura tinyana*, no. 129; *Ḥiddushei Ḥatam Sofer, Bava Kamma* 27b; *Yeshu'ot Ya'akov, Yoreh De'ah*, no. 1, sec. 2; and *Binyan Ẓion*, 1, no. 104. R. Abraham Benjamin Samuel Sofer, *Teshuvot Ktav Sofer, Yoreh De'ah*, no. 145, demonstrates that the position of *Hafla'ah* is reflected in the position of *Tosafot, Bekhorot* 20a, s.v. *ve-Rabbi Yehoshu'a*, but is contradicted by the view of Ramban and Rosh, *Ketubot* 15b. R. Ovadiah Yosef, *Moriah*, Sivan 5739 cites a number of other early-day authorities who disagree with the position of *Tosafot*, including Rashba, Re'ah, Me'iri and *Shitah Mekubbeẓet, Ketubot* 15b as well as *Maggid Mishneh, Hilkhot Issurei Bi'ah* 15:28.

Shev Shem'ateta, shem'ata, 4, chap. 8, earlier expressed the same concept in somewhat different terms on the basis of analogy to the probity of a single witness.[64] The testimony of two witnesses is required in order to convict a person of a capital or corporal transgression. Nevertheless, the testimony of only a single witness is sufficient to establish that a piece of meat is non-kosher and may not be consumed. Rambam, *Hilkhot Sanhedrin* 16:6, rules that if a single witness testifies to the forbidden nature of a food product the appropriate punishment may be administered, provided that two witnesses subsequently testify to the act of consumption. Punishment can be imposed only upon the testimony of two witnesses who have observed the prohibited act, but the antecedent status of the object used in committing that transgression is entirely distinct from the issue of punishment and can be established even by a single witness. Similarly, status as a father or as a non-*treifah* may be determined antecedently by means of *rov*. Once such status is established for other purposes it is recognized for monetary purposes as well. Thus, argues Rabbi Levanon, since DNA is sufficient in establishing identity on the basis of *rov* for a variety of matters entirely dissociated from financial affairs, it may also be accepted for determining financial issues.[65] *Hafla'ah* goes

---

64 A similar preposition is advanced by *Teshuvot R. Akiva Eger, mahadura tinyana,* no. 108.

65 Rabbi Lerer, *Shurat ha-Din,* IX, questions whether, assuming the father can determine the status of the child on the basis of the principle of *yakkir,* there is indeed any other issue that is to be decided simultaneously with the issue of child support that would make it possible to apply *Hafla'ah*'s position regarding simultaneous application of *rov* for a monetary issue together with a non-financial issue.

Nevertheless, Rabbi Lerer finds one other issue regarding which the *rov* established by DNA evidence dispositive. An unwed mother has credibility to assert that her child's father was not a person in the category of those that would render the child a *mamzer. Bet Shmu'el, Even ha-Ezer* 6:31, rules that the child is also eligible to marry a *kohen*. However *Bet Me'ir,* in concluding remarks to *Even ha-Ezer* 6, citing *Teshuvot Rema,* no. 24 and *Teshuvot Maharshal,* no. 17, expresses doubt regarding that matter. Similarly, *Teshuvot R. Akiva Eger,* no. 91, questions the child's status *viz-à-viz* marriage to a *kohen* when the putative father denies paternity. If so, argues Rabbi Lerer, the *rov* established by DNA

beyond *Shev Shem'ateta* in that *Shev Shem'ateta* speaks of antecedent determination for purposes of religious law on the basis of a single witness or *rov* and later applying that determination in adjudicating financial matters while *Hafla'ah* formulates his thesis as applying even when those disparate issues arise simultaneously. However, *Hafla'ah* himself concedes that his thesis is a matter of dispute among early-day authorities.

4. DNA Evidence as Sufficient to Compel an Oath Denying Paternity

Rabbi Lerer takes note of the right of a plaintiff to demand an oath denying a claim and its application to situations involving an allegation of paternity for purposes of child support and the impact of DNA evidence upon such demand.

The Sages assumed that a person would not institute a frivolous claim before a *bet din* that is entirely without basis in fact. Accordingly, they imposed a *shevu'at heset*, i.e., a rabbinic oath, upon the defendant compelling him to deny the basis of the claim under oath. Consistent with that rule, an unwed mother who claims child support should be entitled to impose an oath of that nature upon the alleged father compelling him to deny paternity.

Teshuvot Rivash, no. 41, distinguishes a suit based upon an allegation of paternity from other claims and rules that such an oath cannot be demanded for three reasons: 1) In establishing the principle of *yakkir* the Torah gave absolute credibility to a presumed father to deny paternity even when such denial confirms the child's status as a *mamzer*. The Sages, contends Rivash, imposed an oath only when both litigants are equally credible and the only issue is satisfying the burden of proof borne by the plaintiff. However, if the claim against the father fails, not because of lack of proof, but because of credibility extended to him by biblical law, the Sages did not attempt to compromise that

---

would be the determinant factor in rendering a daughter permissible to a *kohen*. Thus, the *rov* established by DNA would be simultaneously applicable to determination of both a non-financial issue and to child support.

credibility. 2) A plaintiff can demand an oath only if his claim is based upon an allegation advanced with certainty; he cannot demand an oath to deny a tentative or doubtful claim. The mother may claim with certainty that no person other than the named defendant could have caused her to become pregnant but she is not the claimant in her own right. It is the child who is entitled to support and, in instituting a suit against the father, the mother advances the claim on behalf of her child. The child is in no position to identify his father with certainty. 3) A defendant who concedes that he has cohabited with the plaintiff is nevertheless entitled to the defense that cohabitation is not proof of paternity but an oath to that effect cannot be demanded of him since he cannot attest to a matter that is doubtful. *Mishneh le-Melekh, Hilkhot Naḥalot* 4:2, adds that in some circumstances a defendant may be required to swear that he has no knowledge of any fact that would support the plaintiff's claim, but only because the plaintiff claims that the defendant is privy to such knowledge. However, in a paternity suit it is not possible for the cohabiting male to know with certainty that he is not the father. An oath cannot be demanded to attest to that which is already known.

Tashbaẓ, II, nos. 18–19, takes issue with Rivash in arguing that the mother may assert, *inter alia*, her own claim for compensation for her services as a wet-nurse. *Tashbaẓ* acknowledges that the Torah extends credibility to the father to acknowledge or to deny paternity but argues that such credibility is a) only with regard to matters pertaining to the son and b) only because the son cannot deny the father's assertion. However, the dispute for compensation is between the putative father and the mother and she is in a position to advance her allegation with certainty. In response to the argument that there cannot be an oath to support that which is already known, in this case that the defendant cannot know that he is not the father, *Tashbaẓ* replies that he may demand that, before allowing the case to continue, the mother state under penalty of *ḥerem* that she did not consort with any other male.

Citing *Teshuvot Ḥatam Sofer, Even ha-Ezer*, II, no. 105, *Pitḥei Teshuvah, Even ha-Ezer* 177:12, concludes that in light of the controversy an oath is administered in such circumstances only on the basis of custom and only if there are grounds (*raglayim la-davar*) for assuming that there was a sexual relationship between the parties.

It would appear that even if DNA evidence of paternity cannot be accepted as proof of an obligation of child support such evidence certainly constitutes *raglayim le-davar* that are more than ample to warrant imposition of an oath. In practice, *batei din* do not impose oaths but in lieu of an oath they do impose a solemn *ḥerem*[66] and when they are empowered to do so they may award a settlement equal to a third of the claim.[67]

V. STATUS OF THE CHILD

As shown earlier, the father has standing to declare his child to be a *mamzer* certain on the basis of the principle of *yakkir.* There is a significant controversy among early-day authorities with regard to whether a father enjoys credibility on the basis of *yakkir* even when his statement is contradicted by witnesses. Assuming that DNA evidence were to be accepted as proving or disproving a potential relationship with certainty Rabbi Lerer shows that there would be reason to question whether or not the same controversy would extend to a father's assertion in face of contradictory DNA evidence. However, assuming that DNA evidence is no stronger than a *rov* that issue is moot.

If, however, the husband affirmatively claims paternity in face of contradictory DNA or hematological evidence, the situation becomes more complex. The *rov* serves to establish that the child is a *mamzer.* Ostensibly, the principle of *yakkir* would serve to establish the father's standing to affirm paternity and confirm the legitimacy of the child despite the contradictory *rov*.

Rabbi Deichovsky formulates an argument to the effect that if a question arises with regard to a child's legitimacy on the basis of DNA evidence that doubt can be resolved on the basis of *ḥazakah.* The argument is that *rov be'ilot* and DNA evidence are contradictory

66 See R. Yechiel Michel Epstein, *Arukh ha-Shulḥan, Ḥoshen Mishpat* 87:18.

67 See R. Malkiel Tennenbaum, *Teshuvot Divrei Malki'el,* II, no. 133.

rovs that render a child a *mamzer* doubtful. However, if the child was accepted as the child of the husband on the basis of behavior and comportment, that in itself establishes a *ḥazakah* having the effect of resolving the doubt and establishing the husband as the father. That is so because, prior to the doubt created by DNA analysis, there existed a presumption of paternity based upon behavior and comportment in the wake of the father's earlier acknowledgment of paternity.

Rabbi Deichovsky rejects that position in arguing that a *ḥazakah* established in error is not a *ḥazakah*. To put the matter somewhat differently, he maintains that a *ḥazakah* based upon a presumption later shown to be erroneous must retroactively be recognized as an erroneous *ḥazakah*. The father's acknowledgement, his behavior *vis-á-vis* the child, as well as public perception of a paternal-filial relationship, all came about in error as established by later DNA evidence.

R. Ya'akov Eliezerov, another member of the Ashdod *bet din*, followed by Rabbi Levanon, in the latter's contribution to *Shurat ha-Din*, took issue with Rabbi Deichovsky's contention that DNA evidence has the effect of negating a previously established presumption of paternity based on *ḥazakah*. Although they concede that an erroneously established *ḥazakah* is of no effect, they nevertheless maintain that unless the *ḥazakah* is demonstrated with certainty to have been established in error it remains effective. When a presumption established by *ḥazakah* has not been disproved but has merely become a subject of doubt, the previously established *ḥazakah* has not been eradicated and therefore has not lost its efficacy. The *rov* reflected in DNA analysis, since it is contradicted by *rov be'ilot*, does not definitively demonstrate that the previous *ḥazakah* was established in error. Hence, the earlier *ḥazakah* remains effective and, consequently, the father retains credibility with regard to establishing or denying the legitimacy of the child by virtue of the principle of *yakkir*.

As noted earlier, the Tel Aviv *bet din* recognized the logical entailment of the issues of child support and *mamzerut*, i.e., that if DNA evidence is to be accepted as establishing paternity for purposes of child support DNA evidence should also be recognized for purposes of negating paternity with the result that the child must be regarded as a *mamzer.* On the other hand, if DNA analysis creates a doubt that cannot be resolved with the consequence that a claim for child support is dismissed only because the claim has not been established with certainty, in the case of a married woman, the same evidence should render the child a *mamzer* doubtful.

Later, in a decision of the Jerusalem *bet din, Piskei Din shel Bet ha-Din le-Dinei Mamonot u-le-Birur Yahadut,* V, pp. 187–193, Rabbi Shalom Messas makes the point that a *bet din* must perforce recognize that there are respected authorities who reject the position that DNA evidence must be accepted as a matter of certainty.[68] If so, as a matter of halakhic decision-making, recognition of the controversy prevents a *bet din* from according such evidence more than doubtful status.

Nevertheless, R. Shalom Messas declares that, although DNA evidence is sufficient to create doubt and hence to relieve the husband of obligatory child support, it does not lead to a determination that the child is a *mamzer* certain. *Bet Shmu'el, Even ha-Ezer* 4:29, declares that in the absence of the father's declaration that his son is a *mamzer,* a child known to have been born of an adulterous relationship is a *mamzer* doubtful rather than a *mamzer* certain.[69] Rabbi Messas explains that doubt arises because it is not known whether the wife's paramour was a Jew or a gentile. If the father was a non-Jew the child is not a *mamzer.*[70] Consequently, the status of the child is a *mamzer* doubtful. Rabbi Messas explains that such is the case even in a locale in which the majority of men are Jews. A number of authorities, including *Pnei Yehoshu'a, Kiddushin* 73a, maintain that, although *rov* is a deciding principle, it does not establish a prohibition with certainty. Matters that are decided on the basis of *rov* are prohibited on the basis of doubt rather than on the basis of certainty. With regard to biblical

---

68 See also R. Shalom Messas, *Shemesh u-Magen,* III, *Even ha-Ezer,* no. 17 and *Or Torah* (Tammuz, 5757), pp. 771–779.

69 Indeed, the wife has credibility to identify the child's father as a non-Jew and thereby legitimize the status of the child. See *Shulḥan Arukh, Even ha-Ezer* 4:29.

70 See *supra,* p. 44, note 38.

law only a *mamzer* certain is prohibited, but not a *mamzer* doubtful. It is indeed the case that the Sages prohibited as well marriage between a *mamzer* doubtful and a person of legitimate birth but they did not prohibit such marriage in cases of *sefek sefeka*, or "double doubt."

Consequently, argues Rabbi Messas if DNA evidence contradicts the presumption that the husband is the father the result is a double doubt: 1) DNA serves only as a *rov* establishing that in the majority of instances the husband is not the father, but the possibility remains that the husband is indeed the father. 2) If the husband is not the father perhaps the person who impregnated the wife was a non-Jew. A *safek mamzer* may not marry a woman of legitimate birth but a child whose *mamzerut* is a matter of *sefek sefeka* is not subject to such a restriction. In a letter appended to that decision, R. Ovadiah Yosef concurs in Rabbi Messas' conclusion.[71]

VI. REFUSAL TO AGREE TO DNA TESTING

Assuming that negative DNA evidence is sufficient to absolve the husband from the obligation of child support, in situations in which the husband does not deny paternity with certainty, is the husband entitled to demand a DNA test to substantiate the claim against him? *Teshuvot ha-Rosh, klal* 32, chap. 2. and *Shulḥan Arukh, Even ha-Ezer* 117:2, rule that a woman who has been found to be physically incapable of engaging in marital relations is not entitled to the financial benefits of the marriage. A husband who makes such an allegation may refuse to provide support and maintenance unless and until his contention is refuted by physical examination. Apparently, then, a defendant may demand that dispositive empirical evidence, which, if it exists, would be available upon investigation, be produced to support a claim against him.

71 See R. Ovadiah Yosef, *Or Torah* (Tammuz, 5757), pp. 779–780 and *idem*, *Sefer Zikaron le-ha-Ga'on R. Shiloh Refael* (Jerusalem, 5758), pp. 496–497, as well as Rabbi Yosef's responsum published in *Shemesh u-Magen*, III, *Even ha-Ezer*, no. 18.

However, that precedent serves to establish only that a defendant is entitled to demand a readily obtainable proof to support his denial of a claim against him when such evidence, if forthcoming, would establish the veracity of his denial with certainty. It does not necessarily establish a right to demand evidence that would only cast doubt upon the claimant's allegation. It is certainly true that, in order for a defendant to prevail, it is sufficient for him to produce evidence casting doubt upon the plaintiff's claim; the defendant need not prove his defense with certainty since the burden of proof is on the plaintiff. But there is no precedent establishing that the defendant may demand cooperation in producing evidence that merely raises doubt, but does not conclusively refute, the defendant's denial of the claim. Again, it is presumed that, halakhically, DNA evidence can only cast doubt upon the presumption of the husband's paternity that arises from *rov be'ilot* but that DNA evidence cannot conclusively refute the husband's denial of paternity.[72]

There is, however, a talmudic source that has a direct bearing upon this issue. The Gemara, *Bava Batra* 154a, records a dispute involving the sale of a parcel of real estate by an adolescent who died shortly thereafter. The seller's heirs sought to invalidate the sale upon the claim that the seller had the status of a minor because he had not developed pubic hair prior to his death. One of the litigants demanded exhumation of the body to establish whether or not the decedent had pubic hair and hence whether he had legal capacity to transfer property. From the ensuing talmudic discussion there emerges a principle to the effect that, when there is presumptive evidence favoring a litigant, the opposing party is not entitled to demand confirmation in the form of an examination to uncover further evidence that might either confirm or refute the claim.[73] Similarly, concludes Rabbi Levanon, when there

72 This issue was not addressed in the decision of the earlier-cited decision of the Rabbinical Supreme Court of Appeals. See *supra*, p. 44, note 38 and accompanying text.

73 The inference is from the Gemara's statement that, if the purchasers had an authenticated deed, that itself establishes a presumption of regularity in the transaction and consequently the demand for exhumation to confirm their

exists presumptive evidence of paternity in the form of *rov be'ilot,* the husband cannot demand cooperation in the form of DNA testing of the child[74] on the claim that such evidence might refute his denial of paternity.[75]

VII. CONCLUSION

As any epistemologist would attest, knowledge and ignorance are not dichotomous categories. Knowledge admits of subtlety and degree ranging from mere conjecture to absolute certainty. Legal systems demand varying degrees of certainty for diverse purposes. Halakhah posits variegated standards of evidence, each appropriate to the purpose for which it is employed. DNA analysis, when properly carried out, is not infallible but can establish an extremely high degree of certainty. *Teḥumin,* XXI (5761), 121–123, contains a concise statement in the name of the late R. Samuel ha-Levi Woszner of Bnei Brak detailing the manner in which DNA tests should be performed and the purpose for which properly conducted DNA analysis may be regarded as decisive and purposes for which it must be disregarded. It seems to this writer that those conclusions reflect the consensus of opinion of contemporary halakhic decisors. The statement fails to present a conclusion with regard to child support and omits reference to enforcement of an undertaking to be bound by the findings of a DNA test.

---

claim should be summarily dismissed. The same discussion establishes that when no evidence exists, i.e., the purchasers are in possession but have no substantiating proof of purchase, barring other considerations, the plaintiffs would be entitled to demand cooperation in an investigation to provide evidence substantiating their claim to invalidate the sale.

74 The additional argument advanced to the effect that a paternity test involves an invasive procedure that constitutes a form of "wounding" is simply incorrect. Unlike a blood test, a DNA sample can be obtained without invasion of the child's body.

75 Cf., R. Zevi Yehudah Ben-Ya'akov's discussion of compelling DNA testing to establish a right of inheritance in *Teḥumin,* XXII (5762).

Most significant is the statement that DNA evidence cannot establish status as a *mamzer* or be used to impose penal sanctions "even though from the scientific perspective [DNA] congruity is an absolute determination." That issue will be discussed in chapter 4. DNA evidence can be used for purposes of identifying body parts for burial and identity of a corpse for commencement of prescribed periods of mourning. The statement appropriately qualifies that conclusion in instances in which the deceased leaves a wife who must be declared a widow having halakhic capacity to contract a new marriage. When there is a surviving widow, Halakhah does not permit mourning rituals to commence until there is a finding that the wife is permitted to remarry. Use of DNA evidence to resolve the problem of an *agunah* and for purposes of inheritance will be discussed in chapters 3 and 5 respectively.

Chapter Three

Agunah

I. EVIDENTIARY STANDARDS

Jewish law posits two fundamental principles regarding marriage: (1) A woman lacks capacity to contract a polyandrous marriage; (2) a marriage can be terminated, and the wife's capacity to contract a new marriage restored, only upon death of her husband or divorce. A woman known to have been married retains the status of a married woman until there is halakhically cognizable evidence of termination of the marriage. Agonizing situations of *igun* arise in which a woman is "chained" in a marriage in the sense that she is the bereft of the privileges and the prerogatives of marriage but is not free to seek another consort. The most tragic cases of *igun* are those in which the husband is presumed to be dead but there is no satisfactory proof that death has actually occurred. The wife is left an *agunah*, i.e., "a chained woman," ensnared by marital bonds but bereft of consortium with her partner. The problem became the focus of renewed attention in the aftermath of the destruction of the Twin Towers of the World Trade Center on September 11, 2001, in which a large number of bodies were incinerated or were no longer identifiable.

Ostensibly, biblical law would apply the two-witness rule and permit remarriage only on the basis of the testimony of two qualified witnesses who testify to personal knowledge of the husband's death. In practice, rabbinic enactments sanction remarriage upon the testimony of a single witness, hearsay testimony or some limited forms of circumstantial evidence. Those enactments do not constitute a repeal, modification or variance of biblical law; rather they involve changing "facts on the ground" so that less restrictive rules of evidence become applicable. As stated by the Gemara, *Yevamot* 93b and 115a, the enabling principle is *ishah daika u-minseva*, literally, "a woman investigates and [then] marries." As the Gemara explains, a woman will not enter into a new marital relationship unless and until she is absolutely convinced that her husband is no longer alive. That is not to imply that such is the natural female wont. Quite to the contrary, the Sages enacted provisions that compelled women to become exceedingly cautious in remarrying, *viz.*, they legislated that, in the event of the reappearance of the first husband, the wife be forbidden to continue in a marital relationship with either of the two men, that future issue born of a relationship with either of the men be regarded as *mamzerim* and that she forfeits the *ketubah* together with all rights and prerogatives attendant upon a marital relationship. As explained by the Gemara, *Yevamot* 88a, a woman confronted by the stark prospect of such onerous consequences in case of error will exercise extreme caution in contracting a second marriage. The conditions legislated by the Sages served to ensure that no woman would remarry unless she were absolutely convinced that her first husband was no longer alive. The result is a *ḥazakah* equal in evidentiary probity to the reliability of two witnesses.

Rashba, *Ketubot* 3a, offers an alternative explanation in asserting that, when the relaxed rules of evidence are satisfied, the Sages remedied any resultant onerous error in declaring the husband to be deceased by employing their power to retroactively nullify the first marriage by confiscating the specie or other consideration whose conveyance to the bride is necessary for a marriage to come into existence. According to Rashba, the harsh conditions made consequent upon error in determining the husband's death were designed to ensure that the wife not take advantage of relaxed rules of evidence and the ensuing nullification of her marriage unless she herself was convinced beyond all doubt that her husband was indeed dead.

II. *SIMANIM:* IDENTIFICATORY MARKS

DNA evidence is not required in order to establish that death has occurred. Rather, it serves to establish the identify of a body when death is no longer subject to doubt. The evidence is used to establish the identity of a corpse rather than the husband's demise. In general, judicial proceedings cannot commence unless the parties are identified. The parties may declare their own identities or they may be identified by witnesses. Witnesses to an act, criminal or civil, testify not only to the act but to the identity of the actors, i.e., that the person appearing before the *bet din* is one and the same as the person who performed the act that has become the subject of judicial proceedings. The primary method of establishing widowhood is by means of testimony of witnesses who certify the death of the husband by testifying that they saw and recognized the corpse. Testimony regarding recognition of a corpse necessarily entails testimony that the witnesses had previously known the deceased and can identify the body on the basis of their recognition of the corpse as that of a particular individual known to them during his lifetime. Witnesses testify to the identity of a corpse based simply upon their innate power of recognition. Acceptance of testimony of that nature is predicated upon reliance upon the acknowledgement of the veridical nature of "*tevi'ut ayin*" or "discernment of the eye."

In many situations, either there are no available witnesses who knew the deceased while he was yet alive, or the corpse has deteriorated and is no longer recognizable. DNA, if acceptable for the purpose of establishing the identity of the deceased, would be of singular benefit in alleviating the plight of women who would otherwise be *agunot*.

The Mishnah, *Yevamot* 120a, seemingly excludes all forms of identification other than facial recognition: "There can be no testimony other than with regard to the countenance of the face, including the nose, even though there are identificatory marks on the body or clothing." The notion of "*simanim*," or identificatory marks, in conjunction with the identification of a corpse is related to the halakhic category of identificatory marks that suffice to establish a rightful owner's claim to lost property. That type of evidence suffices to establish proprietorship over lost property only because no other person with a claim of title is in possession of the lost object. *Simanim* do not suffice as evidence in other property disputes.

Nevertheless, the Gemara, *Yevamot* 120b, declares that the identificatory marks excluded by the Mishnah in establishing the identity of the corpse are limited to identificatory marks that are not "*muvhak*," a term best translated in this context as "exclusive" or "singular," but that a *siman muvhak* is acceptable for identification of a corpse. Thus, testimony regarding the presence of an identificatory mark that is highly unlikely to be present on another person's body or clothing would be sufficient to declare the wife to be a widow. Nevertheless, in apparent contradiction, Rambam, *Hilkhot Gerushin* 13:21, rules that a corpse can be satisfactorily identified only if the "forehead, nose and facial countenance" are extant and recognized, whereas identificatory marks on the deceased's body or clothing are not sufficient and even identification of a mole (*shuma*) on the body is insufficient to permit the wife to remarry. However, both *Maggid Mishneh* and *Kesef Mishneh* reconcile Rambam's ruling with the statement of the Gemara by declaring that Rambam intended to exclude only "exclusive" identificatory marks but not "extraordinarily exclusive" (*muvhak be-yoter*) identificatory marks. *Kesef Mishneh* adds that Rambam incorporates "*shuma*" in his ruling as an example of the type of identificatory mark that is excluded because, contrary to some authorities who regard *shuma* as more reliable, Rambam deems *shuma* to be merely an "ordinary" exclusive mark, but does not intend to exclude "extraordinarily" exclusive identificatory marks. That understanding of Rambam is reflected in the comments of a host of latter-day authorities.[1]

Left unclear is the precise distinction between a *siman muvhak* and

1 Cf., however, R. David ben Yaḥyah, cited by R. Elijah Mizrachi, *Teshuvot ha-Re'em*, no. 37, who understands Rambam literally and citing Rambam, *Hilkhot Naḥalot* 7:3, explains Rambam as ruling that a *siman muvhak* is fully acceptable insofar as biblical law is concerned, but that the Sages limited acceptable evidence in ruling that only the testimony of at least one witness

a *siman muvhak be-yoter.* R. Elijah Mizrachi, *Teshuvot ha-Re'em,* no. 38, recognizes that there is no identificatory mark that may not also be present on the body of another person but, to be acceptable, the mark must be such that the *siman* in question is "strange" and extraordinary to the point that every person "be certain in his heart that it does not exist in another person in that land and that it has never been heard that another person possessed such a *siman.*" *Teshuvot ha-Re'em* adds that such a limitation does not imply that there can never be an instance in which two people share a common identificatory mark. *Teshuvot ha-Re'em* observes that even the testimony of two eyewitnesses is not infallible but is accepted nevertheless. Hence, it is not surprising that *simanim* are also biblically acceptable even though they are not completely infallible.

Rabbenu Yeruḥam, *Ḥelek Adam ve-Ḥavvah* 23:3, rules that, for purposes of establishing a husband's death, only a singular *siman* in the nature of something certain (*barur*) "that cannot be found on another body" is acceptable. Taken literally, that statement can apply only to a null class because there is no conceivable way to determine that absolutely no other man exhibits an identical identificatory mark. *Teshuvot Mas'at Binyamin,* no. 63, cited by *Bet Shmu'el, Even ha-Ezer* 17:72, regards that statement to be in the nature of hyperbole and that Rabbenu Yeruḥam intended to describe the requisite distinguishing *mark* "as strange and greatly bizarre to the point that it cannot be found in another person other than one in a thousand or two thousand." Rabbenu Yeruḥam was understood literally by *Teshuvot Galya Masekhet, Even ha-Ezer,* no. 8 and *Shulḥan Arukh ha-Rav, She'elot u-Teshuvot,* no. 28, s.v. *e efshar,* but those authorities reject Rabbenu Yeruḥam's position as understood by them because of its extreme nature. *Teshuvot Mas'at Binyamin*'s "one in a thousand" standard is widely cited by latter-day authorities as the threshold level of acceptable statistical improbability.[2]

---

can be relied upon to the exclusion of even a *siman muvhak. Teshuvot ha-Re'em,* no. 38, refutes that interpretation of Rambam.

2 Cf., R. David ben Yaḥyah cited in *Teshuvot ha-Re'em,* no. 37, who categorizes

As a paradigm of an acceptable *siman,* Rashba, *Bava Meẓi'a* 28a, cites an example found in another context, *viz.,* "a hole next to a particular letter of a *get,*" that is acceptable for the purpose of returning the instrument to the wife for use as evidence that the divorce has been effectuated by delivery of the *get* to her because "there is no testimony clearer than this." *Teshuvot Mahari Bruna,* no. 53, offers "a hole piercing a single tooth from one surface to another" as an example of a *siman muvhak. Terumat ha-Deshen,* II, no. 224, portrays a "deeply sunken nose" as a *siman muvhak.*[3]

There is some dispute with regard to other physical anomalies. Me'iri, *Yevamot* 120a, describes an unnatural appendage or the absence of a limb as a *siman she-eino muvhak.* However, Ra'avad, cited by *Shitah Mekubbeẓet, Bava Meẓi'a* 26b and *Teshuvot ha-Rosh, klal* 51, no. 6, followed by Rema, *Even ha-Ezer* 17:24, regard a missing limb or an additional digit as a *siman muvhak.*[4]

Me'iri and *Maggid Mishneh* describe *simanim muvhakim* as the

---

a *siman muvhak* as an identificatory mark that is "strange and idiosyncratic (*zar u-muflag*) to the point that it is clear in everyone's mind that it is not at all to be found on another body in that land and that it has never been heard that another person had a comparable identificatory mark." That definition is probably narrower than the "one in a thousand" criterion posited by *Mas'at Binyamin.*

3 See also R. Israel Isserlein, *Terumat ha-Deshen,* I, no. 239.

4 A recent general survey reports that polydactyly, an additional digit, presents at a frequency of 1 in approximately 700 to 1,000 live births. See H. Ahmed, H. Akbari, A. Emami *et al.,* "Genetic Overview of Syndactyly and Polydactyly," *Plastic and Reconstructive Surgery Global Open,* vol. 5, no. 11 (November, 2017), p. 1. However, an earlier study showed that there is a wide disparity in the incidence of that anomaly between various ethnic groups and geographic populations. Frequency of occurrence ranges from .08% in Japan to 2.71% in Nigeria. The overall rate of occurrence is 12.68 per thousand for African Americans and 1.16 per thousand for Caucasians. Thus, polydactyly is roughly ten times more frequent among Blacks than among Caucasians. See Lewis B. Holmes, *Common Malformations* (New York, 2011), p. 152. See also W.H. Finley *et al.,* "Birth Defects Surveillance: Jefferson County, Alabama, and Uppsala County, Sweden, *Southern Medical Journal,* vol. 87, no. 4 (April, 1994), pp. 440–445. Thus, since the occurrence of an extra digit is less than one in a thousand it would not be considered a *siman muvhak.* It is, of course, quite

equivalent of eyewitness testimony by virtue of biblical law and accepted as such without doubt. The Gemara, *Bava Mezi'a* 18b and 27a as well as *Gittin* 28b, posits talmudic doubt with regard to whether *simanim* are valid as a matter of biblical law or are acceptable as establishing ownership of lost property solely on the basis of rabbinic legislation. Me'iri and *Maggid Mishneh* maintain that the talmudic controversy is limited to ordinary "*simanim muvhakim*" that later came to be known as "*simanim emza'im*," or "*simanim beinonim*," i.e., "intermediate identificatory marks."[5] The highest category of identificatory marks regarded as acceptable beyond cavil should appropriately be termed "*simanim muvhakim be-yoter*" or "extraordinary identificatory marks" but in the course of time have come to be termed "*simanim muvhakim*" in contradistinction to "*simanim emza'im*."

Unlike determining identity of a corpse in order to permit a widow to remarry that, because of the severe nature of the prohibition against adultery, requires *simanim* of the highest category, property may be returned on the basis of intermediate *simanim*. The talmudic controversy is whether such evidence suffices for return of lost property as a matter of biblical law or whether its acceptability is the product of rabbinic edict based upon the rabbinic power of confiscation (*hefker bet din*).

III. DNA AS A *SIMAN*

As noted in the earlier part of this discussion of DNA evidence,[6] *Kezot ha-Ḥoshen* 46:8 asserts that evidence in the highest category of *simanim* is tantamount to testimony of two witnesses and is sufficient as evidence to sustain a plaintiff's financial claim against a person in

possible that the earlier-cited sources reflect varying rates of occurrence among different Jewish populations.

5 *Teshuvot Ẓemaḥ Ẓedek, Even ha-Ezer,* no. 76., widely cited by later authorities, categorizes an intermediate identificatory mark as a characteristic whose frequency of occurrence is statistically no higher than "one in one hundred or in two hundred."

6 See *supra*, pp. 62–63.

possession. *Netivot ha-Mishpat* 46:8 accepts the categorization of the highest category of *simanim* as biblically acceptable evidence but nevertheless finds such evidence to be insufficient to support a financial claim against a *muḥzak* or person in possession.

It is within that framework that one must examine the status of DNA evidence.[7] DNA sequences are idiosyncratically unique to a

---

7 Writing within the context of the acceptability of blood typing in determining issues of paternity for purposes of consanguineous relationships and inheritance, R. Joshua Aaronberg, *Teshuvot Dvar Yehoshu'a,* III, *Even ha-Ezer,* no. 5, summarily dismisses acceptability of scientific evidence regarding genetic transmission of blood types. In espousing that position, he cites *Teshuvot Rivash,* no. 447. (Cf., *supra,* p. 38.) In the course of that discussion, *Dvar Yehoshu'a* asserts, not only that blood typing cannot be accepted as a *siman,* but that it fails to give rise to a doubt "even for purposes of stringency." *Dvar Yehoshu'a* dismisses scientific evidence as inadmissible even when it is not contradicted by talmudic sources.

In addition, *Dvar Yehoshu'a* claims that the Sages asserted that the situations in which they declared paternity to be doubtful as involving a doubt that can never be resolved. The Palestinian Talmud, *Yevamot* 11:7, discusses a situation involving a child born seven months after consummation of his mother's second marriage. The child might be the prematurely-born son of the second husband or a term baby fathered by the first husband. If the child smites either of those two men, he cannot be held culpable because each one is only a doubtful father. But what is the result if he strikes both of them? The issue is whether *hatra'at safek* (a doubtful or conditional admonition) is a valid admonition. It would certainly seem that the second act establishes culpability with certainty since with the act of smiting the second man it becomes clear that the son has committed a capital transgression in performing one of those two acts. Which of the two acts engenders culpability should be irrelevant since, although each of the two admonitions in and of itself is doubtful, nevertheless, in smiting the second man the son knows with certainty that he is now culpable for one of those two acts. However, the Palestinian Talmud rejects this thesis on the basis of the principle that "it is impossible to determine the matter." The standard commentaries interpret that statement as establishing a novel principle, *viz.,* that there can be culpability only if the transgressor knows for which of the acts he is being punished. An example lies in the case of a person who performs a forbidden act of labor on each of the two days of a festival observed in the Diaspora because of doubt. In that situation the day on which *Rosh Ḥodesh* was proclaimed later becomes known with certainty with the result that the transgressor becomes aware of which of

particular person and hence should qualify as a *siman* or an identificatory mark. If found to be tantamount to the highest category of *simanim,* not only would DNA evidence suffice to permit a widow to remarry but, according to *Kezot ha-Ḥoshen,* it would serve to establish paternal identity for purposes of child support as well. Clearly, the incidence of inaccuracy or error with regard to a properly performed DNA identification is far less than "one in a thousand or one in two thousand" posited by *Mas'at Binyamin.* Consequently, the accuracy of

---

the two acts engendered culpability. In the situation involving two possible fathers, the transgressor never discovers for which of the two acts he is held culpable and hence he cannot be punished. *Dvar Yehoshu'a* advances a novel interpretation in explaining that the Palestinian Talmud is not simply stating that, as a matter of fact, the transgressor will never discover which of the two men is his father because no means of determination was available but that it is impossible for him ever to know because, even if a scientifically accepted means of paternity testing were to become available, for halakhic purposes it would have no import.

As additional proof *Dvar Yehoshu'a* cites *Keritut* 17b. The Gemara establishes that a person who is confronted with two pieces of meat, one forbidden *ḥelev* and the second entirely permissible and, because the forbidden status of the *ḥelev* is unknown to him, proceeds to consume one of those two pieces of meat, he is required to offer an *asham taluy* as a sacrifice in tentative expiation of his possible transgression. (See *Keritut* 26b.) The Gemara explains that an *asham taluy* is appropriate only if it is possible that at some future time the status of the forbidden meat that he ate may be determined by as yet unavailable or unrecognized evidence. The Gemara states that, similarly, there is no obligation to offer an *asham taluy* if a person inadvertently struck one of the two men who might be his father. *Dvar Yehoshu'a* assumes that the Gemara is declaring that the rule applies not only in an era in which blood typing is unknown and, therefore, information regarding paternity will not become available during the lifetime of the transgressor but that such evidence, even when forthcoming, is of no consequence.

R. Ben-Zion Uziel, *Sha'arei Uzi'el, sha'ar* 40, chap. 18; R. Israel Veltz, *Teshuvot Divrei Yisra'el, Even ha-Ezer,* no. 18; R. Eliezer Waldenberg, *Ẓiẓ Eli'ezer,* XIII, no. 104; and R. Menasheh Klein, *Mishneh Halakhot,* III, no. 143 and IV, nos. 163 and 164, also refuse to accept the scientific basis of blood typing as a means of disproving paternity. Those authorities would probably dismiss DNA evidence as well. See also R. Moshe Sternbuch, *Teshuvot ve-Hanhagot,* I, no. 896 and *Piskei Din Rabbaniyim,* II, 123–124.

DNA evidence greatly exceeds the threshold of probability necessary to establish the status of DNA as a *siman muvhak be-yoter*.[8]

Nevertheless, R. Yigal Lerer, *Shurat ha-Din*, IX, 47, finds that not to be the case. Rabbi Lerer notes that DNA evidence, since it is not infallible, can be accepted only as a *rov* even though, statistically speaking, it may constitute a "super *rov*."[9] Nevertheless, he finds that DNA can be assigned no greater weight than that assigned to *simanim emẓa'im* or intermediate identificatory characteristics. Rabbi Lerer distinguishes between the nature of DNA as a *siman* and other types of *simanim*. Other *simanim* Rabbi Lerer categorizes as instances of "a natural *rov*, known or perceived by all," whereas the results of a DNA examination, based upon comparison of DNA samples, "is known only to the technician, since it is he himself who establishes the degree of evidence with regard to this test." The presence of a *siman*, he argues, can be confirmed or disconfirmed by all and sundry whereas in determination of DNA evidence others must rely on the judgment and testimony of a technician.

That distinction might appear artificial. Nevertheless, Rabbi Lerer explains that other forms of *umdena*, although based upon comportment of the generality of the populace, are a matter of public knowledge applied by a *bet din* to a particular situation. However, although the general principles of DNA analysis and statistical probability of accuracy are available to any person who interests himself in such matters, in any particular case it is not applied by the *bet din* directly; instead, the *bet din* must rely upon interpretation of the data by a

---

8 DNA is also categorized as a *siman muvhak* by R. David Levanon, *Shurat ha-Din*, V, 82–83; R. Zalman Nechemiah Goldberg, *Kol Ẓvi*, IV (5762), reprinted in *Yeshurun*, XII (Nisan 5762) and *Teḥumin*, XXIII (5763); R. Asher Weiss, *Teshuvot Minḥat Asher*, III, no. 87 and *idem*, *Oraḥ Mishpat* (Jerusalem, 5778), I, 182; and R. Eliezer Igra and R. David Levanon, Rabbinical Supreme Court of Appeals, No. 927675/4, 4 Kislev 5777. R. Joseph Shalom Eliashiv endorsed a decision of a *bet din* convened for the purpose of permitting a resident of Monsey, New York, whose husband perished in the World Trade Center attack to remarry. DNA evidence figures prominently in that decision but is not explicitly categorized as a *siman muvhak* and was also accompanied by other evidence. See *Yeshurun*, XII 506.

9 See *supra*, pp. 62–63.

technician. Since the *umdena* established by the *rov* is not immediately known to the *bet din*, argues Rabbi Lerer, DNA comparison cannot be accepted as the equivalent of eyewitness testimony.

It may be objected that, even accepting Rabbi Lerer's distinction, DNA evidence might be acceptable under certain limited circumstances, e.g., if the members of the *bet din* themselves acquire the technical proficiency necessary to perform DNA tests. Under those circumstances the *bet din* would be relying upon their own knowledge rather than upon the evaluation of an expert. Rabbi Lerer would probably counter that there is scant difference between reliance upon the expert skill of a technician and the *bet din*'s reliance upon their own technical expertise. In the latter case "the judge becomes the witness" but in both cases it is not the bare facts that establish the *rov* but the interpretation of the facts that establishes the *rov*. For reasons that he does not explicate Rabbi Lerer asserts that a *bet din* can act only upon facts conveyed to them but cannot interpret those facts.

If so, the objection can be stated in a more fundamental manner. Other instances of *rov* involve matters that become subject to what is tantamount to judicial notice. The *rov* is the *rov* and 1) requires no further investigation for its acceptance and 2) although there are exceptions to the *rov*, once it has been established, the *rov* itself, as a majoritarian principle, is not subject to error. As has been shown, DNA evidence is subject to some element of subjective judgment in determining the acceptable margin of deviation of variability in determining precision in measurement of alleles and is subject to at least some judgmental error in recognizing a match. It must be emphasized that it is not the likelihood of error in establishing a match or even the subjective nature of the judgment *per se* that diminishes the evidentiary standing of DNA, but it is those aspects of its nature that distinguish DNA evidence from the testimony of witnesses. DNA evidence is based upon judgment rather than solely upon testimony regarding a direct visual phenomenon.[10]

---

10 It is reported that DNA matching can now be performed by computer. If so, it might be argued that the element of subjective judgment is effectively eliminated. Nevertheless, it must be remembered that a "match" does not mean

R. Asher Weiss alludes to the fact that there is a fundamental difference between identification of a lost object or a corpse on the basis of *simanim* and reliance upon DNA for purposes of identification. *Shulḥan Arukh ha-Rav, Teshuvot,* no. 28, s.v. *ve-zu,* explains that the efficacy of *simanim* in identifying a lost object or an unidentified corpse is not contingent simply upon the unlikelihood that two persons or two objects would both manifest the same identificatory mark. That probability may be low, but not necessarily low enough to suffice for purposes of evidence. However, *simanim* are employed as evidence only in conjunction with another high improbability, namely, that two people or two objects not only possess an identical *siman* but also that both persons lost precisely those unique objects or that not only do two individuals share an identical distinctive mark but that the two people having the same mark disappear without a trace. In determining statistical probability of misidentification by means of *simanim,* there are two distinct probabilities, namely, a) common identificatory mark and b) loss of each object by different people or disappearance of two separate persons that must be considered. The probability of misidentification is equal to the probability of the first multiplied by the probability of the second, i.e., the probability of the existence of two items or two persons sharing a common identificatory mark multiplied by the probability that two people would lose objects having the same *siman* or multiplied by the probability that the identity of a person bearing that mark would be unknown at the time of his death. Such probabilities are highly remote. When the probability of such events occurring twice within a quite narrow timeframe is also considered, the resultant statistical probability of those chance occurrences occurring virtually simultaneously is so

---

absolute identity in all respects. Absolute identity does not exist. Identity of length, for example, is defined with allowance for a small band of deviation. See *supra,* pp. 3–5. The amount of allowable deviation is a matter of judgment. That judgment is programmed into the computer and, consequently, the computer's results must also be regarded as "subjective." Other factors affecting reliability of DNA reported in that discussion apply to computerized matching as well. See *supra,* pp. 3–12 and 49–53.

remote as to be absurd. It is even conceivable that the probability of such an occurrence is less than the probability of two unrelated persons possessing matching strands of DNA.[11]

---

11 Rabbi Weiss also argues that if *simanim muvhakim be-yoter* were accepted by the Sages as the equivalent of eyewitness testimony on the basis of *sevara,* as was the position of *Shakh, Ḥoshen Mishpat* 267:7, then DNA can also be accepted on the basis of *sevara*. However, since later decisors apparently fail to follow *Shakh*'s view with regard to this matter, the point is moot. See *infra,* p. 91, note 15.

R. Harel Devir and Eren Hendel, *Assia,* Nos. 107–108, vol. 27, no. 3–4 (Ḥeshvan 5778), pp. 60–62, argue that the mere certainty of DNA matching rises to the level of an *umdena de-mukhaḥ,* or clear circumstantial evidence. It is likely that R. Isaac Ha-Levi Herzog, in a letter cited by R. Aryeh Frimer and published in *Sefer Assia,* v, 196, also regarded DNA as a form of *umdena.* That surmise arises solely from the fact that Rabbi Herzog offers no analysis of the halakhic foundation of DNA evidence.

However, Rabbi Weiss does not regard *simanim* as a type of super *rov.* He accepts the position of those who maintain that *simanim* are biblically recognized as a novel type of evidence equivalent to the testimony of two witnesses, with the result that, in his opinion, *simanim* are sufficient evidence for all purposes, including substantiation of financial claims such as child support. He further accepts DNA as a *siman* rather than as an empirical generalization construed as a *rov.*

Nevertheless, Rabbi Weiss refuses to accept DNA evidence for the purpose of establishing *mamzerut* because *Teshuvot R. Akiva Eger,* no. 100, equates determination of *mamzerut* with criminal proceedings involving capital punishment.

However, it seems to this writer that a close reading of each of the sources that equate an *umdena de-mukhaḥ* with eyewitness testimony employ that concept in establishing that a particular act has occurred, e.g., circumstantial evidence that intercourse has occurred or that a ring has been transferred from the groom to the bride. In each of those situations a conclusion of fact is drawn contextually with regard to the occurrence of a particular act. DNA comparison yields no evidence with regard to any act; it is a means of establishing identification. "The majority of animals are kosher" is not an *umdena.* It is an empirical generalization based upon observation. It is a *rov* rather than an expression of certainty. Both *umdena* and *rov* differ from "*anan sahadei* – we are witnesses" in that the latter is both a general principle and does not posit exception. DNA identification is made on the basis of applying a *rov* to a particular situation. But unless there is a logical basis that

IV. FURTHER OBJECTIONS TO ACCEPTANCE OF DNA AS A *SIMAN*

In a contribution to a symposium devoted to the issue of acceptability of DNA evidence published in *Yeshurun*, XII (Nisan 5762), pp. 493–495, Rabbis Samuel Mordecai Gersten and Judah Shereshevsky advance a number of possible objections to recognition of DNA matching as a *siman* of dispositive import:

> (1a) DNA nucleoids are both infinitesimally small and colorless with the result that they cannot be directly perceived by visual observation. The issue is whether a characteristic that cannot be directly perceived can be regarded as a *siman*.

In response, it may be pointed out that there are numerous areas of Halakhah that are dependent upon visual observation. There is significant rabbinic literature demonstrating that in each of those areas optical enhancement or magnification in the form of corrective lenses, a magnifying glass, a telescope or a microscope is regarded as tantamount to direct visual observation and does not debar or vitiate the authenticity of the resultant visual phenomenon for matters of Halakhah.[12] Moreover, there are a host of authorities who find that

---

renders it impossible for any two people to possess identical DNA sequences (in which case the principle would rise in status to at least that of *umdena*) it cannot be concluded that such is not the case in any particular situation. In any particular situation there are no eyewitnesses and no circumstantial evidence establishing that the situation in question is not an exception of which the *rov* admits. The function of an *umdena de-mukhaḥ* is to establish a particular occurrence. That is not possible with regard to any matter which admits of both a major and minor class and the issue is to which of the two classes a particular matter should be assigned. Categorizing DNA evidence as an *umdena de-mukhaḥ* is tantamount to a claim that DNA establishes identity with certainty because no two people can have the same DNA.

12 See *Contemporary Halakhic Problems*, I, (New York, 1977), pp. 213–215. See also *Petaḥ ha-Dvir*, no. 224, sec. 10, regarding pronouncing a blessing upon seeing a monarch through a telescope and R. Ya'akov Moshe Toledano, *Meshiv Nefesh*, II, no. 244, regarding the blessing pronounced upon observing through a telescope a site at which one has experienced a miracle. See also *Tiferet*

identification of a corpse by means of a photograph of a body, or even comparison of a photograph of a body, with a photograph taken while the person is still alive, to be satisfactory.[13] Indeed, the Israeli Defense Forces photograph fallen soldiers whenever there is a possibility that identification by visual inspection of the body may not be possible within the requisite three-day period before facial features change.[14]

(1b) In employing some methods of DNA analysis, the DNA, to be observed, must be treated with a radioactive material, with fluorescent materials that produce particular light waves or by staining the nucleoids. In such instances as well the issue is whether a characteristic that cannot be directly perceived qualifies as a *siman*.

Technically, this point is well taken. Nevertheless, a distinction does not always make a difference. The essential nature of a *siman* is that it is highly unlikely to be present on two bodies. Distinctive physical marks are the most prevalent of such criteria. Nevertheless, if any given object or person were to be endowed with a certain rare causative characteristic (in the case of a person both in life and in death), e.g., a natural capacity to glow in the dark, logically, that capacity should qualify as a *siman*. DNA analysis is based upon recognition that each person's DNA is unique in its ability to produce an idiosyncratic, albeit nonvisual, manifestation under certain given circumstances. Consequently, DNA evidence should logically also qualify as a *siman*.

Yisra'el, Nega'im 2:11; *Teshvuot Shem Aryeh, Even ha-Ezer,* no. 112; R. Joseph Rosen, *Teshuvot Ẓofnat Pa'aneaḥ* (New York, 5714), I, no. 13; and R. Betzalel Stern, *Be-Ẓel ha-Ḥokhmah,* II, no. 16, sec. 4.

13 See, *inter alia,* R. Naphtali Zevi Yehudah Berlin, *Teshuvot Meshiv Davar,* III, no. 23; R. Zevi Hirsch Orenstein, *Birkat Reẓeh,* no. 3; R. Isaac Elchanan Spektor, *Teshuvot Ein Yiẓḥak, Even ha-Ezer,* no. 31; R. Binyamin Aryeh Weiss, *Teshuvot Even Yekarah,* I, no. 19; as well as *Oẓar ha-Poskim,* V, 17:24, secs. 40–45. Cf., R. Samuel Engel, *Teshuvot Maharash,* III, no. 11 and R. Ovadiah Yosef, *Teshuvot Yabi'a Omer,* VI, *Even ha-Ezer,* no. 3, sec. 3.

14 See R. Alexander Joshua Levinson, *Sugyot be-Ẓava u-Mishtarah* (Jerusalem, 5763), p. 254.

(2) Two DNA samples taken from a single individual are not absolutely identical. Identification of two samples as coming from a single person is based upon the extremely high statistical improbability of the samples not having a common source.

As has already been explained, DNA evidence is generally regarded as predicated upon the principle of *rov*. The objection to employment of a *rov* in granting an *agunah* permission to marry will be discussed in conjunction with objection number 4.

(3) In their conventional form, *simanim* are found on a body and the body is judged to be that of a person known to have possessed an identificatory mark. Identification is made on the basis of the presumption that no other person manifests a similar *siman*. DNA matching in cases of an unidentified corpse begins, not with examination of DNA taken from the decedent, but with DNA known to have been derived from a particular individual and serves as a *siman*. The DNA taken directly from the body is then compared with that *siman*. In conventional identification by means of a *siman*, the physical *siman* is first observed on the body itself rather than on a body or entity external to that which must be identified.

Indeed, comparison of two signatures of the same individual, a method employed for authenticating legal instruments, will show some slight discrepancies. Nevertheless, a signature can be authenticated by means of comparing it to another signature known to be that of a particular individual. In that case as well, it is the extraneous document which serves as the *siman*. However, in signature comparison the authenticity of the already identified signature is fully acknowledged. Any deviation is in comparing the as yet unauthenticated second signature to another already acknowledged signature whereas in DNA analysis even the fragment whose source is known with certainty manifests subtle internal variations with the result that there are minor variations within each of the two DNA segments.

In response it may be said that comparison of signatures is relied upon to authenticate legal documents despite the accepted fact that no two signatures of even a single individual are precisely the same.

The underlying presumption is that such variations are so slight and so subtle as not to be recognized in the usual course of events. Presumably, there is not simply a single such variation between two signatures but multiple variations of that nature. If so, whether such variation takes place in one signature or in two signatures should be of no consequence. Arguably, then, infinitesimal variations even between different segments of a single DNA segment may also be ignored.

> (4) Identification on the basis of DNA matching is based upon the presumption that no two people have identical DNA sequences. That, however, is an empirical generalization in the nature of a *rov*. The reliability of DNA analysis as a *siman* can be no stronger evidence than *rov* upon which it is based. However, *rov* is not a sufficient basis upon which to permit an *agunah* to remarry.

DNA evidence is indeed based upon the fact that, although there is no evidence that no two people can possibly have the same DNA sequences nor is there even a claim to that effect, it remains true that the likelihood of two people having identical DNA is remote in the extreme and hence there is a *rov* to the effect that no two people share a common DNA pattern. But that is the nature of all *simanim*. It cannot be said that it is either logically or empirically impossible for two people to manifest an identical *siman* or DNA sequence.

Nevertheless, *Shakh, Ḥoshen Mishpat* 267:7, maintains that *simanim muvhakim be-yoter*, e.g., a hole next to a particular letter in a *get*, were regarded by the Sages as tantamount to eyewitness testimony for purposes of identifying a *get* even though a *rov*, e.g., the majority of persons who enter a huge body of water and do not reappear must have perished, is not accepted. The distinction must lie in the fact that a "super *rov*" is as reliable as eyewitness testimony. If so, the *rov* involved in DNA analysis is comparable to the *rov* underlying acceptance of *simanim muvhakim be-yoter*. However, although *Shakh*'s position was accepted by *Netivot ha-Mishpat* 46:8, it was rejected by many major latter-day authorities.[15] *Rov* itself is insufficient proof for financial matters or for establishing the death of a husband.

---

15 See, *inter alia*, *Keẓot ha-Ḥoshen* 46:8, 259:2 and 297:1 as well as *Teshuvot R.*

(5) DNA analysis is based upon size and location of nucleoids. Size and location are categorized as "*simanim geru'im*" or "inferior identificatory marks." Rema, *Even ha-Ezer,* 17:24, rules that the presence of "even a hundred" such identificatory marks in combination is insufficient proof.[16]

In rebuttal it may be argued that it is not size or location of nucleoids that constitute the *siman* but the repetition of sequences of particular size and location that is the *siman.*[17] Such repetition may well be a *siman muvhak.*[18]

R. Samuel ha-Levi Woszner, *Teḥumin,* XXI (5761), 123 and *Yeshurun,* XII, 535,[19] distinguishes between DNA taken from a cadaver that is matched with DNA known to have belonged to a particular person and DNA taken from a corpse and compared with that of a close relative. Matching DNA taken from a corpse with DNA known to have been that belonging, not to a relative but to that person himself, he regards as a "*siman beinoni*" and "close to a *siman muvhak.*" In Rabbi Woszner's opinion such DNA comparison may be relied upon only if additional circumstantial evidence is available. Identification on the basis of comparison with a collateral DNA sample taken from a close relative is regarded by Rabbi Woszner as only a "*siman beinoni.*"[20] R. Alexander

---

Akiva Eger, no. 107. See also R. David Levanon, *Shurat ha-Din,* V (5759), 84 and R. Yigal Lerer, *Shurat ha-Din,* IX (5765), 46–47.

16 See *infra,* p. 107, note 41 and accompanying text.

17 A comparable example would be a birthmark or pigmented blotch on the skin. A single unremarkable spot of that nature is a *siman garu'a,* but an unusual pattern or configuration of such spots might be considered by some authorities as an acceptable *siman.* See *Ozar ha-Poskim,* vol. V, *Even ha-Ezer* 17:24, sec. 194:10 and sec. 199, *Luaḥ ha-Simanim,* sec. 71.

18 Cf., R. Eliyahu Levin, *Yeshurun,* p. 504. A similar argument has been made for accepting fingerprint evidence. Fingerprints are comprised of a configuration of swirls and lines none of which in themselves constitute a *siman.* See *Ozar ha-Poskim,* vol. V, *Even ha-Ezer* 17:24, and sec. 199, *Luaḥ ha-Simanim,* sec. 62. See also *Pitḥei Teshuvah* 17:106–107 and *Mishpatim Yesharim,* no. 39.

19 Reprinted as well in *Seridim,* No. 20 (5762), pp. 18–21. Rabbi Woszner's statement also bears the endorsement of the late R. Nissim Karelitz of Bnei Brak. See also *Teḥumin,* XXXV (5775), 211.

20 The distinction presumably lies in the fact that all DNA fragments derived from

Joshua Levinson, *Sugyot be-Ẓava u-Mishtarah* (Jerusalem, 5763), p. 277, reports that "In practice, the ruling is that [DNA] examination is considered to be close to a *siman muvhak*." In context, Rabbi Levinson is referring to comparison of the DNA of a soldier with that of one of his parents.[21]

Thus we find 1) authorities who accept DNA analysis as a *siman muvhak;* 2) authorities who accept DNA analysis as a *siman beinoni;* 3) authorities who regard DNA analysis as a *siman beinoni "karov le-siman muvhak"* (approximating a *siman muvhak*); and 4) authorities who maintain that DNA does not at all rise to the level of a recognized *siman*.

V. *SIMANIM* AS DISTINCT FROM *TEVI'UT AYIN*

The acceptability of DNA evidence is also discussed by R. Zalman Nechemiah Goldberg in a contribution to *Kol Ẓvi*, IV (5762), in the context of the World Trade Center tragedy. That material is also published in *Yeshurun*, XII, 506–512, together with critical comments authored by Rabbi Eliyahu Levin and Rabbi Goldberg's response.[22] Rabbi Goldberg regards DNA evidence as a *siman muvhak*, but his reasoning is not entirely clear to this writer because he seems to conflate two separate types of evidence, *viz.*, *simanim* and *tevi'ut ayin*.

Rabbi Goldberg introduces his discussion by noting that past experience renders the likelihood of error in DNA analysis infinitesimally small but cites the quite logical objection of an anonymous scholar to the effect that confirmatory results in the examination of even an extraordinarily high number of situations does not logically mandate the outcome of any subsequent case. In other words, empirical generalization is of limited predictive value.

---

a common source will be completely identical. Relatives inherit DNA from different progenitors with the result that some parts of the DNA are identical while others are not. See, however, *infra*, p. 112, note 49 and accompanying text.

21 Similarly, in a decision of the Supreme Rabbinical Court of Appeals, No. 927675/4, 4 Kislev 5777, Rabbi Eliezer Igra categorizes comparison of the DNA of two brothers as a *siman muvhak*. Cf., R. David Levanon's opinion in that case.

22 The same material is presented by Rabbi Goldberg in an article published in *Teḥumin*, XXIII (5763) 110–119.

The response to that objection would seem to be that an empirical *rov* such as "The majority of animals are not *treifot*" is not predicated upon examination of every single animal. *Rov* does not require examination of every member of a class; it is a principle based upon examination of a limited number of representative members of a class and applied to the entire class as a frankly acknowledged empirical generalization. This type of *rov* is termed a "*rubba de-leita kamman* – a *rov* that is not present before us." That is precisely why contemporary *batei din* have categorized DNA evidence acceptable only as an application of the principle of *rov* and, consequently, refuse to entertain such evidence in disputes regarding financial matters in support of a plaintiff's claim.[23]

Instead, Rabbi Goldberg responds that DNA may be relied upon even though the presumption that no two people have identical DNA sequences is based solely upon an empirical generalization. In support of that position he cites the principle of *tevi'ut ayin*. Identification on the basis of facial features, which, asserts Rabbi Goldberg, is based upon the antecedent premise that the countenances of no two individuals are identical, although certainly no one has examined every human being in order to reach such a conclusion. The same, he claims, should be true of DNA evidence as well.

However, instead of providing an elucidation of the rationale for the acceptance of DNA he has drawn attention to a more formidable problem, namely, what is the conceptual basis for acceptance of *tevi'ut ayin*? The simplest resolution of that difficulty would be a candid recognition that acceptance of *tevi'ut ayin* with regard to identification constitutes halakhic acceptance of idiosyncratic physiognomy as akin to a law of nature. Two separate talmudic statements lend themselves to such an interpretation:

---

23 See *supra*, p. 42. See also *Piskei Din shel Bet ha-Din le-Dinei Mamonot u-le-Birur Yahadut*, V, 191ff. and 248ff. as well as VIII, 386; and *Teḥumin* IV (5743), 431ff. and XXI (5761), 21ff. Cf., R. David Levanon, *Shurat ha-Din*, V, 82–83 and Rabbinical Supreme Court of Appeals, No. 927675/4, 4 Kislev 5777.

> ... For man stamps many coins with a single seal and all are like one another. But the Holy One, blessed be He, stamps every man with the seal of Adam and not a single one is identical to his fellow.... And why are those countenances unlike one another? So that a person should not see a beautiful domicile or beautiful woman and say, "It is mine." (*Sanhedrin* 38a)
>
> One who sees multitudes of Israel recites, "Blessed is He who discerns secrets (*Ḥakham ha-Razim*)" for their intellects are not similar to one another and their countenances are not similar to one another. (*Berakhot* 58a)

Rabbi Goldberg, however, regards the notion that every person possesses unique facial features as no more than an uncompelled empirical generalization.

Nevertheless, Rabbi Goldberg does not recognize a fundamental qualitative difference between *simanim* and *tevi'ut ayin.* Instead, he analyzes the technical difference between *simanim* and *tevi'ut ayin* and depicts the difference as a variation of degree rather than a difference in kind. In effect, Rabbi Goldberg asserts that *tevi'ut ayin* is a more sophisticated and more precise type of *siman* and implies that a *siman* based upon such a high degree of precision is "a super *siman*" accorded its own classification and its own status as *tevi'ut ayin.*

But Rabbi Goldberg's thesis does not serve to address the actual problem. If *tevi'ut ayin* is simply an amalgam of *simanim geru'im,* or weak identificatory marks, how can it be acceptable? How can DNA evidence acknowledged to be no more than an aggregate of *simanim geru'im* be entertained as evidence? As already noted, Rema, *Even ha-Ezer,* 17:24, rules that no number of *simanim geru'im* combine to serve as the equivalent of a single acceptable *siman.* Moreover, the very nature of a *siman* is that it is objective in nature, readily described and cognitively communicated.

Rather than resolving the doctrinal problem inherent in acceptance of *tevi'ut ayin,* Rabbi Goldberg presents an *argumentum ad absurdum* for accepting DNA evidence. In effect his argument seems to be that any apparent defect present in DNA evidence is also inherent in *tevi'ut ayin.* Hence, if DNA evidence is not acceptable, *tevi'ut ayin* should be unacceptable as well.

It seems to this writer that *tevi'ut ayin* is fundamentally different from *simanim* in both nature and function.[24] The resolution of the problem posed by Rabbi Goldberg must lie in the fact that *tevi'ut ayin* serves only to establish personal identity, i.e., that the person appearing before the *bet din* is the same person who is the subject of the testimony, or that the body witnesses have observed is the remains of a man whose whereabouts is otherwise unknown. Recognition of a *siman* in the form of a hole adjacent to a particular letter of a *get* requires no knowledge of the size or shape of the hole. In contradistinction, recognition in the form of *tevi'ut ayin* is based upon recognition of a combination of characteristics, including size, shape and irregularity, etc. Put somewhat differently, *tevi'ut ayin* establishes that the person appearing before the *bet din* or the corpse that witnesses have identified manifests the *Gestalt* of the person they observed on an earlier occasion and not someone else. DNA evidence does not at all establish personal identity; it establishes either that two strands of DNA were taken from the same person or have a common progenitor. Those strands of DNA, however, remain discrete and distinct. Comparison of two DNA samples does not serve to establish the identity of either DNA sample. DNA is used to compare different entities so that inferences can be made and conclusions drawn; DNA is superfluous and redundant in terms of establishing the identity of any single entity. Hence, *tevi'ut ayin* is not relevant to understanding the nature of DNA as a *siman.*

Apart from being a legal provision established by Sinaitic law or rabbinic enactment establishing it as one of the manifold rules of evidence, *tevi'ut ayin* is a psychological phenomenon far more subtle than identification of *simanim*. It is inherently the case that two similar objects are more likely to share a common *siman* than a person is likely to misidentify an individual already known to him. *Tevi'ut ayin* is not

24 That distinction is supported by the fact that the Gemara, *Ḥullin* 95b, ponders which of the two is more reliable. The question implies that the two are different in kind rather than in degree.

at all comparable to identification of a suspect in a police lineup. In the latter case, the suspect is "identified" by a victim who may well have been traumatized during the commission of a criminal act, who may have caught a glimpse of the perpetrator for only a fleeting moment and who may have been subtly or not so subtly prompted to identify one of those presented for examination. T*evi'ut ayin* as evidence accepted by Jewish law is not confounded by emotional experience or psychological pressure. *Tevi'ut ayin* is a nuanced process resulting from the presence of subliminal recognition of countless numbers of *simanim,* none of which is a *siman muvhak* or even definable, but in the aggregate those phenomena are much more reliable than even a *siman muvhak be-yoter.* Although any particular identification on the basis of *tevi'ut ayin* is based upon what the eye discerns, those visual phenomena need not, and usually cannot, be articulated by the person making the identification. Identification by means of *tevi'ut ayin* is an intuitive phenomenon rather than a rational process and is accorded greater evidentiary deference than mere *simanim.*

The distinction of *tevi'ut ayin* is fully supported by the scientific literature. Facial recognition requires the combined activity of a large-scale neuro network. The neuro activity and cognitive mechanism of face recognition have been the subject of intense study by neuroscientists.[25] It is estimated that a person can remember and recognize some five-thousand faces.[26] Much of what is known regarding the process and mechanism of facial recognition has been learned from the

---

25 See V. Bruce and A. Young, "Understanding Face Recognition," *British Journal of Psychology,* vol. 77, no. 3 (1986), pp. 305–327; R. Jenkins *et al.,* "How Many Faces Do People Know?" *Proceedings of the Royal Society: Biological Sciences,* vol. 285, 1888 (10 Oct. 2018), doi 10, 1098/rspb.s018.1319; B. Rossion "Understanding Face Perception by Means of Prosopagnosia and Neuroimaging," *Frontiers in Bioscience* (Elite Edition), vol. 6, no. 2 (2014), pp. 258–307; J.V. Haxby *et al.,* "the Distributed Human Neural System for Face Perception," *Trends in Cognitive Science* vol. 4, no. 6 (2000) pp. 223–33; J.V. Haxby *et al.,* editors, *Oxford Handbook of Face Perception* (New York, 2011); and K. Grill-Spector *et al.,* "The Functional Neuroanatomy of Human Face Perception," *Annual Review of Vision,* vol. 3 (2017), pp. 167–96.

26 See "How Many Faces Do People Know?" See *supra,* note 25.

study of prosopagnosia, also known as face blindness. Prosopagnosia is derived from the Greek words *"prosopon,"* meaning face,[27] and *"agnosia,"* the medical term for recognition impairment. It is estimated that as many as one in fifty individuals suffers from some form of the malady.[28] The malady, which may be congenital or the result of brain damage, was known in antiquity and was extensively described by Dr. Joachim Bodamer in a landmark study of two individuals with face recognition deficits.[29]

Prosopagnosia is a disorder in the recognition of faces while the perception of them is retained. The disorder may be more or less severe but involves disruption of perception of faces that are seen but not recognized as faces belonging to a particular person. In another manifestation of the illness some individuals have no trouble recognizing faces but cannot identify objects. Halakhah also recognizes *tevi'ut ayin* with regard to objects and provides for return of a lost object to a *talmid hakham* on the basis of *tevi'ut ayin*. Bodamer cites a much earlier writer who, in 1876, described a person who was unable to recognize people but recognized and identified an object correctly.[30]

Bodamer observed that the presence of prosopagnosia as a malady enables us to deduce that in the normal process of perception there must be a stratum of function that carries out the perception of faces without distinguishing between the acts of seeing and recognition. A person suffering from this disorder has no difficulty perceiving a nose, lips, mouth, etc., which together constitute a physiognomy, but is incapable of perceiving them as a structured picture singling out a

---

27 Jastrow regards the word *"parẓof"* in the Mishnah to be an adaptation of the Greek *"prosopon."*

28 See "Understanding Prosopagnosia," Faceblind.Org. www.faceblind.org/research/ 1/6, 2/6, accessed 9 September, 2019.

29 See Joachim Bodamer, "Die Prosopagnosia," *Archiv fur Psychiatrie und Nervenkrankheiten*, vol. 179 (1947), pp. 6–53. A partial translation and commentary authored by Hadyn D. Ellis and Melanie Florence, "Bodamer's (1947) Paper on Prosopagnosia" was published in *Cognitive Neurology*, vol. 7, no. 2 (1990), pp. 81–105.

30 *Ibid.*, p. 82.

particular person. Bodamer theorizes that the perception of faces is possible only through operation of a particular independent structure of the occipital brain. Bodamer describes cases in which sufferers have no trouble recognizing faces and people but have object agnosia. Bodamer takes this phenomenon as evidence that recognition of objects and faces belong to different visual-gnostic categories that can be disturbed separately or together.[31]

The two patients described in detail by Bodamer were victims of trauma that resulted in bilateral occipital damage. In all subsequent cases in which a postmortem exam was carried out bilateral occipital temporal lesions were found.[32] Bodamer argues that a normally functioning brain is endowed with specific face-processing and object-processing mechanisms, making it possible to recognize particular individuals and objects.[33]

If so, acceptance of *tevi'ut ayin* as a basic and independent form of evidence is readily understood. As Bodamer also realized, facial recognition is meaningful only if it is antecedently assumed that physiognomy is idiosyncratic. The very notion of halakhic acceptability of *tevi'ut ayin* impliedly relies on that concept as an antecedent premise. This does not at all imply that *tevi'ut ayin* is infallible. Halakhah mandates acceptance of eye-witness testimony despite candid recognition that witnesses may err or commit perjury. The same is true with regard to *tevi'ut ayin.*

This serves to illuminate the rule requiring return of lost objects to a *talmid ḥakham* upon identification of an object by means of *tevi'ut ayin. Tevi'ut ayin* with regard to objects is the product of a particular visual-gnostic formation. As such, *tevi'ut ayin* constitutes a form of evidence comparable to eyewitness testimony. All persons would have credibility to identify lost objects and demand their return but for the consideration that there is a strong motive to falsely identify

---

31 *Ibid.*, p. 96.

32 See J.C. Meadows, "The Anatomical Basis of Prosopagnosia," *Journal of Neurology, Neurosurgery, and Psychiatry*, vol. 37, no. 5 (1974), pp. 489–501.

33 "Bodamer's (1947) Paper," pp. 83 and 91.

an object for pecuniary gain and thereby preclude return of the lost object to its rightful owner. A *talmid ḥakham* is not suspected of a falsehood. Nevertheless, no person can testify with regard to a matter in which he has a pecuniary interest. Consequently, a *talmid ḥakham* cannot prevail on the basis of *tevi'ut ayin* against a person in possession with claim of title. But the finder of a lost object has no claim of title and, typically, no other individual has asserted a claim of title; hence, a *talmid ḥakham* may recover his property upon recognition in the form of *tevi'ut ayin.*

It cannot be objected that a DNA technician's testimony based upon *tevi'ut ayin* should not be accepted because such credibility is extended only to a *talmid ḥakham.* Acceptance of *tevi'ut ayin* in validation of a claim to a lost object is limited to a claimant who is a *talmid ḥakham* not because only a *talmid ḥakham* has the capacity of *tevi'ut ayin;* others possess that ability as well, but others are suspected of advancing a false claim in anticipation of acquiring personal gain. A DNA technician has no potential for such gain; hence the *tevi'ut ayin* of a technician who is not a *talmid ḥakham* should also be acceptable. The *tevi'ut ayin* involved in DNA evidence is, of course, a form of object recognition rather than facial recognition.

There is little question that *simanim* and *tevi'ut ayin* are disparate forms of evidence[34] and hence Rabbi Goldberg's transposition of principles of *tevi'ut ayin* to *simanim* is not appropriate.[35] The distinction

34 Cf., however, the cryptic comments of *Pri Megadim,* Introduction to *Hilkhot Ta'arovot, Klal Simanim u-Tvi'ut Ayin,* s.v. *ve-da.*

35 Cf., R. Ezekiel Landau, *Teshuvot Noda bi-Yehudah, Even ha-Ezer, Mahadura Kamma,* no. 51, who comments, "But in truth a *siman muvhak be-yoter* is considered to be exactly as *tevi'ut ayin*... and there is no difference between them even in executing a murderer." In that statement, *Noda bi-Yehudah* is equating the efficacy of two types of evidence rather than their intrinsic nature. See also Rashi, *Ḥullin* 79a, s.v. *simanim,* who writes, "There is no clearer evidence than a *siman muvhak.*" R. Elijah Mizrachi, *Teshuvot ha-Re'em,* no. 38, understands Rashi as stating that *simanim muvhakim* are tantamount to witnesses. *Shakh, Ḥoshen Mishpat* 167:7; *Teshuvot R. Akiva Eger,* no. 107; R. Joseph Saul Nathanson, *Teshuvot Sho'el u-Meshiv, Mahadura Kamma,* I, no. 146,

between the two is pithily expressed by R. Iser Zalman Meltzer, *Yagdil Torah,* vol. 1, no. 2 (Tevet 5669), who categorizes *simanim* as "evidence" (*ra'ayah*) whereas *tevi'ut ayin* he categorizes as "recognition and knowledge of the matter itself" (*yedi'ah be-eẓem ha-davar).* Requiring elucidation, however, is the distinction drawn by Reb Iser Zalman between *ra'ayah* and *yedi'ah*. Undoubtedly, *ra'ayah* connotes evidence in the form of establishing facts from which inferences may be drawn whereas *yedi'ah* refers to facts immediately known either by *a priori* cognition or by means of sensory perception.

Perception of a *siman,* in and of itself, is no more than a visual phenomenon. The value of a *siman* lies in the fact that its presence enables conclusory judgments to be made. A *siman*'s rarity of occurrence combined with other knowledge enables further conclusions to be drawn. Thus, if *siman* X is present on a corpse and only Y is known to possess such a physical characteristic, it may concluded that the corpse is the body of Y. The same is the case in a situation in which an identificatory mark is present in a lost object and a person comes forward claiming to have lost an object baring an identificatory mark of that nature. Since the *siman* is rare and its presence unlikely to be known to anyone other than the object's rightful owner, the lost object is deemed to be the property of the individual presenting the *siman.* In each of these examples the scenario begins with a visual perception which sets in motion a process of reasoning. Thus, the *siman* serves as a *ra'ayah* or evidence from which a conclusion may be drawn.

Tevi'ut ayin is a quite different phenomenon. One looks at a face or an object and immediately realizes the identity of the person or object. No mediating reasoning process is required. The distinction is comparable to the different ways of determining that an object is yellow in color. One may measure the wavelength of light reflected by an object and identify that wavelength with the wavelength known to be reflected by the color yellow. One can thereby identify the color of the object as yellow without ever having seen the object. Or, one

disagree with *Noda bi-Yehudah* and rule that a *siman muvhak* is not admissible in capital cases.

may simply gaze at the object and pronounce, "This is yellow." The first method involves an intricate reasoning process; the second requires no reasoning whatsoever. J.S. Mill described color and the like as "simple qualities" because they are perceived immediately without mediation of reason.[36]

Tevi'ut ayin is loosely comparable to a simple quality: It is a perception, but it is more than a perception. "Yellow" is the word we assign to a particular visual phenomenon. The perception is the same for all people, including those who speak no language and have heretofore never seen a yellow object. *Tevi'ut ayin* is a perception, but it is a perception immediately associated by the brain with an earlier perception of the same qualitative nature. Think of a person who sees a yellow object and describes it as "canary yellow." That more nuanced identification of the color is not a deduction; it is an immediate identification of a present visual perception with an earlier perception of the same nature.

Put somewhat differently, a *Gestalt* is an amalgam of countless minor and subliminal *simanim* immediately perceived by the brain. A *siman* is clearly recognized and can be readily articulated. *Tevi'ut ayin* is the product of countless indescribable phenomena that are subliminal in nature but which in the aggregate is far greater than the sum of its parts. Such a perception is synonymous with *yedi'ah,* i.e., immediate awareness or knowledge, in contradistinction to *ra'ayah,* or evidence from which knowledge can be gleaned.

All eyewitness testimony is based upon witnesses' knowledge that the accused is indeed one and the same as the perpetrator whose act they observed. This is dramatized in the courtroom when the prosecuting attorney asks a witness if the accused is in the courtroom and, if so, to point him out to the members of the jury. Little wonder, then, that *tevi'ut ayin* is depicted as tantamount to eyewitness testimony. The subject matter of eyewitness testimony is communication

---

36 See John Stuart Mill, *A System of Logic, Ratiocinative and Inductive, Book III of Induction, Chapter XXII, Of Uniformities of Co-Existence Not Dependent on Causation,* sec. VI.

of knowledge acquired by sensory perception, not of the witnesses' conclusion based on such perceptions.

It is indeed the case that only people have *tevi'ut ayin* that is recognized by Halakhah and that machines such as computers cannot have *tevi'ut ayin*. That is certainly true if *tevi'ut ayin* is a neuro-phenomenon. If so, it may well be objected that if a computer is used to establish a DNA match the results cannot be accepted as evidence in the nature of *tevi'ut ayin*. While that may be so, it would seem that *tevi'ut ayin* might still be applied if, after identification by means of computer, the match is confirmed visually. The function of the computer would serve to spare much time and effort necessary to eliminate possible matches. The function of the computer would be to identify the samples which could be presented to a human observer for purposes of a determination of whether or not they match by application of *tevi'ut ayin*. It would be the confirmatory judgment of the human observer that would be admissible in a *bet din*.

Earlier it was shown that in various decisions the Israeli Rabbinical Courts have ruled that the conclusions of DNA analysis can be accepted only on the basis of the principle of *rov*.[37] One of the implications of that position is that DNA cannot be used in financial disputes to substantiate a plaintiff's claim. Similarly, a *rov* cannot establish a presumption that a man has perished and hence that his wife is free to remarry. Thus, although the majority of persons who enter a seemingly boundless body of water (*mayim she-ein lahem sof*) and do not emerge fail to do so because they have drowned in the water, still the wife is not permitted to remarry because some such individuals may survive and emerge on a far distant bank beyond eyesight. *Simanim muvhakim* are defined as identificatory marks that are not present in more than one person in a thousand. If so, *simanim muvhakim* represent no more than a *rov*. If *simanim* establish no more than a *rov*, how can *simanim* suffice to permit a widow to remarry?[38]

---

37 See *supra*, pp. 52–53.

38 *Noda bi-Yehudah, Even ha-Ezer, Mahadura Kamma*, no. 51, s.v. *ve-ho'il*, asserts that only *simanim muvhakim* are biblically acceptable, i.e., *simanim muvhakim*

R. Moshe Zev Margolies, *Mar'ot ha-Ẓove'ot* 17:24, cites a number of early-day authorities who regard *simanim* to be as reliable as eyewitness testimony. *Mar'ot ha-Ẓove'ot* himself suggests that the acceptability of *simanim muvhakim* is based upon an explicit biblical source. The Gemara, *Bava Meẓi'a* 27a, declares that the inclusion of the word *"ḥamor"* (donkey) in Deuteronomy 22:3, the biblical passage regarding return of lost objects, teaches that a donkey must be returned upon an identification of its saddle despite the fact that a person other than the owner may have found the saddle and placed it upon his own donkey and then proceeded to lose both donkey and saddle or that the saddle alone might have been lent to another person who lost it. If so, *simanim* constitute a novel form of evidence limited to return of lost objects.

---

constitute a novel, biblically established form of evidence that stands on par with testimony of eyewitnesses by virtue of biblical fiat.

Noda bi-Yehudah proceeds to raise the objection that, if such is indeed the case, the testimony of witnesses who do not recognize the perpetrator but identify him on the basis of physical *simanim muvhakim* should suffice for conviction. *Noda bi-Yehudah* responds that reliability of *simanim muvhakim* constitutes a novel category of evidence derived from the biblical obligation to return lost property on the basis of *simanim*. Hence, *simanim muvhakim* are accepted only in situations analogous to those present with regard to restoration of lost property, namely, where no party is in a position to assert with any degree of certainty that the conclusion reached on the basis of proffered *simanim* is false. *Simanim* are accepted to establish widowhood precisely because no one has any basis to proclaim that the corpse has been misidentified. However, an alleged perpetrator, identified solely by *simanim*, is in a position to deny with certainty that the identification is correct.

According to *Noda bi-Yehudah*'s novel view, it might be argued that DNA comparison would be acceptable as a *siman* in establishing the identity of a corpse as well.

VI. DNA AND FINGERPRINT EVIDENCE AS *TEVI'UT AYIN*

Despite the foregoing, it seems to this writer that DNA can be accepted, neither as a *siman muvhak* nor as a *siman* analogous to *tevi'ut ayin,* but as actual *tevi'ut ayin*. Putting aside questions of credibility, *tevi'ut ayin,*as stated earlier, is an independent and discrete category of evidence whose halakhic efficacy is comparable to eyewitness testimony. The validity of *tevi'ut ayin* extends to objects no less so than to people. Accordingly, it is arguable that DNA should be accepted as simply another instance of *tevi'ut ayin*. Recognition of the repeated appearances of an idiosyncratic DNA sequence in a strand of DNA is comparable to, and no less reliable than, recognition of a phenotype of a facial countenance. Although computers are used to match size, position and other characteristics of the various alleles, that process is necessary in order to limit the time and travail necessary to examine countless matching possibilities. Once the computer has found a match human confirmation is not required. However, it seems to be the case that if two DNA fragments are placed side by side a trained eye would have no difficulty in declaring them either to match or not to match. Indeed, at the end of the process of identification, images of the DNA fragments being compared are available. Such an identification process is no different from identification by means of comparing two photographs; it is, however, far more accurate. DNA recognition is actually *tevi'ut ayin* on the microcosmic level.[39]

Acceptance of DNA analysis as *tevi'ut ayin* serves to obviate the objection that DNA evidence represents a form of *rov* which is not acceptable evidence for permitting remarriage but also dispels the second major problem with regard to acceptance of DNA as a *siman,* i.e., that an identificatory sign such as measurement, weight or location

39 It has earlier been contended that enhancement of an image by means of magnification, staining or the like does not preclude identification by means of a *siman*. The same should be true of comparison of two samples of any substance even when both are enhanced in an identical manner. Any measurements that are taken serve only to confirm that there is no error in the visual identification.

is termed a "*siman garu'a*" and unacceptable as evidence no matter how many such congruent factors may be present.[40]

The essence of DNA evidence is identity of size and location of the allele. Each of those characteristics is a *siman garu'a*. Earlier it was noted that if DNA is regarded as a *siman muvhak* it is only because of the unique, repetitive sequencing of multiple alleles. The

---

40 A *siman beinoni*, or intermediate *siman*, is also not acceptable but there is significant controversy with regard to the acceptance of a coalescence of several such *simanim*. *Teshuvot ha-Baḥ ha-Ḥadashot*, no. 65, cites the son of *Mas'at Binyamin* who rejects not only a combination of *simanim geru'im*, but even multiple intermediate identificatory marks for purposes of permitting an *agunah* to remarry. However, *Bet Shmu'el, Even ha-Ezer* 17:73, citing *Mas'at Binyamin*, rules that the presence of a multiple number of *simanim beinonim* is sufficient, as do *Taz, Even ha-Ezer* 17:30, and *Keẓot ha-Ḥoshen* 65:11. *Bet Shmu'el* cites *Ḥelkat Meḥokek* as disagreeing. Cf., however, *Ḥelkat Meḥokek* 17:43. *Noda bi-Yehudah, Even ha-Ezer, Mahadura Tinyana*, no. 66, also accepts that view provided that the *simanim* are "*keẓat muvhakim*," i.e., somewhat idiosyncratic, and gives as an example the instance of a person whose right ear was disproportionate to his left ear and who was also missing a finger on the right hand. See also R. Isaac Elchanan Spektor, *Teshuvot Ein Yiẓḥak, Even ha-Ezer*, no. 20, *anaf* 3, sec. 12. Those authorities maintain that two intermediate *simanim*, taken together, constitute a *siman muvhak*. For additional sources see *Pitḥei Teshuvah, Even ha-Ezer* 17:106.

Presumably, the rationale for accepting a combination of two intermediate *simanim* is that there is a significantly low statistical probability that two people manifest any particular intermediate *siman*. Hence, the likelihood that two individuals manifest two separate *simanim beinonim* is the probability of the occurrence of the first *siman* in two people multiplied by the probability of the occurrence of the second *siman* in two people. For example, *Ẓemaḥ Ẓedek, Even ha-Ezer*, no. 76, regards inordinate height as a *siman beinoni*. As defined earlier, the frequency of occurrence of a *siman beinoni* must be less than one in a hundred or one in two hundred. Presumably, inordinate obesity also constitutes a *siman beinoni*. The chances that two individuals manifest both of those *simanim*, i.e., extraordinary height as well as inordinate obesity, equals one in a hundred multiplied by one in a hundred, or one in ten thousand. Thus, the presence of two *simanim beinonim* has the statistical reliability of at least as great as that of a *siman muvhak* which is defined by *Mas'at Binyamin* as one in a thousand or one in two thousand. Hence, for many authorities two such *simanim* combine to become one *siman muvhak*.

notion that a particular sequence and repetition of what are otherwise *simanim geru'im* do not have evidentiary weight greater than a single *siman garu'a* is not without precedent but cannot be regarded as unassailable.[41]

However, recognition of DNA matching as a form of *tevi'ut ayin* obviates the problem. DNA analysis is tantamount to visual comparison of diverse DNA strands under a microscope. A positive identification appears when the strands appear to be identical to the eyes of the technician; his measurements serve merely to confirm his presumption. The perception is not of measurement of a number of alleles but is a form of comparison quite similar to *tevi'ut ayin* with regard to a countenance. A countenance is distinctive because of unique size, arrangement and contour of myriad portions of the face. No aspect of any portion of the countenance qualifies either as a *siman muvhak* or as the subject of *tevi'ut ayin,* but the countenance is uniquely identifiable as a whole even though individually the parts are not unique and even nondescript. If so, DNA comparison is actually a form of *tevi'ut ayin* rather than a *siman.*

It further seems to this writer that fingerprint evidence is no different from DNA. Although fingerprint identification is often categorized as a *siman muvhak,*[42] such categorization is subject to objections akin to those that have been expressed with regard to DNA evidence. In particular it may be objected that the presumption that no two people possess an identical fingerprint is no more than an empirical generalization in the nature of a *rov*. Fingerprint comparison is, however, actually a form of *tevi'ut ayin* rather than a *siman.*[43]

---

41 See *supra*, p. 92, note 16 and accompanying text.

42 See *Oẓar ha-Poskim,* V, 24:17, sec. 62. See also R. Yehoshu'a Moshe Mereminsky, *Ha-Pardes,* Tishri 5714. Cf., *Sugyot be-Ẓava u-Mishtarah,* pp. 296–297. R. Ovadiah Yosef, *Teshuvot Yabi'a Omer,* VI, no. 3, sec. 20, relies upon fingerprint comparison only in conjunction with other circumstantial evidence. A similar view is attributed to Rabbi Joseph Shalom Eliashiv in *Sugyot be-Ẓava u-Mishtarah,* p. 295.

43 R. David Levanon in a parenthetical comment, *Shurat ha-Din,* V, 82, questions why fingerprint evidence should not be regarded as actual *tevi'ut ayin.* He

It may be surprising to some, but fingerprint evidence is fundamentally a product of visual judgment on the part of highly trained human examiners. Little is known concerning the perceptual or neural processes involved in making those comparisons or even about which characteristics of fingerprint pairs make comparisons easy or difficult. The early steps involved in fingerprint analysis are manual and automated. The vast number of fingerprints with which a latent print must be compared make it necessary to submit a fingerprint to a database for automated preliminary comparison. The computer returns a list of potential matches many or most of which can be quickly excluded. The rest require scrutiny by a human observer. The examiner must look closely at a latent print, compare it to the print found in the database and decide whether the prints match or do not match.

There is no formalized process for those steps. "There is no method or metric, or specification of which features should be used for comparison, or any general measure for what counts as sufficient information to make a decision. Examiners rely on their experience and training rather than formal methods or quantified rubrics at each stage of the process."[44]

Fingerprint examination is similar in nature to the reading of an electrocardiogram by a cardiologist. The electrocardiogram records the electrical activity of each heartbeat in what a layman might term a series of hills, ridges, valleys and bumps. The trained eye of a physician can readily determine that the pattern is unexceptional because he recognizes as identical to the countless normal heartbeats he has previously observed on similar cardiograms; he may spot anomalies that lead him to diagnose underlying problems; or, putting the patient's cardiogram side by side with earlier recorded cardiograms, he can

---

leaves the question as a matter requiring investigation (*ẓarikh iyun*). Strangely, Rabbi Levanon does not raise the same question with regard to DNA matching.

44 Philip J. Kelman *et al.*, "Forensic Comparison Matching of Fingerprints: Using Quantitative Image Measures for Estimating Error Rates through Understanding and Predicting Difficulty," PLOS One. 2014; 9(5): e94617. Published online 2014 May 2. Doi: 10. 1371/journal.pone.0094617.

readily determine how they differ and draw appropriate conclusions. In examining the cardiogram, the cardiologist is applying cardiac *tevi'ut ayin.* However, unlike other forms of *tevi'ut ayin,* only a *talmid ḥakham* – that is, a cardiologist or fingerprint specialist – has such *tevi'ut ayin.*

In short, fingerprint analysis is not an exact or precise scientific process; it is remarkably similar to the *tevi'ut ayin* involved in facial recognition. One recent study revealed a false positive rate of 3%.[45] The rate of error reflects the subjective nature of fingerprint evaluation; it is precisely the subjective nature of the process that constitutes *tevi'ut ayin.* Paradoxically, subjective *tevi'ut ayin* is of greater halakhic evidentiary value than an empirical generalization.

Regardless of the merits of the conflicting views, it is quite apparent

---

45 *Ibid.*

It should be noted that recent studies have confirmed the role of bias in fingerprint matching. Bias may arise because of awareness of the seriousness of the matter under consideration, time constraints, knowledge of previous determinations by another examiner, stereotypical preconceptions and a host of other factors. See Sarah Stevenage and Alice Bennett, "A Biased Opinion: Demonstration of Cognitive Bias on a Fingerprint Matching Task Through Knowledge of DNA Test Results," *Forensic Science International,* 276 (July 2017), 93–106. Such bias also exists in comparing facial components of a perpetrator and a suspect if the observer is led to believe that the suspect is guilty. See S.D. Charman *et al.,* "Exploring the Diagnostic Utility of Facial Composites: Beliefs of Guilt Can Bias Perceived Similarity Between Composite and Suspect," *Journal of Experimental Psychology: Applied,* 15 (2009), 76–90. A natural and well-intentioned bias to free an *agunah* cannot be denied and should not be overlooked. Measures, some obvious and some not so obvious, can be taken to eliminate bias. See S.M. Kassin *et al.,* "The Forensic Confirmation Bias: Problems, Perspectives, and Proposed Solutions," *Journal of Applied Research in Memory and Cognition,* 2 (1) (2013), 42–52 and "Cognitive Bias Effects Relevant to Forensic Science Examinations," *Forensic Science Regulator* FSR-G-217 Issue 1 (2015). Hopefully, it is not necessary to emphasize that the members of a *bet din* relying upon the *tevi'ut ayin* herein described will consult with experts in order to assure that measures have been taken to eliminate all possible bias. See S.A. Cole, Implementing Counter-Measures Against Confirmation Bias in Forensic Science, *Journal of Applied Research in Memory and Cognition,* 2, (2013), 61–62. Cf., *supra,* p. 25, note 39.

that significant disagreement exists with regard to whether DNA analysis is tantamount to a *siman muvhak*. Rabbinic scholars who have addressed the issue have not taken into account the consideration that, empirically, both fingerprint comparison and DNA matching are actually forms of *tevi'ut ayin* – a factor that would free a woman from the bonds of *igun* beyond cavil.

VII. IDENTIFICATION BY MEANS OF COLLATERAL DNA

Rabbi Woszner's distinction between identification on the basis of different samples of DNA derived from the same person and collateral identification on the basis of DNA shared by blood relatives appears tenuous.[46] Assuming that a *siman muvhak* is an identificatory sign not found with the frequency of more than one in a thousand, reliability of DNA matching with accuracy of more than one in a thousand would qualify as a *siman muvhak*. Current estimates of reliability of DNA matching both for establishing identity and for establishing a consanguineous relationship are far higher.

However, if DNA is accepted as *tevi'ut ayin* rather than as a *siman*, that distinction becomes entirely cogent. Facial recognition is defined by the Mishnah as recognition of the "countenance and nose," i.e., an entire phenotype. Alleles, as has been argued, are the microscopic analogue of a countenance and, as such, identifiable on the basis of *tevi'ut ayin*. Two fragments of DNA taken from the same person will be identical and immediately recognized as such by a trained observer. However, DNA samples taken from a father and a son will never be identical because a child inherits only one half of the complement of chromosomes from his father; consequently, there cannot be more than a fifty percent match between DNA of parent and child. The percentage of DNA shared by more distant relatives can be readily predicted by applying elementary principles of genetics but will steadily attenuate with the reduced degree of consanguinity. While

46 See *infra*, p. 111, note 48.

comparison of full complements of identical alleles and recognition of their identification can be categorized as *tevi'ut ayin*, comparison of only a number of alleles cannot be categorized in that manner any more so than comparison of half a face with a full face can qualify as *tevi'ut ayin*.[47]

The reason is rooted in the very nature of *tevi'ut ayin* as distinct from other forms of cognition. As has been explained, *tevi'ut ayin* involves a particular neuro-mechanism that renders such recognition the equivalent of perception of a simple quality such as the color yellow. Neither the power of deduction nor the faculty of reason nor the gift of imagination is involved. Recognition is intuitive; it is not mediated by the intellectual faculty. Recognition arrived at by the perception of less than a full physiognomy involves fleshing out the immediate perception by deduction, analogy and/or imagination. That type of recognition is an entirely different neuro-phenomenon and involves different regions of the brain. It is not akin to an immediate sensory perception. Comparing a full set of alleles with a set in which only half or less are identical gives pause to the neuro-mechanisms involved. The cognitive conclusion is not immediate; the brain must first sort out the common alleles from among the disparate ones. That process involves rational analysis of whether the common alleles that are present meet the criteria for identification and degree of relationship. That process involves discernment and judgment that cannot be spontaneous. In short, that process is qualitatively different than *tevi'ut ayin* and one must assume that it involves different neuro-centers within the brain. It is certainly not akin to the simple quality of yellow described by J.S. Mill or to the knowledge of *ezem ha-davar* postulated by R. Iser Zalman Meltzer.[48]

---

47 See *Shulḥan Arukh, Even ha-Ezer* 17:24 and *Ḥelkat Meḥokek* 17:41.

48 It is indeed the case that, strictly speaking, DNA contained with each of the chromosomes that comprise the entire genome should be required to make an absolutely positive identification on the basis of *tevi'ut ayin* just as only the physiognomy of the entire face must be compared with the picture of previous perceptions of that physiognomy stored in a person's memory makes *tevi'ut ayin* possible. But surely one can conceive of a neuro-system in which

Despite the foregoing, it can be argued that comparison of a lesser number of alleles shared by a father and a son, by two brothers etc., may be halakhically acceptable as sufficient to establish a familial relationship – not on the basis of *tevi'ut ayin* alone but on quite different grounds.

The earlier-cited text of *Sanhedrin* 38a declares:

> ... For man stamps many coins with a single seal and all are like one another. But the Holy One, blessed be He, stamps every man with the seal of Adam and not a single one is identical to his fellow...

One may ask: Are the Sages informing us that the Omnipotent One utilizes a single mold but, unlike a comparable humanly-fashioned artifact, He manipulates that artifact to create dissimilar beings each time He gives life to a human child or are the Sages declaring that, at the time of creation the divine mold was originally fashioned or "programmed" to produce an idiosyncratic countenance each time a child is endowed with a phenotype?[49]

---

comparison of a profile with a profile, rather than a full countenance with a full countenance, would be equally reliable because a more highly developed neuro-system would be capable of experiencing the same neuro-perception even when exposed to a lesser stimulus or "trigger." Only a small number of alleles are actually compared in DNA matching because research has determined that comparison of a greater number of alleles does not result in a higher degree of accuracy. Assume that visual perception of eyebrows alone, ears alone, or a nose alone were as accurate as perception of a full countenance including the nose. Certainly, were that the reality, *tevi'ut ayin* would have been defined by the Mishnah as predicated upon observing that aspect of the countenance alone. That is indeed the conclusion that science has reached in its determination of microscopic *tevi'ut ayin* of genetic material, *viz.*, perception of x number of alleles is as reliable for purposes of immediate recognition and examination of additional "features," i.e., additional alleles, because additional alleles contribute little to the phenomenon of visual identification.

49 Unique countenances were not necessarily a hallmark of human beings in the earliest generations of man. Since Eve was created from Adam's rib it would seem that they shared a single genotype. Change, including change in the chromosome controlling gender, presumably occurred by means of genetic mutation. Mutations which are rather common in genetic transmission

It is generally assumed by medieval Jewish philosophers that, subject to miraculous and providential intervention, laws of nature were embedded in the universe from the moment of creation. The dictum of the Sages concerning the idiosyncratic nature of human physiognomy is quite consistent with that scheme. The appearance of individual countenances is controlled by multiple genes. Because of random combination of multiple genes and the phenomenon of genetic mutation of individual genes, facial appearance changes from generation to generation albeit while usually preserving familial resemblance to a greater or lesser extent. Man was created with forty-six chromosomes. Laws of nature ordained by the Deity provide for every child to inherit twenty-two matching chromosomes from each parent plus an additional chromosome from each parent that determines gender. Diversity among human beings is largely attributable to the random nature in which those matching pairs of chromosomes are divided so that only twenty-three chromosomes are present within each somatic cell and by which matching pairs of chromosomes are reassembled in the fusion of sperm and ovum. The randomness of inheritance of the multiple genes governing physical appearance guarantees a near infinity of possible phenotypes. Man was created and made subject to the rules of genetic inheritance, so that, *inter alia,* each person's appearance must be unique.

It has earlier been shown[50] that *Tosafot, Shevu'ot* 34a, establishes the principle that, given the laws of nature as postulated premises, circumstantial evidence in the form of necessary deductive conclusions based upon those laws constitutes proof positive for all halakhic purposes. *Tosafot*'s assertion is manifest in the distinction between *mayim she-yesh lahem sof* and *mayim she-ein lahem sof* as reflected in the following scenarios: A man enters a body of water and does

---

occurred over a period of generations. The Gemara, *Bava Meẓi'a* 87a, makes it quite clear that in the days of Abraham individual physiognomy was unique and that it was necessary for God to "change" Isaac's countenance so that he became immediately recognizable as the child of Abraham.

50 See *supra*, pp. 16–20.

not emerge. If the opposite shore is beyond visual perception, we do not permit the woman to remarry because of the possibility that the husband may have survived, emerged on the opposite side and then absconded. However, if the opposite bank is within sight and the husband does not reappear, we conclude as a matter of certainty that he perished in the water and permit his wife to contract a new marriage. In neither case has anyone seen a dead body. In the first case, it is highly unlikely that the husband swam across a body of water so vast that the other side is not within eyeshot, emerged alive, and later disappeared without a trace. Although circumstantial evidence of the husband's death is compelling, nevertheless, since it is within the realm of possibility that the husband is still alive, the wife cannot be declared a widow. In the second case, since were the husband to have emerged on the other side of the body of water he would have been seen, the circumstantial evidence of his non-appearance is acceptable. What assurance is there that the husband has not survived and is yet alive under water? Perhaps the husband tunneled under the opposite bank and emerged beyond eyesight. Perhaps the husband emerged but became invisible. Since those hypothetical conclusions are rendered impossible by the laws of nature, the circumstantial evidence dictates the only logical conclusion that is consistent with those laws, namely, that the husband drowned in the water but the body has not been found.

The laws of genetics dictate that an equal number of chromosomes are derived from each parent and that each of a paired set of chromosomes is contributed randomly by each parent. Accordingly, it is possible to determine in advance how many of the original chromosomes present in any particular progenitor will be present in each member of every succeeding generation. Consequently, the phenomenon of a particular number of identical DNA alleles shared by two individuals serves to establish not only the existence of a blood relationship but also the degree of that relationship.

A conclusion of that nature does not have the immediacy of *tevi'ut ayin*. It does arise from the *tevi'ut ayin* that establishes the commonality of a certain number of alleles. However, since such comparison is analogous to comparing half a countenance with half a countenance that comparison, in itself, proves nothing. However, reflection upon the number of alleles perceived to be shared in the context of known patterns of genetic behavior allows reason to make certain deductions. Those conclusions are logically deduced from the laws of nature governing genetic transmission. The result is a form of deductive evidence based upon established laws of nature that *Tosafot* declare to be recognized by Halakhah as absolute proof for all purposes. If so, DNA evidence in instances of DNA comparison of samples derived from different individuals, although it is not valid as a simple form of *tevi'ut ayin,* serves as the basis for applying deductive reasoning brought to bear upon information gleaned by *tevi'ut ayin.*

VIII. EXHUMATION FOR THE PURPOSE OF OBTAINING DNA

Teḥumin XXII (5762), pp. 412–426, features an article by Rabbi Zevi Yehudah Ben-Ya'akov discussing use of DNA evidence for resolving questions of inheritance. In that contribution Rabbi Ben-Ya'akov also addresses the issue of exhumation of a body for the purpose of obtaining a DNA sample on the basis of which the decedent's wife may be permitted to remarry. The prohibition against exhumation is recorded in *Semaḥot* 13:5 and in the Palestinian Talmud, *Mo'ed Katan* 2:4. Exceptions are provided in order to reinter the body on property belonging to the deceased or to transfer the remains from an ignominious location to a dignified grave.

The commentaries identify the narrative recounted in I Samuel 28:15 describing how Samuel was raised from the grave by a sorceress as the scriptural source for the prohibition against exhumation. Samuel exclaimed in distress, "Why did you cause me to tremble by raising me?" *Bet Yosef, Yoreh De'ah* 363, followed by *Shakh, Yoreh De'ah* 363:1, and *Taz, Yoreh De'ah* 363:1, explains that disturbing the repose of the deceased is distressful to them as alluded to in Job 3:13, "I slept, then it was restful for me." Two reasons are given for such distress: 1) pain experienced by the deceased as a result of disturbance of the corpse;

and 2) trepidation on the part of the deceased in the form of *ḥerdat ha-din,* i.e., anxiety on the part of the deceased because he fears that he is being summoned for Heavenly judgment.

R. Judah Leib Graubart, *Teshuvot Ḥavalim ba-Ne'imim,* II, no. 72, suggests that it may be the case that the alternate reasons underlying the prohibition against exhumation are rooted in those two separate scriptural passages and that they differ in their ambit. *Ḥavalim ba-Ne'imim* assumes that "pain" is experienced only by actual movement of the body whereas even uncovering the body disturbs the repose of the deceased by causing *ḥerdat ha-din.* Accordingly, *Ḥavalim be-Na'imim* surmises that "perhaps whether such fear is caused only by actual exhumation or even by exposure of the corpse depends upon which of the reasons serves as the source of the prohibition." The incident involving Samuel serves to establish only that actual "raising" and removal of a body from its grave is prohibited; even uncovering the corpse for examination *in situ* as described in Job disturbs the repose of the deceased because of fear of divine judgment.

However, R. Ẓevi Hirsch Ashkenazi, *Teshuvot Ḥakham Ẓevi,* no. 50, cites Job 3:13 as establishing a prohibition against disturbing the repose of the dead quite independent of any fear of judgment and finds such repose to be occasioned by any movement of the remains from place to place even in a sealed coffin. That appears to be the opinion of *Bet Yosef, Yoreh De'ah* 363, as well. Moreover, *Ḥakham Ẓevi* finds even uncovering the corpse to be prohibited for yet a third and probably more serious reason, namely, the prohibition against *nivul ha-met,* i.e., ignominious behavior that constitutes desecration of the corpse.[51]

R. Ezekiel Landau, *Teshuvot Noda bi-Yehudah, Yoreh De'ah, Mahadura Kamma,* no. 89, cites the verse "but his flesh shall pain him" (Job 14:22) as establishing that the dead experience pain only until their

---

51 R. Meir Simchah ha-Kohen of Dvinsk, *Or Sameaḥ, Hilkhot Semaḥot* 14:16, expresses doubt with regard to whether the prohibition of *nivul ha-met* is biblical or rabbinic in nature but, citing *Shabbat* 85a, regards it as associated with the verse "You shall not move the boundary of your fellow" (Deuteronomy 19:14).

flesh has entirely decomposed but do not experience pain when it is only their bones that are displaced. *Noda bi-Yehudah* explains that the fear and distress caused to the deceased arises because of dread of punishment to which they may be subjected, as suggested by *Ḥakham Ẓevi*, no. 50, but that upon total decomposition of the flesh there is no further punishment and hence no occasion for fear.[52] However, R. Shalom Schwadron, *Teshuvot Maharsham*, II, no. 343, does not accept that distinction. In addition, R. Mordecai Benet, *Parashat Mordekhai, Yoreh De'ah*, no. 24, takes issue with *Noda bi-Yehudah* in arguing that, even granting *Noda bi-Yehudah*'s contention regarding fear of judgment, the entirely separate prohibition of *nivul ha-met*, or desecration of the corpse, applies even to bones alone, as is evident from the comments of *Or Zaru'a, Hilkhot Aveilut*, no. 419. Indeed, it is quite evident from the discussion of the Gemara, *Bava Batra* 154a, that desecration of

52 R. Zevi Hirsch Ashkenazi, *Teshuvot Ḥakham Ẓevi*, no. 47, cites R. Gershon Metz, author of *Avodat ha-Gershuni*, who maintains that minors are not subject to judgment and hence do not experience fear of impending judgment, as well as the opposing view of R. David Oppenheim. R. Gershon Metz' opinion was later published by R. David Oppenheim in the latter's *Nish'al Dovid, Yoreh De'ah*, no. 27. Citing the *Zohar* and *Ḥesed le-Avraham, ma'ayan* 5, *nahar* 3, *Ḥakham Ẓevi*, no. 50, asserts that even minors are subject to fear of judgment. See also R. Shlomoh Kluger, *Ha-Elef Lekha Shlomoh, Yoreh De'ah*, no. 299, and R. Abraham Samuel Benjamin Sofer, *Teshuvot Ktav Sofer, Yoreh De'ah*, no. 183. Cf., R. Moshe Schick, *Teshuvot Maharam Shik, Yoreh De'ah*, no. 354, who declares that "fear of judgment" is limited to the twelve-month period following death. See the responsum of R. David Oppenheim, published as an addendum to *Teshuvot Ḥavvot Ya'ir* and included in his *Nish'al Dovid, Yoreh De'ah*, no. 27, who suggests that there is no fear of judgment on the part of a person who dies prior to attaining the age of twenty but rejects that view and asserts that there is no distinction between an adult and a minor. See R. Ezekiel Landau, *Teshuvot Noda bi-Yehudah, Yoreh De'ah, Mahadura Tinyana*, no. 164, and *Ktav Sofer, Yoreh De'ah*, no. 183, who disagree and maintain that even minors below the age of thirteen experience fear of judgment. R. Judah Aszod, *Teshuvot Mahari Asad, Yoreh De'ah*, no. 347, asserts that even abortuses and non-viable neonates experience fear of judgment. See also *Teshuvot Bet Leḥem Yehudah*, no. 363; *Teshuvot Yosef Omeẓ*, no. 37; *Teshuvot Seridei Esh*, II, no. 125; and *Sedei Ḥemed, Asifat Dinim, ma'arekhet aveilut*, no. 3.

the corpse is an independent reason for prohibiting exhumation and that such consideration applies even to mere visual observation of the uncovered remains.[53] Rabbi Ben-Ya'akov draws attention to *Teshuvot Ḥakham Ẓevi,* no. 50, from which it is clear that the distress caused to the deceased and their "fear of judgment" are two independent reasons for not disturbing the remains of the deceased.

Rabbi Ben-Ya'akov himself asserts that within three days of death, during which time the countenance has not undergone deterioration, there is no ignominy in merely observing the face of the deceased for purposes of identification. However, it would appear that, although opening a grave within the first three days following death and removing a miniscule DNA sample[54] without moving or disturbing the remains may not involve a violation of either *nivul ha-met* or occasion fear of judgment, it would nevertheless constitute disturbance of the repose of the deceased according to *Bet Yosef, Ḥakham Ẓevi* and later authorities who cite the verse in Job, "it was restful for me," as the basis of the prohibition and apply it literally.

The fundamental question of whether the prohibitions involved in exhumation are superseded by the need to identify a corpse so that the wife may be enabled to remarry is the subject of controversy between R. Eleazar Flekeles, a disciple of *Noda bi-Yehudah* and author of *Teshuvah me-Ahavah,* and R. Samuel Landau, a son of *Noda bi-Yehudah* and author of *Teshuvot Shivat Ẓion.* The responsa of both authors are published in the latter's *Shivat Ẓion,* nos. 64–66. R. Eleazar Flekeles asserts that, in light of the fact that the Sages assiduously strove to remedy the plight of the *agunah,* the grave may be uncovered "for such an important matter...particularly since it is also for the honor [of the deceased] so that his progeny will mourn and recite *kaddish.*" This position is also espoused by R. Joseph Saul Nathanson, *Teshuvot Sho'el u-Meshiv,* I, no. 231.

Shivat Ẓion disagrees and argues that the sole "honor" that justifies

---

53 See also the earlier-cited responsum of R. David Oppenheim and the responsum of R. Jacob Reischer, *Teshuvot Shevut Ya'akov, Yoreh De'ah,* no. 103.

54 See R. Moshe Feinstein, *Iggerot Mosheh, Yoreh De'ah,* II, no. 151.

opening a grave is the honor of burial in an ancestral plot or in the Land of Israel. Moreover, although the Gemara, *Bava Batra* 154b, recognizes the right of purchasers who have expended funds in acquiring property to demand exhumation in order to establish the decedent's legal majority by examining the corpse for the presence of pubic hair and hence his capacity to convey real property, the wife has no comparable claim against the deceased. *Shivat Ẓion*, no. 66, reaffirms the halakhic points he made in his earlier responsum but retracts his previous ruling because there is no guarantee that the attempt at identification will be successful. If the endeavor does not prove to be successful, the deceased, a complete stranger who is under no duty and who derives no benefit from the exhumation, will have been treated ignominiously without justification.

R. Abraham Benjamin Samuel Sofer, *Teshuvot Ktav Sofer, Yoreh De'ah*, no. 174, agrees that the corpse may not be defiled solely for the benefit of the widow but nevertheless finds reason to permit opening the grave. He argues that the grave may be uncovered in order that benefit may accrue to the deceased, including the spiritual merit that would accrue to the deceased through release of his widow from levirate obligations by means of *ḥaliẓah*.

Moreover, *Ktav Sofer* finds that, if the wife would otherwise be an *agunah* and there are also surviving sons, disinterment yields a benefit for the deceased. In a situation in which a wife is not permitted to remarry it is forbidden to observe mourning practices and sons may not recite *kaddish* lest the wife and prospective suitors erroneously believe that she is eligible to remarry as a widow. Thus, releasing the wife from the chains of *igun* results in benefit to the deceased in that it renders it permissible for the decedent's son to recite *kaddish* for the repose of his father's soul.

Ktav Sofer fully recognizes that should there be no affirmative identification subsequent to exhumation there will have been a miscarriage of Halakhah in the disrespectful treatment of an anonymous stranger without concomitant benefit to him. Accordingly, *Ktav Sofer* limits dispensation to open the grave to situations in which there is an *umdena*, i.e., reason to assume, that the corpse is that of the husband or that "intermediate" identificatory marks have been observed but those identificatory marks in themselves are insufficient evidence to permit the widow to remarry only because of the severity of the prohibition against adultery.[55] Such evidence, however, argues *Ktav Sofer*, is acceptable for other purposes of Halakhah, including suspension of the prohibition against violation of a corpse. The result is an almost paradoxical situation: Intermediate identificatory marks do not constitute evidence of sufficient strength to permit a wife to remarry nor can exhumation of a corpse be sanctioned for purposes of identification because the attempt at identification may fail. But intermediate identificatory marks do give rise to the degree of certainty necessary for other halakhic purposes, including the need to exhume the corpse in the anticipation that a more positive identification will indeed be available. Similarly, avoidance of the transgression of adultery requires a higher degree of certainty by virtue of rabbinic decree but the already available level of certainty is sufficient to obviate the prohibition against disturbing the dignity of the corpse in order to obtain the level of evidence necessary to permit the wife to remarry.[56]

---

55 See *supra*, p. 81.

56 See also *Oẓar ha-Poskim*, v, 17:24, sec. 200:19.

Chapter Four
Mamzerut

I. DNA AS EVIDENCE OF *MAMZERUT*

The question of whether a child can be declared a *mamzer* on the basis of DNA analysis is complex. *Teshuvot R. Akiva Eger,* no. 101, rules that principles of evidence and procedure for making such a determination are comparable to those governing capital cases. Consequently, the two-witness rule applies and testimony may be heard only in the presence of the putative *mamzer.* The various contemporary writers who regard DNA to be comparable to a *siman*[1] do not accept such evidence for purposes of awarding child support and certainly not for determination of *mamzerut.*

However, the issue of declaring the child to be a *mamzer* certainly does arise if DNA is regarded as tantamount to an *umdena de-mukhaḥ*[2] or to *tevi'ut ayin*[3] and hence as acceptable evidence to substantiate the claim of a plaintiff in financial matters. Nor does acceptance of DNA analysis as only a manifestation of *rov* serve to obviate the problem. DNA evidence does serve to generate doubt. Although, even according to *Pnei Yehoshu'a, Kiddushin* 73a, s.v. Rashi, and 75a, s.v. *ve-rami,* who maintains that only a *mamzer* certain is biblically categorized as a

1 See *supra,* pp. 81–82.
2 See *supra,* p. 59.
3 See *supra,* pp. 95–97.

mamzer and that *rov* does not establish the requisite degree of certainty for that purpose, nevertheless, *rov* does serve to establish status as a *mamzer* doubtful who is forbidden to contract a marriage with a person of legitimate birth by virtue of rabbinic decree.

Many writers cite the comment of *Reshash, Bava Batra* 58a, indicating that R. Bena'ah did not choose to apply R. Sa'adia Ga'on's blood test in order to disprove a filial relationship[4] because there is no halakhic obligation to engage in such an endeavor.[5] However, as has been noted,[6] it is far from clear that R. Sa'adia Ga'on's test is halakhically conclusive. More significantly, since marriage between a *mamzer* and a person of legitimate lineage involves a biblical transgression why is there no obligation to resolve the matter in instances of doubt?

Declaring DNA evidence to be in the category of a *siman muvhak*, R. Asher Weiss, *Teshuvot Minḥat Asher*, III, no. 81, regards DNA evidence as acceptable with regard to all noncriminal matters. Rabbi Weiss accepts the view of *Shakh, Ḥoshen Mishpat* 297:1, and *Netivot ha-Mishpat* 46:8, as opposed to that of *Keẓot ha-Ḥoshen* 46:8, 259:2 and 297:1 and *Teshuvot R. Akiva Eger*, no. 107, in affirming that, as a matter of biblical law, singular identificatory marks are recognized as tantamount to the testimony of two witnesses and hence are sufficient to support a plaintiff's monetary claim. Accordingly, he intimates that DNA evidence should constitute adequate proof of paternity for the purpose of establishing an obligation of child support. Although the Israeli Rabbinical Courts disagree with that position and do not recognize DNA evidence as dispositive, they do acknowledge that it gives rise to doubt.

Logical consistency should require that, in the case of a married woman, the selfsame evidence demonstrating that the husband is not the father should also establish that the child is a *mamzer* certain or – if the possibility that the wife's paramour was a non-Jew is to be

4 See *supra*, pp. 33–35.

5 See *Ḥelkat Meḥokek, Even ha-Ezer* 2:9.

6 See *supra*, p. 34, note 12.

entertained – a *mamzer* doubtful.[7] Rabbi Weiss, however, declines to accept that conclusion. In justifying that reluctance, he presents a number of considerations. One is that the tests are carried out by a technician and the results subsequently conveyed to the *bet din*, usually in writing. Rabbi Weiss objects to reliance upon that form of testimony because (1) *Shulḥan Arukh* and Rema, *Ḥoshen Mishpat* 28:11, rule in accordance with the opinion of Rashi who maintains that only oral testimony is admissible; (2) two witnesses are required; and (3) frequently, the technician is not a halakhically qualified witness. Rabbi Weiss regards DNA evidence as intrinsically sufficient for all purposes but, since the *bet din* does not itself have knowledge of the DNA results, it must be apprised of such findings by means of acceptable testimony and, generally, such testimony is not forthcoming.

That argument is hardly dispositive. First, if the usual rules of evidence govern with regard to conveyance of the results of the DNA test to the *bet din*, the *bet din* should also be unable to award child support and the like in the absence of the testimony of two qualified witnesses. Of course, if the putative father voluntarily accepts the accuracy of the results, further testimony would not be required insofar as the father's financial obligations are concerned. However, the father has no standing to enter a waiver on behalf of the child that would enable the *bet din* to declare the child to be a *mamzer*. It would then seem that other earlier-cited authorities who are willing to rely upon blood typing and DNA evidence would agree that two qualified witnesses would be required 1) to establish the provenance of the DNA sample, 2) to observe the testing process and 3) to testify to the authenticity of any written information conveyed to the *bet din*. Although the witnesses need not have the technical expertise to carry out the test themselves, they must acquire the knowledge necessary to understand the nature of the test in order to certify the results. If those conditions are satisfied, according to those authorities, child support might be assessed against the father – but, logically, the child must be declared a *mamzer* as well.

---

7 See *supra*, p. 44, note 38.

Rabbi Weiss' second objection is that the testing process is subject to human error. Rabbi Weiss acknowledges that the possibility of human error is present in all instances of eyewitness testimony, nevertheless, although such evidence is fallible, the two-witness rule mandates acceptance of the testimony of two qualified witnesses. However, claims Rabbi Weiss, although the technician can testify to the results of the tests he has conducted, he cannot possibly testify that no error has occurred because statistical evidence shows that some error does occur.

That argument is not compelling. The technician certainly does testify to the absence of error. He knows full well that error does occur but, nevertheless, he must be prepared to testify that he did not err and that, in effect, if at times error does occur it must be on the part of other technicians. Eyewitnesses cannot, and need not, testify that witnesses never err. Indeed, witnesses may err and may even commit perjury.[8] Implicit in the testimony of witnesses is that, despite the fallibility of human faculties, they themselves have not erred and they themselves have not committed perjury. The technician may have erred, but all witnesses may err. Witnesses can testify only to what they believe to be true. The technician similarly testifies to that which he believes to be true regarding the DNA sample he has examined. If so, it should follow that if DNA evidence is sufficient to compel child support it should establish the child's status as a *mamzer* as well.

II. *MISHPAḤAH SHE-NITME'AH NITME'AH*

Some writers have sought to apply the principle of "*mishpaḥah she-nitme'ah nitme'ah* – a family that has become intermingled remains intermingled" formulated by the Gemara, *Kiddushin* 71a. R. Moshe Sternbuch, *Teshuvot ve-Hanhagot*, I, no. 896, reports that he was consulted by a physician who in the course of performing a routine blood test discovered that the child's blood type was incompatible

---

8 See Rambam, *Hilkhot Yesodei ha-Torah* 7:7; *Hilkhot Yesodei ha-Torah* 8:2; and *Hilkhot Sanhedrin* 24:1. See *supra*, p. 12.

with that of his presumed father. The physician questioned whether he was obligated to disclose that the child is a *mamzer*. Rabbi Sternbuch replied that, since the child was recognized in the community as the son of the mother's husband and a *ḥazakah* had already been established, the principle of *mishpaḥah she-nitme'ah* formulated by the Gemara applies; consequently, the child cannot be relegated to the status of a *mamzer* other than on the basis of "absolute proof."

That brief response presents a number of difficulties: (1) nonpaternity established on the basis of blood typing represents conclusive application of scientifically based Mendelian principles and seemingly is the type of circumstantial evidence accepted by *Tosafot, Shevu'ot* 34a as admissible even in capital cases;[9] and (2) *mishpaḥah she-nitme'ah* is a widely misunderstood principle. It applies only in situations in which there is a cloud over a family because it is known that a *mamzer* has married into the family but no particular individual is known to be a *mamzer*.[10] It does not apply when a specific individual is known to be a *mamzer* or even a *mamzer* doubtful.[11] Furthermore, Rema, *Even ha-Ezer* 2:5, declares that it is proper to disclose the identity of even a possible *mamzer* to "*ẓenu'in*," i.e., persons who are discrete and would themselves not wish to marry a person whose genealogy is under a cloud. Moreover, Rema rules that the matter is not to be disclosed publicly only if the possible *mamzer* has already married but that if the person is as yet unmarried his status should be revealed and publicized so that others will not enter into marriage with him.[12]

The formulation of the cryptic and much misunderstood doctrine "*mishpaḥah she-nitme'ah nitme'ah*" ascribed by the Gemara, *Kiddushin* 71a, to R. Yitzchak reads: "The Holy One, blessed be He, performs an

---

9 See *supra*, pp. 16–20.

10 See *Ḥelkhat Meḥokek, Even ha-Ezer* 2:9 and *Bet Shmu'el* 2:19.

11 Some authorities limit this rule to a family into which an unidentified doubtful *mamzer* has married; others extend the rule to include a *mamzer* certain as well. See *Oẓar ha-Poskim*, I, 2:5, sec. 34.

12 See also R. Yechiel Michel Epstein, *Arukh ha-Shulḥan, Even ha-Ezer* 2:26; R. Menasheh Klein, *Mishneh Halakhot*, IX, no. 238; *Piskei Din Yerushalayim le-Dinei Mamonot u-Birur Yuḥasin*, XII (Jerusalem, 5770), pp. 414–417.

act of charity on behalf of Israel, for a family that has become intermingled remains intermingled." The Gemara introduces that dictum with an elucidation of Malachi 3:3, "And He shall sit as a refiner and as a purifier of silver." The prophet is understood by the Gemara as declaring that families whose lineage has been contaminated by persons disqualified from entering into marriage with persons of legitimate birth, e.g., *mamzerim*, but who succeeded in contracting prohibited marriages because of their wealth will not be separated from the community of Israel; rather, "since they have become intermingled, (i.e., unrecognized), they will remain intermingled." Rambam understands that comment as referring to individuals of illegitimate lineage but who are presumed by the public to be of legitimate birth. Rambam, *Hilkhot Melakhim* 12:2, states:

> He [Elijah] will come neither to declare the pure impure nor the impure pure; neither to disqualify those who are presumed to be of legitimate descent nor to pronounce qualified those who are deemed to be of illegitimate descent; but to bring peace to the world, as it is said: "And he shall turn the hearts of the fathers to the children" (Malachi 3:24).

Rambam makes it explicitly clear that this principle is applicable only upon the coming of the Messiah 1) by recording the principle in *Hilkhot Melakhim* rather than in his codification of the laws pertaining to forbidden marriages and 2) in declaring explicitly in the very next paragraph, *Hilkhot Melakhim* 12:3:

> *During the days of the messianic king,* (emphasis added) when his kingdom has been established and all of Israel has gathered around him [the entire nation's] line of descent will be established by his mouth on the basis of the prophetic spirit which shall rest upon him, as it is said: "He shall sit as refiner and purifier...."

Thus, Rambam declares that the dictum of *mishpaha she-nitme'ah nitme'ah* will be applied by the Messiah. The obvious inference is that it has no application prior to the arrival of the Messiah. However, Rabbenu Nissim, in his commentary on *Kiddushin* 71a, disagrees with Rambam and emphasizes that no halakhic provisions will be suspended upon the coming of the Messiah. He understands R. Yitzchak as teaching that, just as Elijah will not identify illegitimate families even though their identities will have been revealed to him, so also we should not, and dare not, do so.[13]

Shiltei ha-Gibborim, ad locum, citing Ri'az, carefully distinguishes between individuals of known tainted lineage and persons whose status is not publicly established. According to *Shiltei ha-Gibborim,* R. Yitzchak's dictum is limited in application to persons who have become recognized as individuals of legitimate birth. The verse in Malachi serves to confirm their legitimacy, both future and present. Nevertheless, Rabbenu Nissim concludes, "However, perhaps it is proper to reveal [their disqualification] to discrete persons because the Holy One, blessed be He, causes His presence to rest only upon the genealogically pure families of Israel." This is also the position of many early-day authorities and is codified in *Shulḥan Arukh, Even ha-Ezer* 2:5.

---

13 Rabbenu Nissim's major point is that, contrary to some authorities, since Halakhah remains constant, the status of a *mamzer* certain will not change in the messianic era. Citing Rambam's forceful declaration to the effect that Halakhah will not be modified in the messianic era, Rabbenu Nissim concludes that just as the messiah will not identify unknown *mamzerim* we must not do so either. It is possible to read Rabbenu Nissim as ascribing that position to Rambam himself. See R. Moshe Feinstein, *Iggerot Mosheh, Even ha-Ezer,* IV, no. 9, sec. 2. However, in context, Rambam is cited by Rabbenu Nissim only to contradict other authorities who maintain that even *mamzerim* certain will be accepted by the messiah. Rabbenu Nissim's concluding remark asserting that consistency demands that the identity of a doubtful *mamzer* should not be revealed in our day, just as it will not be revealed by the messiah, is not necessarily to be understood as ascribed to Rambam by Rabbenu Nissim. The inference from Rambam's words is quite the opposite. Nor would Rambam necessarily accept Rabbenu Nissim's argument that the messiah will not use prophetic insight to reveal the status of a doubtful *mamzer* represent a change in the Halakhah that currently requires us to do so. We, in our day, are similarly not obligated to employ prophetic insight to reveal the status of a *mamzer* doubtful, nor are we capable of doing so. Thus, no change in Halakhah will occur.

Ḥelkat Meḥokek, Even ha-Ezer 2:9, and *Bet Shmu'el, Even ha-Ezer* 2:19, emphasize that the restriction against revealing illegitimate lineage is limited to a particular individual who has come into possession of information not known to others. However, when the *irur,* or challenge to the legitimacy of the family, is widely known, it is obligatory to conduct an investigation into their lineage; otherwise, it is forbidden to enter into marriage with a member of such a family.

It might be possible to understand those authorities as interpreting R. Yitzchak's dictum to be inclusive of all unidentified persons of illegitimate birth who are otherwise subject to marital restrictions, including situations in which the unidentified individual is a *mamzer* certain. However, *Ḥelkat Meḥokek* and *Bet Shmu'el* as well as subsequent latter-day authorities fail to do so. Those authorities limit the ambit of R. Yitzhak's statement to situations in which the unidentified individual is a *mamzer* doubtful. According to those authorities, the prohibition against marrying into a family one of whose number is a *mamzer* certain remains firmly in place and will remain in effect even subsequent to the advent of the Messiah. Why, then, is a person in possession of personal knowledge of illegitimacy not obligated to reveal that information in order to prevent transgression?[14]

Both *Ḥelkat Meḥokek* and *Bet Shmu'el* limit application of this rule to a situation in which 1) the cloud of illegitimacy extends only to a single unidentified member or to a small number of unidentified members of a family and 2) the illegitimacy of the person or persons is not known with certainty but is merely a matter of doubt. The result is a *sefek sefeika,* or a "double doubt." In instances of *sefek sefeika* there is no infraction whatsoever. Elijah himself will not be in a state of doubt; as a prophet he will be fully aware of all genealogical information but "the Torah is not in heaven" (Deuteronomy 30:12) and issues of doubt

14 Indeed, Rema, *Yoreh De'ah* 265:4, records that it is customary to proclaim a male child's status as a *mamzer* at the time of his circumcision. In some locales it was even the practice to name the baby "*Kidor,*" an illusion to the verse "*ki dor tahpuḥot hemah*" (Deuteronomy 32:20) which, in turn, is understood as a reference to licentiousness. See *Yoma* 83b.

must be resolved solely by means of natural human intelligence and prowess.[15] Accordingly, Elijah will not reveal instances of illegitimacy. Since the identity of a *mamzer* doubtful will never become known, each member of the family is permitted to marry without restriction. Since that is the normative Halakhah, no person may cast aspersion upon members of the family by publicizing the existence of an inconsequential *sefek sefeika* that does not pose an impediment to marriage. Consequently, there is certainly an obligation to disclose the status of an identifiable *mamzer* certain, or even of an identifiable *mamzer* doubtful, in order to prevent transgression and to prevent a *sefek sefeika* with regard to the entire family from arising with the passage of time.

In defense of those who invoke the principle *mishpaḥah she-nitme'ah nitme'ah* in support of nondisclosure it must be said that the dictum is often used as a *bon mot* rather than a halakhic justification. Used in that sense, *mishpaḥah she-nitme'ah nitme'ah* is conclusory in nature and applied in situations in which halakhic doubt has been resolved permissively on adequate grounds and consequently there is no reason to air the matter publicly. In such contexts, the import of the aphorism is "Let sleeping dogs lie." In the present context it does not explain why it is unnecessary to seek available genetic information in order to avoid transgression.

III. *ḤAZAKAH* AS DETERMINATIVE

In an article published in *Shurat ha-Din*, v, 66–90, R. David Levanon addresses, *inter alia*, the question of the reliability of DNA evidence in establishing that a child is a *mamzer*. The anecdote recorded in

---

15 See R. Elchanan Wasserman, *Kuntres Divrei Soferim*, no. 5, sec. 5, who asserts that a prophet lacks credibility with regard to matters of fact only in proceedings in which the two-witness rule is applicable. Cf., *Tosefet Yom ha-Kippurim*, *Yoma* 75a; R. Ẓevi Hirsch Chajes, *Torat ha-Nevi'im*, chap. 2 and addendum as well as R. Abraham Israel Rosenthal, *Ke-Moẓe Shalal Rav* (Jerusalem, 5762), v, 337–338. As noted earlier, *Teshuvot R. Akiva Eger*, no. 107, states that two witnesses are required to determine status as a *mamzer*.

Sefer Ḥasidim regarding acceptance of absorption of blood by a bone as evidence of paternity is certainly far less scientifically reliable than DNA evidence. Nevertheless, *Eliyahu Rabbah* and *Teshuvot Rivash* accept that test as conclusive confirmation of a filial relationship.[16] Although he takes passing notice of anonymous sources that question the scientific basis of the test, R. Abraham Price, *Mishnat Avraham, Sefer Ḥasidim*, I, no. 291, ascribes extravagant reliability to that test in categorizing it as regarded by the Gemara as constituting an *anan sahadei*. Earlier, the Tel Aviv *bet din* accepted evidence in the form of incompatible blood types as constituting a *rov* but found that, in the case of a married woman, there is a contradictory *rov* in the form of *rov be'ilot*.[17]

In point of fact, it was probably not necessary for R. Sa'adia's examination to yield a positive proof of the absence of a filial relationship in order for the child whose blood was not absorbed to be disinherited. Consequently, there is no evidence that R. Sa'adia would regard hematological evidence as an absolute proof of illegitimacy. In all likelihood, the claim of the son whose blood was absorbed had already been established as a matter of public knowledge in the deceased's original place of domicile and was merely confirmed by the blood experiment. That fact was presumably known to R. Sa'adia, albeit not to the non-Jewish king. Hence, the son was already an heir certain. It was not necessary for the non-absorption of blood of the putative son to be accepted as proof positive of the absence of a father-son relationship for him to be disinherited. Even if failure of the experiment generated only a doubt with regard to the existence of an additional paternal-filial relationship, any other claimant would have been disinherited; his status would have been that of an heir doubtful whereas the newly-arrived son was an heir certain, since there was no evidence to contradict the already established paternal-filial

16 See *supra*, p. 34, note 11 and p. 38.

17 See *supra*, p. 52 and the decision of the Rabbinical District Court of Ashdod, *Piskei Din Rabbaniyim*, XIII, 51–68, with regard to DNA evidence.

relationship. The son whose blood was absorbed would have prevailed on the basis of the halakhic principle *ein safek moẓi midei vadai.*[18]

In an earlier-cited decision of the Rabbinical District Court of Ashdod, *Piskei Din Rabbaniyim,* XIII, 51–68,[19] R. Shlomoh Deichovsky tentatively argues that if a child's legitimacy is challenged on the basis of DNA evidence the issue can be resolved on the basis of *ḥazakah.* The argument is that *rov be'ilot* and DNA evidence are contradictory *rovs* that render a child a *mamzer* doubtful. However, if the child was earlier accepted as the child of the mother's husband on the basis of behavior and comportment, that in itself establishes a *ḥazakah* having the effect of resolving the doubt by establishing the husband as the father. In the case before the *bet din,* because, prior to the doubt created by DNA analysis, a presumption of paternity had been established in the wake of the husband's original acknowledgment of paternity. Rabbi Deichovsky rejects that conclusion in arguing that a *ḥazakah* established in error is not a *ḥazakah.* To put the matter somewhat differently, he maintains that a *ḥazakah* based upon a presumption later shown to be erroneous must retroactively be recognized as an erroneous *ḥazakah.* The husband's acknowledgement of paternity, as manifested by his behavior *vis-à-vis* the child and the resultant public perception of a paternal-filial relationship, all came about in error as established by subsequent DNA evidence. If so, in light of contradictory *rovs,* it should follow that the child has the status of a *mamzer* doubtful.

R. Ya'akov Eliezerov, another member of the Ashdod *bet din,* followed by Rabbi Levanon in his contribution to *Shurat ha-Din,* takes issue with Rabbi Deichovsky's contention that DNA evidence has the effect of negating a previously established presumption of paternity based on *ḥazakah.* Although they concede that an erroneously established *ḥazakah* is of no evidentiary value, they nevertheless maintain that, unless the *ḥazakah* is demonstrated with certainty to have been

---

18 For explanation of that principle see *infra,* p. 149, note 5 and accompanying text.

19 See *supra,* pp. 52–53.

established in error, the *ḥazakah* remains effective as a nonprobative presumption. Rabbi Eliezerov and Rabbi Levanon contend that when a presumption established by *ḥazakah* has not been successfully rebutted but has merely become a subject of doubt, e.g., by application of a contradictory *rov*, the previously established *ḥazakah* has not lost its procedural efficacy.[20] According to those authorities, the

---

20 Rabbi Deichovsky's explanation is complex and nuanced and is propounded in order to explain a fundamental difficulty with regard to mistakenly established *ḥazakot*. For example, a woman has virtually absolute credibility in informing her husband that she is a menstruant. At the same time, she can withdraw her statement upon offering an *amatla*, or cogent reason, for her original misstatement. If, however, her status became known in her social circle, e.g., she donned garments known to be worn by her only during her menstrual periods, such comportment gives rise to a *ḥazakah* that she cannot readily negate unless she can credibly claim that her conduct was born of genuine error. Unlike a mere verbal statement that can be withdrawn as having been false if the original deceit is acknowledged but explained (e.g., she felt unwell and did not wish to engage in intercourse) she cannot negate a resultant *ḥazakah* even if it arose only because of her misleading act unless she can establish that she acted in actual error. Thus, she cannot claim that she wore inappropriate clothing simply because other laundered clothes were not available. Unless there was an incontrovertible error in its establishment, a *ḥazakah* generates a halakhic status that cannot be explained away. Rabbi Deichovsky explains that the *ḥazakah* controls because the woman could have prevented its inception by "seizing a cymbal in her hand" and explaining to her friends that she was wearing those clothes only because she had no others and thereby would have prevented a *ḥazakah* from arising; if that option was not available to her, e.g., she believed that a particular stain rendered her a *niddah* but subsequently discovered that her presumption was incorrect, her error made it impossible for her to prevent a *ḥazakah* from arising. A *ḥazakah* arising as a result of such error has no halakhic import.

It seems to this writer that this analysis has an impact upon child support subsequent to DNA testing as well. A husband who treats a child as his own until a DNA test shows otherwise can certainly contest liability for child support by asserting that, since the facts revealed to him by DNA testing were previously unknown to him, he acted out of unavoidable error in allowing a paternal-filial relationship to be presumed. However, if the husband was earlier aware of the fact that the child was not his but, by virtue of his comportment allowed a public perception to that effect to arise by virtue of his failure to

rov reflected in DNA analysis, since it remains contradicted by *rov be'ilot*, does not definitively demonstrate that the previous *ḥazakah* was established in error. Hence, the *ḥazakah* remains effective and, consequently, the father retains the prerogative of establishing the illegitimacy of the child on the basis of the principle of *yakkir*.[21]

In a concurring opinion in a case before the Rabbinical District Court of Haifa,[22] and in an article published in *Teḥumin*, XXXV (5775), 212, R. Yizchak Zevi Ushinsky suggests that, although *Bet Shmu'el, Even ha-Ezer* 2:2,[23] maintains that a single witness is insufficient to establish matters of lineage, he would agree that DNA analysis, in and of itself, is sufficient to determine a maternal-filial relationship. Rabbi Ushinsky compares DNA evidence to the acceptance of comportment as mother and child, *viz.*, "a child following a woman in the marketplace," as proof of a maternal-filial relationship.

However, the comparison of DNA evidence to comportment as mother and child is inapt. The latter is a *ḥezkat hanhagah*, i.e., comportment that is recognized by the public as emblematic of a maternal-filial relationship; it is only after that relationship has been publicly demonstrated and hence antecedently established that it becomes the premise for consequential matters, e.g., punishment for striking a parent, incest, etc. If, as *Bet Shmu'el* asserts, a single witness

---

negate that perception, according to Rabbi Deichovsky's analysis, the *ḥazakah* will control and cause him to remain liable for child support.

21 The distinction may perhaps be captured by a somewhat different formulation. *Ḥazakah* may operate either as a *birur*, i.e., an evidentiary rule, or as *din*, i.e., a judicial presumption that might be categorized as "halakhic inertia." The value of a *rov* arising from an erroneously established *ḥazakah* loses all evidentiary value when contradicted by a second *rov*. An unknown conflict between two *rov*s does not disprove the application of either *rov*; the conflict serves only to neutralize the *birur* or evidentiary capacity of the *ḥazakah* arising in its wake. However, since the fact established by the *ḥazakah* has not been disproved, the status of the *ḥazakah* as *din*, i.e., non-evidentiary establishment of a presumed status, is not affected unless and until the erroneous presumption is conclusively rebutted.

22 No. 954915–1, 20 Elul 5773.

23 Cf., however, *Oẓar ha-Poskim* 2:2, sec. 4.

cannot testify to legitimacy for purposes of marriage it is because of the principle of *ma'alah asu be-yuḥasin,* i.e., a rabbinic stringency designed to protect against forbidden marriages when the status of the individual seeking to marry has not been previously established by means of *ḥazakah*. There is no reason to assume that, for *Bet Shmu'el,* in the absence of a *ḥazakah, rov* is any more acceptable than the testimony of a single witness. Consequently, there are no grounds to assume that the *rov* reflected by DNA analysis should suffice in itself to create a presumption of a paternal relationship unless accompanied with, or followed by, a behavioral *ḥazakah*.

IV. DOUBLE DOUBT

Earlier, in chapter 2, section V, R. Shalom Messas' position regarding *sefek sefeika,* or "double doubt," was discussed in detail. Briefly summarized, Rabbi Messas asserts that the controversy regarding the admissibility of DNA evidence gives rise to a status of halakhic doubt. In addition, assuming that the husband is not the father of the child, a doubt arises with regard to whether conception occurred as the result of cohabitation with a Jew or a non-Jew. If the father was a non-Jew, the child is not a *mamzer.* The Sages did indeed prohibit marriage between a *mamzer* doubtful and a person of legitimate birth. However, asserts Rabbi Messas, the Sages did not prohibit such marriage in cases of *sefek sefeika* or "double doubt."

R. Shlomoh Aviner, *Assia,* No. 67–68, vol. 17, no. 3–4 (Shevat 5761), pp. 99–100, similarly rules that DNA evidence cannot establish *mamzerut* because of the confluence of a number of considerations:

1. Whether DNA evidence is sufficient with regard to establishing paternity is a matter of halakhic controversy.
2. DNA evidence is circumstantial in nature and, although *Tosafot* regard circumstantial evidence that is deductive in nature to be acceptable even in capital cases, that position is rejected by Mei'ri and *Yad Ramah.*[24]

24 See *supra,* pp. 16–20.

That consideration arises only if the logically prior issue of whether a two-witness rule applies with regard to establishing *mamzerut* is resolved in the affirmative.[25] Only if that position is accepted antecedently can the issue of whether deductive circumstantial evidence is tantamount to two witnesses be considered. If the two-witness rule does not apply, the controversy between those early-day authorities is moot. Basically, this issue is simply one facet that enters into the controversy regarding sufficiency of DNA evidence rather than an independent doubt.

3. The father of a child may be a non-Jew, in which case the child is not a *mamzer*.
4. DNA evidence, although highly reliable, is nevertheless subject to error.

If Rabbi Aviner's allusion is to empirical error, that point is integral to the controversy regarding whether DNA can be accepted on the basis of *rov*. If the allusion is to human error on the part of the technician, the response is that all eyewitness testimony is subject to human error.[26]

5. DNA evidence, by its nature, is based upon microscopic genetic fragments.

Rabbi Aviner regards all subclinical phenomena as entirely beyond the cognizance of Halakhah. Moreover, Rabbi Aviner actually considers this consideration as dispositive, thereby rendering other arguments superfluous.

Rabbi Aviner's final argument is akin to the more limited argument advanced by Rabbis Samuel Mordecai Gersten and Judah Shereshevsky, *Yeshurun*, XII, 493–495, to the effect that only a physical characteristic observed by the naked eye qualifies as a *siman*.[27] Rabbi

25 See *Teshuvot R. Akiva Eger*, no. 124, s.v. *gam yesh*, discussed *infra*, p. 189. See also *infra*, p. 181, note 24. R. Akiva Eger's view is impliedly rejected by the many decisors who examine the applicability of other categories of evidence.

26 See *supra*, p. 124.

27 See *supra*, p. 88.

Aviner's argument is much broader: "For the Torah was given in conformity with human reflection (*al da'at bnei adam*) in accordance with usual halakhic truths." It is indeed true that halakhically cognized criteria are based on normally perceivable phenomena and that subclinical phenomena are ignored because "the Torah was given neither to angels nor to owners of microscopes or telescopes," as stated by Rabbi Aviner. That is true with regard to definitional matters, e.g., identity of a *sherez̩*, a gap in a letter of a Torah scroll or a spot on an *etrog* etc.,[28] but there is no reason to assume that it applies to either evidence or knowledge based upon subclinical evidence. If "knowledge" – as distinct from eyewitness testimony – is sufficient, it is, to be sure, human knowledge that is required, but the method by which evidence is discovered and the knowledge that is thereby acquired should be entirely irrelevant. The issue is only whether circumstantial evidence can give rise to an *umdena, anan sahadei* or the like.

There is no reason that the instrumental factors that give rise to "knowledge" cannot be subclinical. Rabbi Aviner argues that a person who would not have been declared a *mamzer* in days gone by cannot be categorized as a *mamzer* upon invention of the microscope. That argument is a *non sequitur.* A person identified as a *mamzer* by qualified witnesses would not be declared a *mamzer* if witnesses did not come forward. Nor would that person be declared a *mamzer* had witnesses not been present to observe the occurrence to which they testify. Knowledge derived from DNA analysis may not have been available in earlier epochs but that knowledge, when available, is human knowledge, not angelic knowledge and not "microscopic" knowledge.

Thus, upon closer scrutiny, Rabbi Aviner's arguments are reducible to Rabbi Messas' contention that the validity of DNA testing

28 See J. David Bleich, *Bioethical Dilemmas,* II (Southfield, Michigan, 2006), 213–215, and *idem, Contemporary Halakhic Problems,* VI (Jersey City, 2012), 203–217 and 271–274. Cf., also R. Shlomoh Auerbach, *Minḥat Shlomoh: Tinyana* (Jerusalem, 5760), no. 100, sec. 7. According to the position attributed to Rabbi Auerbach in that source there is no question that Halakhah would take cognizance of DNA evidence placed on a slide and examined under a microscope.

in establishing *mamzerut* is a halakhic *sefek sefeika*, i.e., controversy regarding acceptability of DNA evidence and doubt arising from the possibility that the child's father is a non-Jew. Rabbi Aviner's argument also assumes as a silent premise that marriage to a person whose status as a *mamzer* rests upon a *sefek sefeika* is entirely permissible.

V. SHOULD DNA TESTING BE PERFORMED?

Certainly, if DNA evidence does not suffice to determine absence of paternity for any halakhic matter, there is no reason to undertake such testing.[29] A husband's right to demand a DNA test in conjunction with

---

29 Disclosure of *mamzerut* by a physician as a possible violation of the Hippocratic Oath is discussed by *Ẓiẓ Eli'ezer*, XIII, no. 81 and no. 104, sec. 1.

In 1983, the President's Commission recommended that misattributed paternity be disclosed to both husband and wife. See President's Commission for the Study of Ethical Problems in Medicine and Biomedical and Behavioral Research, *Screening and Counseling for Genetic Conditions: A Report on the Ethical, Social, and Legal Implications of Genetic Screening, Counseling, and Education Programs*, Washington, DC: U.S. Government Printing Office, 1983, pp. 60–61. However, in 1994 the Committee on Assessing Genetic Risks of the Institute of Medicine recommended that only the mother be informed and that misattributed paternity not be disclosed to her husband, on the grounds that "genetic testing should not be used in ways that disrupt families." See Committee on Assessing Genetic Risks, Institute of Medicine, *Assessing Genetic Risks: Implications for Health and Social Policy*, ed. Lori B. Andrews, Jane E. Fullarton, Neil A. Holtzman and Arno G. Motulsky, Washington, DC, 1994, pp. 6, 23, 38, 70, 100, 127, 163 and 175. The American Society of Human Genetics has recommended that information concerning paternity not be provided to a child's parent unless there is a clear medical benefit for the child. See American Society of Human Genetics Board of Directors and American College of Medical Genetics Board of Directors, "Points to Consider: Ethical, Legal, and Psychosocial Implications of Genetic Testing in Children and Adolescents," *American Journal of Human Genetics*, vol. 57, no. 5 (November, 1995), pp. 1233–1241. In 2015, the American Society of Human Genetics issued a position statement recommending that healthcare providers avoid disclosure of misattributed parentage unless there is a clear medical benefit that outweighs the potential harms.

See J.R. Botkin, J.W. Belmont, J.S. Berg *et al.*, "Points to Consider: Ethical,

his refusal to provide child support has already been discussed.[30] The remaining issue is whether a DNA test should be performed solely in order to determine the status of the child as a *mamzer* certain or as a *mamzer* doubtful and, the concomitant question of the effect of such testing, if performed, upon the status of the child.

The issue of whether a DNA test should be performed if it would lead to unwelcome identification of a *mamzer* has not been addressed directly in the rather extensive literature dealing with DNA and Halakhah. However, the Rabbinical District Court of *Ẓefat*, composed of R. Chaim Bazak, R. Yo'ezer Ariel and R. Shlomoh Shoshan,[31] did recently issue a ruling in a different matter that addresses similar considerations.

An unmarried woman became pregnant by means of artificial insemination using semen that was obtained from a donor (AID). In an earlier decision dated 17 Cheshvan 5778, the *bet din* of *Ẓefat* ruled that anonymous sperm donations are forbidden because of the possibility of future incestuous relationships but that *post factum* a child born as a result of such a procedure might enter into a valid marriage since the likelihood of an incestuous marriage is remote. The issue before the *bet din* was whether a young woman born of AID and her prospective groom should undergo a DNA test before a

---

Legal, and Psychosocial Implications of Genetic Testing in Children and Adolescents," *American Journal of Human Genetics*, vol. 97, no. 1 (July, 2015), pp. 6–21. More recently, the Connecticut Supreme Court, in *Doe v. Cochran*, 332 Conn. 325 (2019), ruled that a physician "owes a duty of care to an identifiable third party." See also Moshe Y. Prero, Meghan Strenk, Jeremy Garrett *et al.*, "Disclosure of Misattributed Paternity," *Pediatrics*, vol. 143, no. 6 (June, 2019).

The issue of whether the right to privacy includes "a right not to know" is a topical issue in contemporary bioethics. See, *inter alia*, Graeme Laurie, "Recognizing the Right Not to Know: Conceptual, Professional, and Legal Implications," *Journal of Law, Medicine & Ethics*, vol. 42, no. 1 (Spring, 2014), pp. 53–63 and Jonathan Herring and Charles Foster, "'Please Don't Tell Me': The Right Not to Know," *Cambridge Quarterly of Healthcare Ethics*, vol. 21, no. 1 (January, 2012), pp. 20–29.

30 See *supra*, pp. 71–73.

31 No. 112395/1, 20 Adar 5778.

marriage license is issued in order to assure that no consanguineous relationship exists.

The *bet din* recognized that there is no barrier to the daughter's marriage to any unmarried member of the overwhelming majority of eligible male suitors. The principle of *rov* serves to determine that any particular prospective groom is not a member of the class of forbidden relatives. The issue is whether it is permissible to rely upon *rov* or whether, when possible, there is an obligation to investigate further rather than to rely upon *rov*. The *bet din* marshalled a number of well-known sources indicating that such an investigation is required.

The Gemara, *Ḥullin* 3b, posits a presumption to the effect that a majority of persons who undertake the slaughter of an animal are proficient in the laws governing the procedure. Nevertheless, a prospective slaughterer must undergo an examination to determine his knowledgeability regarding such matters before he is entrusted with carrying out the procedure. However, if the slaughterer was not tested prior to slaughter of the animal and is presently unavailable to be tested subsequent to the slaughter of the animal, *post factum* the slaughtered animal is regarded as kosher in reliance upon the *rov*. Quite evidently, at least in some cases, it is not appropriate to rely upon *rov* when the facts can readily be established with certainty.

The rule with regard to reliance upon *rov* is clarified in a number of sources:

1) Animals suffering from certain anatomical anomalies, either congenital in nature or the result of trauma, are *treifot* and hence non-kosher. Unless there is evidence to the contrary, the animal is presumed to be kosher because the majority of animals do not suffer such defects. Nevertheless, unless they have been lost, examination of the animal's lungs is required. Rashi, *Ḥullin* 12a, s.v. *Pesaḥ*, and *Shakh, Yoreh De'ah* 39:2, explain that there is a *mi'ut ha-moẓuy*, or "prevalent minority," of animals that suffer from adhesions and other pulmonary anomalies. The rule formulated by those authorities is that in face of a "prevalent minority" reliance upon *rov* is appropriate only *post factum*. Otherwise, an examination or investigation should be undertaken in order to determine the salient facts with certainty.

2) The Gemara, *Pesaḥim* 9a, discusses whether a person who leases a dwelling on the fourteenth day of Nisan may assume that the search for *ḥameẓ* has already been carried out. It is to be presumed that the majority of property owners carry out the search for *ḥameẓ* at the designated time, *viz.*, the eve of the fourteenth day of Nisan. However, the Gemara states that if the lessor is available one should not rely on such a presumption; rather, the lessor must be asked whether the domicile has actually been inspected for the presence of *ḥameẓ*. One member of the *Ẓefat bet din*, R. Yo'ezer Ariel, cites *Mishkenot Ya'akov, Yoreh De'ah*, no. 17, who rules that a minority of ten percent constitutes a *mi'ut ha-moẓuy* but that a lower percentage may be ignored.[32] The proportion of children born of AID is extremely small and does not rise to the level of a *mi'ut ha-moẓuy*. Consequently, DNA testing to exclude the possibility of consanguinity is not necessary.

Moreover, *Pri Megadim*, in his introduction to *Yoreh De'ah* 39, demonstrates that if the matter requires "*toraḥ gadol*," or "great travail," no examination is necessary.[33] Rema, *Yoreh De'ah* 102:3, equates

32 That is also the position of *Teshuvot Dvar Shmu'el*, no. 260. See also R. Shlomoh Zalman Auerbach, *Minḥat Shlomoh, Tinyana*, no. 63. That figure is derived from a presumption recorded in the Mishnah, *Bava Batra* 93b, to the effect that ten percent of wine turns to vinegar and hence a buyer has no recourse if less than that quantity of the purchased wine is found to be spoiled. R. Samuel ha-Levi Woszner, *Teshuvot Shevet ha-Levi*, IV, no. 81, objects that, although the source establishes that ten percent is certainly a *mi'ut ha-moẓuy*, a lower proportion might constitute a *mi'ut ha-moẓuy* as well. In response it may be argued, that since there is no confirmatory evidence that such is the case and, consequently, since the obligation to be concerned with a *mi'ut ha-moẓuy* is rabbinic in nature, any doubt is to be resolved permissively. Other authorities, including R. Joseph Shalom Eliashiv, R. Nissim Karelitz and R. Chaim Kanievsky, define *mi'ut ha-moẓuy* as five percent. See J. David Bleich, *Contemporary Halakhic Problems*, VI (Jersey City, New Jersey, 2012), 245, note 72. See also R. Moshe Viya, *Bedikat ha-Mazon ke-Halakhah* I (Jerusalem, 5738), *sha'ar* 2, chap. 4:2, note 3. In the second edition of that work, I (Jerusalem, 5765), 116, the author cites R. Joseph Shalom Eliashiv as maintaining that *mi'ut ha-moẓuy* is to be defined as four percent.

33 *Shulḥan Arukh, Yoreh De'ah* 184:49, similarly rules that a *sefek sefeika*, or "double doubt" cannot be relied upon if the doubt can be resolved but that there is

expenditure of funds with "travail" in ruling that if a non-kosher utensil has become mingled with kosher utensils the utensils need not be koshered because of the expense involved.[34] Rabbi Ariel concludes that, since DNA testing involves significant expenditure of both time and money, the prospective bride need not seek DNA confirmation of the absence of consanguinity before marrying.

Nevertheless, Rabbi Ariel entertains the possibility that requirements pertaining to a possibly forbidden marriage may be more stringent and hence require investigation and clarification despite the presence of *rov* even though the investigation may be cumbersome and/or require an expenditure of funds. The Gemara, *Nazir* 11b, declares that a person who designates an agent to betroth an unspecified woman on his behalf is prohibited from entering into a marital relationship with all other women because of 1) the presumption that the agent has fulfilled his duty and 2) the resultant possibility that any particular woman he seeks to marry may be a prohibited relative of his presently unidentified wife. *Tosafot, ad locum*, s.v. *asur*, explains that the rule is rabbinic in nature and is predicated upon the stringent nature of prohibitions concerning forbidden marriages.[35]

---

no need to do so if "exertion" is necessary. See also Rashba, *Ḥullin* 53b and R. Shlomoh ha-Kohen of Vilna, *Teshuvot Binyan Shlomoh*, no. 13. Cf., Rema, *Yoreh De'ah* 110:9, who rules that there is no obligation to investigate matters subject to a *sefek sefeika*. See *Contemporary Halakhic Problems*, VI, 343–354, regarding whether the pregnant wife of a *kohen* who contemplates coming into contact with a corpse is required to undergo a sonogram in order to ascertain that she is not carrying a male fetus who would be subjected to defilement.

Shulḥan Arukh, Oraḥ Ḥayyim 14:4, rules that one may borrow a *tallit* belonging to another person without permission and Rema, *Oraḥ Ḥayyim* 649:5, similarly rules that one may borrow the four species on *Sukkot* without permission because of a presumption that people are pleased to have *mizvot* performed with their possessions. Nevertheless, *Mishnah Berurah* 14:13 and 649:34, rules that if the owner is present one should not rely upon that presumption "since the matter can readily be clarified."

34 See also R. Shlomoh Luria, *Yam shel Shlomoh, Ḥullin*, chap. 8, no. 87.

35 See *Bi'ur ha-Gra, Even ha-Ezer* 4:99, who posits an identical concern with regard to foundlings and with regard to a person whose father is unknown.

However, *Arukh ha-Shulḥan, Even ha-Ezer* 4:58, points to a further comment of *Tosafot, ad locum,* indicating that the prohibition in the case of the earlier described agent is in the nature of a rabbinic penalty for having created a potential pitfall by giving the agent absolute discretion to act on his behalf. *Arukh ha-Shulḥan* notes the absence of a similar restriction because of fear of a consanguineous marriage in the case of a child whose parents are unknown. *Arukh ha-Shulḥan* contends that the two cases are dissimilar in that the principal who designated the agent and granted him unrestricted power is deserving of a penalty for having acted incorrectly but that a foundling is not guilty of any infraction and hence not deserving of punishment. Similarly, contends Rabbi Ariel, a woman who avails herself of artificial insemination with the semen of an anonymous donor may deserve to be penalized, but a child born of that procedure is entirely innocent.

Moreover, Ramban, *Gittin* 64a, is of the opinion that the restriction upon the principal is not a rabbinically imposed penalty but is biblical in nature. The restriction, according to Ramban, is biblical because the principle of *rov* does not apply. The principle of *rov* applies only in situations in which the person or object upon whom doubt devolves has become separated from other members of his or its class; *rov* does not apply in instances in which the subject of doubt remains *kavu'a,* i.e., *in situ.* Ramban maintains that the principle of *rov* does not apply in the case of an unidentified bride because the bride is in a status of *kavu'a,* i.e., she remains stationary and is sought out by the groom.[36] Nevertheless, *Ḥelkat Meḥokek* 35:33 and *Bet Shmu'el* 35:67 apparently reject Ramban's position. Furthermore, Rabbi Ariel correctly points out that Ramban maintains that the principle of *rov* is not applicable in the case of an unidentified bride because a woman is stationary in the sense that she has a permanent dwelling and even if she goes abroad she returns to that dwelling. Thus, the identity of the bride is always a matter of *kavu'a.* In contradistinction, the sperm donor presents his specimen in a clinic or in a physician's office and the

36 Cf., however, *Tosafot, Nazir* 12a, *s.v. asur*; *Rabbenu Nissim, Gittin* 30b; and *Bet Yosef, Even ha-Ezer* 35:11.

act of insemination takes place in that or a similar locale. The semen assuredly does not return to its earlier site. Thus, the identity of the sperm donor is always subject to determination by means of *rov*.

Despite the foregoing, R. Chaim Bazak points to the rule recorded in *Shulḥan Arukh, Even ha-Ezer* 2:11, to the effect that a man may not maintain wives in two separate cities lest his progeny, unmindful of their shared paternal relationship, enter into a marriage with one another with the result that "a brother may marry his sister." Rabbi Bazak asserts that this halakhic provision demonstrates that, despite the presence of a *rov*, the Sages prohibited all marriages that might conceivably lead to a consanguineous relationship. Rabbi Ariel responds that any such rabbinic decree is directed solely against the person who causes a possibility of consanguinity to arise. There is no corresponding rule to the effect that a person who becomes aware that his father had an unidentifiable family in another city is in any way restricted from entering into a marriage on the basis of reliance upon *rov*. Similarly, he argues, there can be no restriction upon a child born of AID impeding him from marrying freely in reliance upon *rov*.

Rabbi Bazak cites *Bi'ur ha-Gra, Even ha-Ezer* 4:99, in demonstrating that *rov* is of no avail in any situation involving a possibly consanguineous relationship. Biblical law would permit a *shetuki*, i.e., a person whose father is unknown but whose mother has declared that she was impregnated by an unidentified male with whom she might have contracted a legitimate marriage, to marry a woman of legitimate birth. Nevertheless, *Shulḥan Arukh, Even ha-Ezer* 4:37, rules that the child is prohibited from marrying any woman who might be a consanguineous paternal relative. The class of such individuals includes any woman whose father or brother was alive at the time that the person's mother became pregnant as well as any divorcée or widow since the woman in question might have been his father's wife or the wife of a paternal uncle. *Bi'ur ha-Gra* equates that situation with the case of a person whose agent is presumed to have betrothed a woman of unknown identity on his behalf. In equating the two situations, *Bi'ur ha-Gra* implies that there is a global decree prohibiting any possibly consanguineous relationship.

Similarly, R. Pinchas ha-Levi Horowitz, *Giv'at Pinḥas*, no. 5, rules that a person whose mother has declared him to be the legitimate child of an otherwise unidentified father is also forbidden to marry a woman who had a male consanguineous relative living in the city at the time his mother conceived. The concern is that such a relative may have been the child's father and hence that person's close blood relatives are forbidden to the child. *Arukh ha-Shulḥan, Even ha-Ezer* 4:58,[37] *Teshuvot Maharam Minẓ*, no. 95, and *Teshuvot Noda bi-Yehudah, Even ha-Ezer, Mahadura Kamma*, no. 7, disagree with *Bi'ur ha-Gra* and *Giv'at Pinḥas*. Rabbi Bazak concedes that, even according to the authorities who rule stringently in such instances, a problem arises only because the father lived in the same town as the mother and hence, at least by virtue of rabbinic decree, *rov* does not pertain because the father returns to his place of domicile and is considered to be *kavu'a* as is the case with regard to an unidentified bride betrothed by an agent on behalf of his principal.

Nevertheless, as noted earlier, Rabbi Bazak recognizes that the Sages prohibited a person from establishing families in different locales whose identities are unknown to each other "lest a brother marry his sister." The Sages prohibited that practice despite the presence of a *rov* and despite the fact that members of the minor class of prohibited marriage partners are *eino maẓuy*, i.e., not at all numerous. Without citing sources, Rabbi Bazak suggests that the reason for that edict is that, unlike other situations in which application of *rov* can at worst result in a one-time transgression, incestuous marriage results in ongoing transgressions and thus even a remote possibility was interdicted by the Sages. Rabbi Bazak then argues that the same concern is present in pregnancy resulting from AID and, accordingly,

---

37 *Arukh ha-Shulḥan* notes that a minor female whose father has died is not prohibited from marrying in consideration of the fact that her father may have given her in marriage to a consanguineous relative of her prospective husband. For that matter, she is not prohibited from marrying any and all persons because of the possibility that her father deprived her of capacity to enter into a marriage by contracting a marriage on her behalf during his lifetime.

the self-same rabbinic prohibition pertains. Therefore, he concludes that DNA testing is required to eliminate that concern.[38]

Although in his opinion it is not strictly necessary, Rabbi Ariel strongly advises that DNA testing be performed in cases of AID in order to determine paternity and thereby prevent possible incestuous marriages. However, both Rabbi Ariel and Rabbi Bazak agree that, although a *rov* should not be relied upon when an investigation would resolve any existing doubt, the father of the prospective groom has credibility to declare that he has never been a sperm donor. Consequently, they further assert, that if such a declaration is made, there is no remaining doubt. Hence, there is no need for further investigation and, accordingly, no need for DNA confirmation of the absence of consanguinity.[39]

---

38 The third member of the *bet din,* R. Shlomoh Shoshan, concurred with Rabbi Bazak's opinion. Rabbi Shoshan cites Rashi, *Ketubot* 2a, regarding the ordinance requiring marriages to be solemnized on Wednesday so that, if the groom finds the bride not to be a virgin, he will have immediate recourse to a *bet din* that normally sits on Thursday. The ordinance reflects a rabbinic concern despite the presence of a double doubt: a) perhaps the hymen was ruptured accidentally and there was no adultery; and b) perhaps the loss of virginity was due to rape rather than consensual adultery. *Tosafot,* s.v. *she'im,* assume that the concern was primarily with regard to a *kohen* to whom the wife would be prohibited even in cases of rape with the result that there is but a single doubt but the edict was made uniform and extended to all men on the basis of *lo plug.* It is to be inferred that *Tosafot* understood Rashi as maintaining that the decree was specifically extended to encompass situations of *sefek sefeika,* not because of *lo plug,* i.e., a desire to enact a uniform edict admitting of no exceptions, but because the Sages did not wish to rely upon *sefek sefeika* or *rov* when the underlying issues can be investigated and clarified.

The identical rebuttal applies to Rabbi Shoshan's proof as well. The Sages did not enact a broad ordinance eliminating reliance upon *rov* and *sefek sefeika* in all conceivable situations. They enacted particular ordinances for particular cases; *rov* remains definitive in any situation in which there is no specific legislation. Otherwise, *Tosafot* would have no reason to invoke and dismiss the consideration of *lo plug. Tosafot*'s understanding of Rashi serves to contradict Rabbi Shoshan's reliance upon Rashi in establishing his point and, in fact, contradicts Rabbi Shoshan's conclusion.

39 Cf., R. Pinchas ha-Levi Horowitz, renowned as the author of *Hafla'ah,* in his

Although unstated by Rabbi Bazak, it might follow from his position that a person who designates an agent to betroth an unspecified woman on his behalf should be permitted to marry freely provided that the parties undergo DNA testing to eliminate the possibility of consanguinity. Nevertheless, assuming that DNA matching is valid because its accuracy is predicated upon the principle of *rov*, it is not at all clear that, having enacted an ordinance negating reliance upon *rov* of the male populace in determining that the possibility of an incestuous relationship need not be considered, the Sages were willing to permit reliance upon another *rov* in order to escape the onus of their original decree. Moreover, whatever the underlying rationale, the prohibition against having "wives in every port" is quite specific and there is no evidence that the edict was intended to encompass every future contingency in which only a far-fetched concern of an incestuous relationship might arise.

The foregoing notwithstanding, the argument advanced in the majority opinion of the Rabbinical District Court of *Ẓefat* recognized that the obligation to investigate underlying facts despite the presence of a *rov* is limited to situations that do not involve undue travail or a significant financial expenditure. If indeed, as the majority asserts, the Sages suspended the reliance upon *rov*, at least before the fact, even when the result is disqualification from entering into any marriage, such an edict was enacted only to avert the possibility of incest. There is no evidence that such an edict was issued in order to prevent the lesser transgression of consorting with a *mamzer*. Consequently, since DNA testing involves both significant inconvenience and a financial burden, DNA testing (or even R. Sa'adia's test described by *Reshash, Bava Batra* 58a) need not be undertaken in order to establish that a person is not a *mamzer* doubtful or even a *mamzer* certain.

Netivot la-Shevet, cited in *Oẓar ha-Poskim*, I, 4:37, sec. 173, who rules that a person alive at the time of a child's conception has credibility to deny that he impregnated an unwed mother with the result that her son may marry that person's female relative.

Chapter Five

Familial Relationships

I. INHERITANCE

1. DNA to Establish a Right of Inheritance

Identification of a body is necessary not only to permit a widow to remarry but also to distribute a person's estate to the heirs. The Gemara, *Yevamot* 107a, records a dictum of Rav Pappa to the effect that evidence sufficient to enable a wife to remarry also suffices to establish death for purposes of inheritance. If DNA evidence is accepted for the purpose of permitting a widow to remarry, it follows that it should also suffice for purposes of inheritance. However, Rambam, *Hilkhot Naḥalot* 7:1, rules that an estate cannot be assigned to heirs other than upon "*ra'ayah berurah*," or "clear evidence" of the death of the ancestor. R. Isaac ben Sheshet, *Teshuvot Rivash*, no. 155, appropriately interprets the term "clear evidence" as excluding the testimony of a single witness and the like. If so, Rambam's ruling contradicts the principle established by Rav Pappa. R. Simon ben Ẓemaḥ Duran, *Tashbaẓ*, I, no. 77, explains that Rambam understood Rav Pappa's dictum as having been rejected in the course of the ensuing discussion presented in the Gemara.[1] *Tashbaẓ*, I, no. 82, explains that the testimony of a single witness is accepted for the purpose of establishing widowhood

1 See also R. Shlomoh Kluger, *Ḥokhmat Shlomoh*, *Ḥoshen Mishpat* 284:1.

because the matter is a *milta de-avida le-igluyei,* i.e., a matter that will eventually become known to everyone. The rationale is that a person will not place himself in a situation in which he will be exposed as a liar; hence, he will not testify untruthfully when it is certain that the falsity of his testimony will be discovered. R. Yitzchak Schmelkes, *Teshuvot Bet Yiẓḥak, Even ha-Ezer,* II, no. 12, secs. 12–13, explains that the credibility of a single witness in such circumstances is not absolute but is based upon the principle of *rov,* i.e., the majority of people will not allow themselves to be caught in a lie.[2] Thus, since the underlying principle is *rov* and since evidence based upon *rov* is insufficient for adjudicating financial matters, a single witness is not sufficient to establish pecuniary rights to an estate.[3]

However, *Teshuvot Noda bi-Yehudah, Even ha-Ezer, Mahadura Kamma,* no. 33, advances the novel view that the talmudic discussion, *Yevamot* 107a, concerning the testimony of a single witness as sufficient for purposes of establishing a widow's capacity to enter into a new marriage is an elucidation of an entirely different principle. According to *Noda bi-Yehudah,* the Gemara is explaining why the hearsay evidence of a single witness is given credence when repeated to the *bet din* by the wife herself. The underlying principle, asserts *Noda bi-Yehudah,* is *ishah daika u-minseva,* i.e., a presumption that a woman will not enter into a new marital relationship unless she has investigated and is fully convinced that her husband is deceased. *Ishah daika u-minseva*

2 Cf., *infra,* p. 162, note 29 and accompanying text.

3 R. Naphtali Zevi Judah Berlin, *Ha'amek Davar,* Numbers 27:8, develops a novel thesis in explaining why a *milta de-avida le-igluyei*or any other form of *giluy milta* is not sufficient for purposes of inheritance. The conventional explanation is that inheritance occurs *nolens volens,* i.e., the estate passes to heirs automatically, and hence, any role played by the *bet din* is only ministerial in nature. *Ha'amek Davar,* however, points to the phrase "and you shall cause his inheritance to pass to his daughter" (Numbers 27:8) which seems to connote that the *bet din* plays an active role in assigning an estate. According to *Ha'amek Davar,* resolution of a dispute regarding an estate is not a mere declaration of fact but a judicial fiat. As such, the standard of evidence is the two-witness rule.

is limited to establishment of license to remarry but is not sufficient grounds to commence distribution of an estate. In contrast, asserts *Noda bi-Yehudah,* the personal testimony of a single witness before a *bet din* is accepted on the basis of a different principle, namely, credibility of a single witness with regard to a *milta de-avida le-igluyei.* The latter principle, asserts *Noda bi-Yehudah,* is biblical in nature and regarded as absolute rather than as the product of the principle of *rov.* As such, it is sufficient for adjudication of financial matters.

According to *Noda bi-Yehudah,* a single witness to the death of an ancestor is biblically acceptable evidence sufficient to vest title to the estate in the heirs. That is so, according to *Noda bi-Yehudah,* because biblical law extends absolute credibility to a single witness regarding a *milta de-avida le-igluyei.* On the other hand, the rules of evidence do not allow monetary recovery on the basis of *rov.* Assuming that reliance upon DNA matching is based on the principle of *rov,*[4] *Noda bi-Yehudah* would agree that DNA evidence is not sufficient proof of death for distribution of an inheritance. The question of whether it is possible for a putative heir of a person whose demise has been conclusively established to advance a claim to share in an estate on the basis of DNA matching is more complex.

Among the rules applicable to distribution of an estate is that a doubtful heir cannot disinherit an heir certain in whole or in part. The applicable principle is known as *ein safek moẓi midei vadai* or "the doubtful cannot displace the certain."[5] Accordingly, a person whose

---

4 See *supra,* pp. 52–53.

5 Examples of application of the principle *ein safek moẓ'i midei vadai* includes situations in which two individuals with potential interests in an estate perish in a common disaster, e.g., a widow and her son. If the widow died first, the estate would pass to the son and then to his heirs. If the son died first, the widowed mother's estate would pass to her family. The widow's family definitely survived and are heirs certain but it is doubtful that the son survived the mother with the result that the son and his heirs are heirs doubtful. Heirs doubtful cannot claim against heirs certain.

A similar result will occur if a father and his sole issue, a married daughter, perish in a common disaster. If the father died first, the estate would pass to

relationship to the deceased is uncertain cannot claim a share of the estate to the detriment of known heirs. Persons known to be children of the deceased are heirs certain; the claimant who alleges that he is also a son is unknown and hence an heir doubtful. As such, he has no claim against an heir certain. The issue is whether DNA evidence can establish a claimant's status as an heir. Obviously, if DNA evidence is probative on the basis of *umdena*,[6] *tevi'ut ayin*[7] or other proof regarded as absolute, a claimant who presents DNA evidence would be recognized as an heir certain.[8]

However, if DNA evidence is accepted only on the basis of the

---

the daughter and through the daughter to her husband. If the daughter died first, the estate would pass to the father's closest paternal relatives. Those in hereditary succession to the father certainly survived and hence are heirs certain. The daughter's husband is an heir only if the father died before his daughter. Therefore, the husband is only an heir doubtful who cannot claim against heirs certain.

Yet another illustration is the case of a father who dies leaving two children, a son and a hermaphrodite. The son is an heir certain whereas the hermaphrodite is doubtfully a male and doubtfully a female. The hermaphrodite, as an heir doubtful, cannot claim against the son who is an heir certain. See *Shulḥan Arukh, Ḥoshen Mishpat* 280:7.

6 See *supra*, pp. 59–63.

7 See *supra*, pp. 93–110.

8 R. Zevi Yehudah Ben-Ya'akov, *Mishpatekha le-Ya'akov*, V, 136–137, concludes that if DNA constitutes a *siman muvhak be-yoter* it may be used to establish a claim to inheritance.

Rabbi Ben-Ya'akov further cites *Teshuvot Avodat ha-Gershuni*, no. 110, who addresses the case of an unknown person residing in a distant locale who claimed to be an heir to an estate. It was known that the deceased had a son who left the family home at a young age. Decades later, when he appeared subsequent to his father's death no one recognized him but two witnesses testified that they could identify him on the basis of his voice. *Avodat ha-Gershuni* did not accept voice recognition as a form of *tevi'ut ayin de-kala* because it could not be confirmed by actual *tevi'ut ayin*. Rabbi Ben-Ya'akov infers that voice recognition would be acceptable but for the fact of "contradiction" by virtue of the witnesses' inability to confirm their identification by visual recognition. Rabbi Ben-Ya'akov then proceeds to form an analogy between DNA evidence and uncontradicted vocal recognition. The analogy to *tevi'ut ayin de-kala* is

principle of *rov*, a person so identified cannot be regarded as an heir certain. By the same token, no blood relationship between the decedent and any male member or members of his family can be established other than by reliance upon a *rov*, namely, *rov be'ilot aḥar ha-ba'al*. Consequently, the claims of other heirs are no more definite than a claim based upon DNA evidence. In each case the claim is predicated upon a *rov*. It might be argued that the claims of the known heirs and the claim of a putative heir based upon DNA evidence, since they are all based on *rov*, are equal in nature.

However, the statement of the *bet din* of Rabbi Woszner, published in *Teḥumin*, XXI, 123,[9] contains a ruling to the effect that a person cannot claim a share of an inheritance on the basis of DNA evidence. That ruling flows from recognition that DNA evidence involves invocation of the principle of *rov* together with recognition that application of *rov* is insufficient to displace a person in possession because known heirs are deemed to be in possession. Rabbi Woszner presumably regards the individuals previously known to be heirs as being in possession because of a *ḥazakah* that arises from their presumed relationship to the deceased. Rabbi Woszner similarly rules that a person cannot be excluded from inheritance of an estate on the basis of DNA evidence. Presumably, his reasoning is that all presumptive heirs are regarded as being in possession and the *rov* reflected in DNA evidence is not sufficient to substantiate a financial claim against an adversary who is in possession.

Rabbi Woszner further rules that when it is known that no potentially identifiable heir exists, a person can claim an inheritance on the basis of DNA evidence. In such circumstances, seizure of the estate by a non-heir is of no avail because it is only against possession accompanied by claim of rightful title that *rov* cannot prevail. That ruling also flows from the principle that *rov* is of sufficient weight to substantiate a financial claim when the claim is not advanced to dispossess a person

---

both inapt and unnecessary. For a discussion of DNA identification as a form of *tevi'ut ayin* see *supra*, pp. 96–104.

9 See *supra*, p. 92.

in possession. *Rov* can prevail against seizure of property that would otherwise be *res nullius*.

Rabbi Woszner's ruling with regard to establishing a claim to recognition as an heir on the basis of DNA analysis was impliedly rejected by the Israeli Supreme Rabbinical Court of Appeals. That *bet din* also tangentially addressed another intriguing question.

2. DNA Evidence Contradicted by Eyewitness Testimony

Imagine a situation in which an unknown individual claims to be the long-lost son of a deceased person and hence entitled to inherit the decedent's estate. Assuming that DNA evidence is acceptable for disproving a relationship between a putative heir and a progenitor, and that such evidence is produced. What would be the effect of absence of a DNA match in a situation in which witnesses appear and testify to their personal recognition of the claimant as a previously unknown relative? That issue was addressed tangentially in a decision of a panel of the Israeli Rabbinical Supreme Court of Appeals comprised of Rabbi Eliezer Igra, R. Eliyahu Heishrik and R. David Levanon.[10]

The fact pattern of the case is intriguing. A person, apparently of means, died intestate. A number of cousins claiming to be the sole heirs were awarded the estate. Subsequently, the *bet din* was informed that the deceased had a son who had emigrated to South America several decades earlier. The *bet din* annulled the earlier award and sent an emissary, a former chief rabbi of Uruguay who was proficient in Spanish, to South America to conduct an investigation. That delegate found ample documentary evidence establishing the existence of a hitherto unknown son. He then proceeded to convene a *bet din* in Argentina for the purpose of hearing the testimony of witnesses who had been personally acquainted with the son during his stay in Argentina and also testified that they remembered having attended the *bar miẓvah* of the son decades earlier together with the son's parents. One of the witnesses further testified that he himself had been the tutor who prepared the son for the latter's *bar miẓvah*.

10 No. 927675/4, 4 Kislev 5777.

The Rabbinical District Court of Haifa awarded the entire estate to the son, assessed the costs of the investigation as well as court costs against the false claimants, imposed a fine upon them payable to the treasury of the State of Israel and delivered the *bet din* file to the Israeli civil authorities for possible criminal prosecution. The cousins submitted an appeal to the Rabbinical Supreme Court. The appellees' primary argument was that, in the course of the proceedings before the Rabbinical District Court, the parties had agreed to submit to a DNA test and that the putative son would withdraw his claim to the estate if a DNA test failed to show a relationship between the claimant and the deceased. The test involved matching the DNA of the putative son with the DNA of his recognized cousins. The claimant, if he was indeed the son of the decedent, would have been a blood relative of the cousins and consequently that should have been reflected in at least some shared DNA alleles. That test was not performed. The appellants, particularly in light of the appellee's original undertaking, contended that in the absence of a DNA test the award of the estate to the son was improper.

The appeal was dismissed in a two-to-one decision.[11] R. Eliyahu Heishrik stated succinctly that, in light of eyewitness identification establishing a filial relationship, a DNA test would have been superfluous and, moreover, the *bet din* would have been compelled to ignore any negative result of a DNA test that contradicted the already accepted testimony of witnesses.[12]

In a concurring opinion Rabbi David Levanon entertained the

---

11 The cousins had previously presented a similar claim to an Argentinean court claiming that the decedent was childless. The putative son became aware of those proceedings and opposed the cousins' claim. The Argentinian court ruled in favor of the son. Apparently, the decedent also had property in Israel. After losing their case in Argentina, and recognizing that Israeli secular courts would extend full faith and credit to the judgment of the Argentinian court on the basis of the rule of comity, the cousins bypassed the Israeli probate court and claimed the remaining property by means of a proceeding before a rabbinical court.

12 That assertion is not self-evident. If DNA reflects an immutable law of nature

possibility that DNA evidence might be accepted by Halakhah as invariably accurate but finds no need to seek confirmation in the form of DNA matching in light of the testimony presented by the witnesses.[13] In a dissenting opinion, R. Eliezer Igra rather unconvincingly argued that the agreed-upon test should be conducted and the case remanded to the Rabbinical District Court for further deliberation based upon the totality of evidence.

Both Rabbi Levanon and Rabbi Heishrik accept DNA testing as establishing a *siman muvhak* even though the test does not serve to establish that two DNA fragments come from the same person but involves samples from different individuals that are never exactly identical but are sufficiently similar that they serve to establish that the persons from whom they were taken had a common progenitor and hence are blood relatives. This is in contradiction to the decision of Rabbi Woszner who maintained that comparison of two DNA samples taken from the same person establishes "a *siman karov le-muvhak*" while comparison of DNA with a DNA sample taken from a relative can be no better than a *siman benoni*.[14]

---

the testimony of witnesses would be dismissed as false. Cf., *Mishmeret Ḥayyim*, no. 37.

13 Both Rabbi Levanon and Rabbi Heishrik dismissed the claim that the appellant is bound by his agreement to submit to a DNA test because at the time of his undertaking to do so no witnesses had come forward. Consequently, the undertaking to submit to a DNA test was an obligation undertaken in error, particularly since there is no obligation to seek confirmation of a matter to which witnesses are prepared to attest. Moreover, the undertaking was one-sided in nature in the sense that the son agreed to forfeit his claim if DNA analysis were to fail to establish a familial relationship but that the cousins' claim might go forward even subsequent to confirmation of the son's claim on the basis of DNA comparison. If so, argued Rabbi Levanon, the son should not be compelled to undergo a test that is only of benefit to his adversary. Rabbi Heishrik added that an undertaking to perform an act that is not coupled with an assumption of a financial liability is an unenforceable *kinyan etan* comparable to a contract for personal services.

14 See *supra*, p. 92. DNA evidence is strongest in establishing that two separate samples come from the same person because in such instances there is a total match between all examined alleles. Accordingly, matching a DNA sample

Rabbi Heishrik found grounds to rule that DNA evidence is to be accepted even if contradicted by witnesses who testify to the existence of a filial relationship. The Gemara, *Bava Meẓi'a* 28a, declares that, if two individuals claim a lost object and one provides identificatory marks while the other brings witnesses testifying to his ownership, the lost object is to be awarded to the person whose claim is supported by witnesses. Rashi, *ad locum*, seems to indicate that this ruling is valid even if *simanim* are a biblically recognized form of evidence. However, R. Shlomoh Luria, *Ḥokhmat Shlomoh, Ḥoshen Mishpat* 267:8, understands Rashi's comment differently and concludes that, if *simanim* are a biblically recognized form of proof, *simanim* are of equal weight to the testimony of witnesses and when contradictory evidence in the form of *simanim* and testimony of witnesses is presented no decision can be made. However, *Shakh, Ḥoshen Mishpat* 267:7, rejects the position of *Ḥokhmat Shlomoh. Teshuvot R. Akiva Eger*, no. 107 and *Teshuvot Ẓemaḥ Ẓedek, Even ha-Ezer*, no. 86, follow the position of *Shakh*.

Quite obviously, the various *batei din* and other authorities who regard DNA to be acceptable evidence solely on the basis of *rov* would maintain that the testimony of witnesses would prevail over *rov*.[15]

---

taken from a corpse with a DNA sample reliably established as having been derived from the same person during the course of his lifetime, e.g., DNA recovered from a toothbrush or the like, is the strongest type of DNA evidence. Matching the DNA of an otherwise unidentified person with that of a parent or other relative will never yield a total match but, when a sufficient number of alleles match, the statistical probability of a relationship – and hence of the identify of an otherwise unidentified body – can be established with an extremely high degree of statistical probability. DNA identification based upon matching a sample of the unidentified person's own DNA with DNA of known provenance is described by Rabbi Wozsner's *bet din* somewhat enigmatically as "more than an intermediate identificatory mark and close to a *siman muvhak*." In a rather imprecise manner, Rabbi Woszner's *bet din* stated that the DNA match should not be relied upon unless there are "additional factors" present as well. Identification on the basis of comparison with DNA of even parents or children is categorized as "no more than an intermediate identificatory mark."

15 See *supra*, pp. 35–36 and pp. 50ff.

3. DNA Evidence to Disprove Heirship

Another issue mentioned *en passant* by Rabbi Levanon but left undiscussed by him is whether absence of any identical allele is halakhically acceptable as disproof of a familial relationship. The genetic science upon which DNA is based is statistical in nature. The reason that DNA cannot establish identity with a hundred percent scientific certainty is primarily because mutations do occur in genetic material with a high degree of regularity. The chances of multiple identical mutations occurring in a manner that would establish a false positive identification are virtually nil. On the other hand, the chance of a series of mutations occurring that would change an allele in a manner that would make it impossible to recognize it as having the same source as an allele in the DNA of a relative seems somewhat more likely. This writer is unaware of any scientific study describing false negatives in DNA testing.[16] In the case before the Rabbinical Supreme Court, that issue would have arisen had DNA analysis been undertaken but failed to disclose a relationship between the son and his cousins. The implication to be drawn would have been that the "son" was not related to the deceased.

4. Compelling Contribution of a DNA Sample for Purposes of Inheritance

Assuming that DNA evidence is sufficient to establish identity for purposes of establishing a claim of inheritance, Rabbi Ben-Ya'akov, *Teḥumin*, XXII, 425–426, questions whether a putative heir can demand that a known heir provide a DNA sample in order for the former to establish his own relationship to the deceased.[17] The hypothetical situation is quite simple: A person is known to be the son of the decedent and that relationship is unchallenged. Another claimant appears and protests

16 Rabbi Levanon added that were DNA to be 100% accurate it would be acceptable even if contradicted by eyewitnesses. *Tosafot, Yevamot* 88a, s.v. *ve-ata gavra*, declare that witnesses have no credibility to contradict "that which is seen and known by everyone." Such testimony is to be peremptorily dismissed as false. Cf., *Netivot ha-Mishpat* 46:7.

17 See also Rabbi Ben-Ya'akov, *Mishpatekha le-Ya'akov*, V, 141–143.

that he is also a son of the deceased and hence an equal heir. Short of disinterring the body, there is no way of comparing the claimant's DNA with that of the deceased. Comparison of the putative son's DNA with the DNA of the acknowledged heir will serve either to confirm or to disprove the existence of a fraternal relationship between them.

Rabbi Ben-Ya'akov cites rabbinic sources justifying a course of action that in modern legal parlance would be called "discovery." Rambam, *Hilkhot To'en ve-Nit'an* 5:7, rules that a litigant who claims that his adversary is in possession of documents that would support the former's claim is entitled to demand that such documents be produced. *Teshuvot ha-Rosh, klal* 68, chap. 25, disagrees and rules that no such demand can be enforced unless the *bet din* has grounds to assume that those documents will indeed support the litigant's claim. Alternatively, "the adversary should show the document to the judges and they will determine if the alleged benefit claimed in this matter is to be found in the document." Rosh notes that it is not at all unreasonable for a person to refuse to produce financial documents in response to an allegation supported only by "mere words" for "a person does not wish to make himself appear wealthy, that everyone know his wealth and fortune."

Sema, Ḥoshen Mishpat 17:14, adopts an intermediate position in ruling that a person who claims that the documents demanded of him do not support his adversary's claim cannot be compelled to produce them. Nevertheless, if his response is that he does not know whether he possesses documents containing such information or that he cannot determine whether or not those documents support his adversary's claim, the *bet din* may compel him to conduct a search for such documents, to deliver documents that support such claim and, if he does not comprehend the import of those documents, to deliver them to the *bet din* for scrutiny. R. Jonathan Eybeschutz, *Urim ve-Tumim* 16:3, rules that a litigant can compel delivery only of documents whose authenticity he challenges in order to examine them for forgery. However, he cannot compel discovery of documents whose authenticity he concedes but which he demands for examination in order to scrutinize them for possible technical flaws.

Rabbi Ben-Ya'akov asserts that, assuming that the DNA evidence is sufficient to substantiate a claim, such a sample is no different than a document and, according to Rambam, may be demanded. Rabbi Ben-Ya'akov further suggests that a DNA sample may be demanded even according to Rosh. He argues that Rosh's objection to compelling discovery applies only to financial documents that may contain information reflecting upon a person's fortune but does not apply to a DNA sample used only for purposes of identification. Rabbi Ben-Ya'akov assumes that a person enjoys a right of privacy regarding the extent of his financial worth but has no similar right with regard to DNA samples designed solely to resolve a disputed familial relationship. That point may not be entirely correct in light of the fact that much significant medical and genetic information that is personal in nature can be gleaned from DNA samples. Privacy of medical and genetic information certainly warrants no less respect than privacy of financial information. *Teshuvot ha-Rosh* does, however, acknowledge that the *bet din* may examine financial documents *in camera*. The same should be true of DNA evidence as well.

Rabbi Ben-Ya'akov would apparently concede that an invasive procedure, such as a blood test, is not at all comparable to delivery of financial documents and therefore cannot be demanded even according to Rambam. Although Rambam does not recognize a right of privacy that takes precedence over another person's possible financial interests, Rambam would presumably agree that the right of bodily integrity is not subservient to an otherwise unsupported countervailing claim. However, in most instances a DNA sample can be obtained without violation of bodily integrity by examining personal items that had been handled by the deceased.

Based upon those assumptions it may readily be concluded that a *bet din* may demand that DNA samples obtainable without violation of bodily integrity be made available for confidential examination by the *bet din*, with the assurance that personal information revealed by examination of the DNA sample having no bearing upon the proceedings be held in confidence by the *bet din*.

II. IDENTITY AS A JEW

In the wake of the vast number of Russian immigrants admitted to Israel under the Law of Return, Israeli rabbinical courts were taxed with verifying the status of many of those immigrants particularly because they arrived with little or no evidence of association with a Jewish community. One available method of proving one's identity as a Jew is establishing the existence of a biological relationship with a maternal relative whose status has already been verified. Unfortunately, in a large number of cases involving Russian immigrants documentary evidence of such a relationship is not available.

Not long ago the Rabbinical District Court of Haifa addressed one such case in a decision authored by R. Yitzchak Zevi Ushinsky.[18] A prospective bride already in the fifth month of pregnancy applied for a marriage license. The bride claimed to be the daughter of a woman recognized as a Jewess but failed to produce any written evidence or oral testimony to support the existence of such a relationship. The question before the *bet din* was whether marriage could be permitted on the basis of a DNA test establishing a maternal-filial relationship.

Rabbi Ushinsky also addressed that problem in *Teḥumin*, XXXV (5775), 211–212. Citing the earlier discussed declaration of R. Samuel ha-Levi Woszner's *bet din* regarding the reliability of DNA matching,[19] Rabbi Ushinsky categorizes that statement as rejecting the reliability of DNA evidence for all matters requiring formal proof but as accepting the results of DNA testing as sufficient for matters that require a lower standard of evidence. There are matters that are in the category of a *milta de- avida le-igluyei* that require evidence only in the nature of *giluy milta*, i.e., establishing a matter that would become evident in the course of events even without testimony. Such matters can be substantiated on the basis of the testimony of relatives, disqualified witnesses and even a single witness. Those matters include confirming the death of a close relative for purposes of observing the laws of

18 No. 954915–1, 20 Elul 5773.

19 See *supra*, p. 151, note 9 and accompanying text.

mourning,[20] establishing the identity of a bride,[21] establishing the identities of a husband and wife in order to execute a bill of divorce[22] or of a brother-in-law and sister-in-law in order to allow the sister-in-law to remarry subsequent to *ḥaliẓah*[23] and establishing the identity of persons named in financial instruments.[24] Rabbi Ushinsky asserts that an individual's identification of a woman as his or her mother is a matter of *giluy milta* and hence, confirmation of Jewish identity can be established on the basis of DNA evidence demonstrating a mother-daughter relationship.

Under the given circumstances, this writer finds it difficult to categorize the matter under discussion as a *milta de-avida le-igluyei.* The general rule is that a person declaring himself to be a Jew has credibility to do so. Ritva and *Nimmukei Yosef, Yevamot* 47a, explain that such credibility is based upon the principle of *milta de-avida le-igluyei* and hence does not require further confirmation. However, *Teshuvot Rivash,* no. 254, and *Noda bi-Yehudah, Even ha-Ezer, Mahadura Kamma,* no. 27, define a *milta de-avida le-igluyei* as a matter that is likely to become known with certainty in the near future even in the absence of presently available supporting testimony. The principle is based upon a psychological assessment that a person will not lie if he faces imminent exposure of his duplicity. That is not the case with regard to a non-Jewish Russian immigrant, whose deception in claiming to be a Jew is unlikely to be exposed imminently, if at all. R. Moshe Mordecai Farbstein, cited in *Teḥumin,* XII, (5751), 40, and R. Ovadiah Yosef, *Teshuvot Yabi'a Omer,* VII, *Even ha-Ezer,* no. 1, sec. 4, state that the principle cannot be applied to Russian immigrants since many of those immigrants stem from locales in which there are few Jews. Consequently, it would be difficult to find anyone capable of rebutting such a claim.[25] Strangely enough, those arguments were advanced by

20 See *Shulḥan Arukh, Yoreh De'ah* 397:1.
21 See *Be'er Heitev, Even ha-Ezer* 42:2.
22 See *Shulḥan Arukh, Even ha-Ezer* 120:3.
23 See *Shulḥan Arukh, Even ha-Ezer* 157:2 and 169:24.
24 See *Shulḥan Arukh, Ḥoshen Mishpat* 49:1.
25 Rabbi Farbstein also rejects the applicability of *milta de-avida le-igluyei* with

Rabbi Ushinsky himself in an earlier-cited decision of the Rabbinical District Court of Haifa of which Rabbi Ushinsky was the author.[26]

Moreover, other early-day authorities advance quite different considerations in support of the rule extending self-credibility to a person claiming to be a Jew.[27] It must be assumed that since those authorities posit a more circumscribed degree of justification they reject the view of Ritva and *Nimmukei Yosef* who maintain that *milta de-avida le-igluyei* is a sufficient basis to justify self-credibility in establishing identify as a Jew.

In his contribution to *Teḥumin* Rabbi Ushinsky cites *Bet Shmu'el, Even ha-Ezer* 2:2, who follows Rashi and Ramah in ruling that testimony of a single witness is insufficient with regard to questions pertaining to matters of lineage. However, *Bet Mosheh,* cited in *Oẓar ha-Poskim* I, 2:2, sec. 4, disagrees with *Bet Shmu'el* and rules that a single witness is sufficient. *Be'er Heitev, Even ha-Ezer* 2:4, cites a number of authorities who maintain that a person of unknown lineage who declares himself to be a Jew must produce sufficiently acceptable evidence. Rabbi Ushinsky infers that *Bet Mosheh* would disagree with *Bet Shmu'el* with regard to the latter matter as well.

In his article published in *Teḥumin,* Rabbi Ushinsky asserts that, even according to *Bet Shmu'el* who rules that a single witness is insufficient to establish status as a Jew, circumstantial evidence "close to certainty" is sufficient for that purpose. Rabbi Ushinsky regards matching DNA as proof "close to certainty" of a Jewish relationship between a woman and her putative Jewish mother.[28]

---

regard to Russian immigrants because, even if witnesses were to testify that the immigrant was known to be a non-Jew, their testimony does not establish the immigrant as a liar. He may readily and believably claim that while yet in the U.S.S.R. he concealed his identity as a Jew because of discrimination and fear of persecution. See *Teḥumin,* XII (5751), 38–41.

26 No. 954915-1, 20 Elul 5773.

27 See *Tosafot, Yevamot* 47a, s.v. *be-muḥzak* and Rambam, *Hilkhot Issurei Bi'ah* 13:9. *Tosafot* explain that the majority of persons claiming to be Jews are indeed Jews and Rambam declares that such credibility is predicated upon a *ḥezkat hanhagah, viz.,* comportment as a Jew as manifest in the observance of *miẓvot.*

28 Not surprisingly, the State of Israel accepts DNA evidence as proof of familial

III. IDENTITY AS A *KOHEN*

Few people heretofore not recognized in their communities as *kohanim* would seek to establish their identity as members of the priestly class.[29] But instances of persons presumed to be *kohanim* seeking to marry divorcées are rampant. Generally, those endeavors involve an attempt to show that the mother of a person heretofore presumed to be a *kohen* was disqualified from marrying a *kohen* with the result that her progeny are *ḥalalim,* or disqualified *kohanim,* not subject to such marital restrictions.

A more direct, but more difficult, way to achieve the same result is to demonstrate that the presumption that the individual's father was a *kohen* is predicated upon an error. Such a finding would result if it could be shown that the putative father, in reality, is not the biological father.

R. Moshe Feinstein, *Iggerot Mosheh, Even ha-Ezer,* IV, no. 12, rules that a person who claims that his mother informed him that she was disqualified from marrying a *kohen* – with the result that her son is a *ḥalal* – may marry a proselyte (and, by the same token, a divorcée) provided that the son has absolute faith in the credibility of his mother. The same would be the case if the mother confides to her son that he is the issue of an adulterous relationship and hence the son could not possibly be a *kohen.* In the eyes of a *bet din* a wife has no credibility to establish her adultery or to render her son a *mamzer.* Nevertheless, *Iggerot Mosheh* advances the novel view that, outside of a judicial framework, when absolutely convinced of an informant's probity, a person may act upon his own subjective reliance on another person's truthfulness.

Although he has no directly supporting proof, *Iggerot Mosheh*

---

relationship for purposes of identification as a Jew, eligibility for citizenship and the privileges of the Law of Return.

29 In one such case brought before the Jerusalem *Bet Din le-Birur ha-Yahadut,* IV, 319–320, the petitioner, born three months after his mother's marriage to a *kohen,* sought a share in the estate of his putative father and to be identified as a *kohen* as well. Citing *Ḥelkat Meḥokek, Even ha-Ezer* 3:12, the *bet din* ruled, that, as a stringency applying to the priesthood, an ordinary *rov* is not sufficient to establish identity as a *kohen.*

assumes that it is precisely this consideration that underlies the rule that, in certain circumstances, the testimony of even a non-Jewish artisan or member of a profession may be relied upon. Ostensibly, the underlying rationale is a presumption in the nature of the *ḥazakah* to the effect that *uman lo mara umnateih,* i.e., a person will not compromise his professional integrity and reputation. It is generally presumed that the *ḥazakah* is the product of a person's concern for financial consequences or professional reputation.[30] *Iggerot Mosheh* maintains that such presumption is not strong enough to establish a *ḥazakah* that would give rise to the rule. However, contends *Iggerot Mosheh,* the awareness by others of that motivating consideration does serve to create psychological reliance and establishes a sense of trust on their part. Those persons may then act upon their own subjective belief in the veracity of the professional.[31] In effect, *Iggerot Mosheh* declares that *uman lo mara umnateih* is not an ancillary factor conferring credibility upon the testimony of an otherwise disqualified witness but a principle that empowers a person to act upon his own informed subjective belief in matters of religious compunction.

Rabbi Asher Weiss, *Teshuvot Minḥat Asher,* III, no. 87, sec. 5, correctly observes that subjective belief may be sufficient for reliance on the part of the person having such conviction but not for others who do not share that trust. The son may have absolute faith in his mother's truthfulness but there is no reason for the son's prospective wife to place similar faith in her future mother-in-law's confession. Prohibitions forbidding a *kohen* to enter into prohibited marital alliances are equally forbidden to the woman with whom he might consort.[32] Hence marriage under such circumstances is effectively precluded.

---

30 As discussed earlier, R. Yitzchak Schmelkes, *Teshuvot Bet Yiẓḥak, Even ha-Ezer,* II, no. 12, secs. 12–13, maintains that this *ḥazakah* is actually a *rov,* i.e., the majority of people will not present false evidence of such nature because of a concern for financial consequences and/or professional standing. See *supra,* p. 148, note 2 and accompanying text.

31 See *Iggerot Mosheh, Yoreh De'ah,* I, no. 54.

32 Cf., however, the opinion of R. Eliezer of Metz, cited by *Tosafot, Nedarim*

Absent credible witnesses, the most direct way of disproving paternity is DNA analysis. The issue is whether DNA evidence may be relied upon to "dekohenize" a son and make it permissible for him to marry a divorcée. It must be presumed that DNA evidence does not suffice in penal matters in which the two-witness rule must be applied to the exclusion of DNA evidence, that is based upon *rov, simanim* or *tevi'ut ayin.* The selfsame two-witness rule also applies to matters pertaining to a *davar she-be-ervah,* i.e., to certain conjugal matters defined by *Tosafot, Gittin* 2b, as including "marriage, divorce and adultery to render a wife forbidden to her husband." It must be presumed that *Tosafot* pointedly omit any reference to either *mamzerut*[33] or to disqualification as a *kohen. Kesef Mishneh, Hilkhot Sanhedrin* 16:6, followed by R. Chaim Ozer Grodzinski, *Teshuvot Aḥi'ezer,* I, no. 5, rules explicitly that matters pertaining to status as a *kohen* are treated as ordinary halakhic matters subject to a single-witness rule. *Tosafot* presumably understand the term "*davar she-be-ervah*" as connoting only matters pertaining to incest and adultery to the exclusion of sexual matters of lesser severity. However, *Pnei Yehoshu'a, Kiddushin, Kuntres Aḥaron,* sec. 91, disagrees and regards disqualification as a *kohen* to be subject to the two-witness rule.[34]

Rabbi Weiss argues that the controversy with regard to whether disqualification as a *kohen* is subject to the two-witness rule is limited to testimony regarding a matter that is literally a *davar she-be-ervah,* i.e., a conjugal matter, e.g., the status of the mother as a potential consort of a *kohen,* but not to matters pertaining solely to genealogical identity of her son, e.g., disqualification of the father as a *kohen.* Issues of genealogical status, he argues, are not sexual matters and hence are not subject to the two-witness rule even according to *Pnei Yehoshu'a.*

However, that analysis does not affect the hypothetical question here presented. The DNA evidence that refutes the presumption that

---

90b, s.v. *hayu,* who maintains that it is only the *kohen* who is subject to such prohibitions.

33 Cf., however, *Teshuvot R. Akiva Eger,* no. 100.

34 Cf., *Or Sameaḥ, Hilkhot Sanhedrin* 16:6.

a *kohen* is the father of a particular child also establishes that the child is a *mamzer.* The authorities who maintain that the two-witness rule applies to disqualification as a *kohen* also maintain the same view with regard to status as a *mamzer* since a *mamzer* is forbidden to enter into a sexual relationship with a person of legitimate birth. If a person cannot be disqualified as a *kohen* other than by concomitantly establishing that he is a *mamzer,* the matter hinges upon a matter of conjugality and, consequently, according to *Pnei Yehoshu'a,* the two-witness rule should apply.

The situation presented to Rabbi Weiss was significantly different. The matter brought to his attention did not allege an adulterous union. The mother claimed that her husband was infertile and that her pregnancy was a result of artificial insemination. Many authorities maintain that a child born of artificial insemination involving a donor is not a *mamzer.*[35] Nevertheless, assuming that the principle of *rov be'ilot* does not pertain in situations of male infertility,[36] the husband

---

35 See Abraham S. Abraham, *Nishmat Avraham, Even ha-Ezer* 1:1, note 4, sec. 2, and Fred Rosner "Artificial Insemination in Jewish Law," *Jewish Bioethics,* ed. Fred Rosner and J. David Bleich, augmented edition (Hoboken, New Jersey, 2000), pp. 129–130.

36 It is not to be assumed that a husband refrains from intercourse with his wife while she undergoes artificial insemination. Nevertheless, it seems to this writer that when it has been medically established that a husband cannot possibly father children, e.g., he produces no sperm whatsoever, the principle of *rov be'ilot* cannot be applied.

However, in many cases involving AID the husband suffers from low or even moderate male infertility, i.e., the husband produces some sperm but has been unsuccessful in impregnating his wife. Conception occurs upon penetration of a single ovum by a single sperm. Normally, well over a hundred million sperm enter the vagina with each ejaculation. The overwhelming majority of those sperm are destroyed with the result that few survive to enter the fallopian tube where conception occurs. The chances of a single sperm making contact with and fertilizing the single ovum present in the fallopian tube are even lower. The greater the number of sperm present in the ejaculate, the higher the probability of achieving pregnancy. In instances of low or moderate male infertility the statistical probability of pregnancy is low but such a result is not at all impossible. Consequently, if the couple engage

is not to be regarded as the father and hence the child cannot be a *kohen*. It is only in a situation of that nature, i.e., a situation in which a child can be "dekohenized" without alleging an improper conjugal relationship, in which it might be argued that *Pnei Yehoshu'a*'s opinion regarding the applicability of the two-witness rule to disqualification of a *kohen* does not pertain.

In a decision of the Jerusalem *Bet Din le-Birur ha-Yahadut*, v, 85, R. David Levanon contends that in situations in which an unwed mother has consorted with both a *kohen* and with a non-*kohen* and those facts are acknowledged by both parties, DNA can establish priestly lineage, again on the basis of the principle of *rov* inherent in DNA matching. Similarly, *rov* as represented by DNA evidence can establish paternity for purposes of levirate obligations even when it is known that the woman has had multiple sexual partners.[37] However,

---

in intercourse during the woman's fertile period there can be genuine doubt with regard to whether the husband or the donor is the father of the conceptus.

The few authorities who regard the child born of AID to be a *mamzer* do not discuss the possibility that the child is a *mamzer* doubtful because of the husband's access. The husband certainly has opportunity for multiple acts of coitus while AID is typically limited to a single insemination per reproductive cycle. If the husband's ejaculates are combined it is even possible that, in the aggregate, the husband has provided more sperm than the donor. But even if that is not the case, it is likely that *rov be'ilot* should be understood as denoting a majority of coital acts likely to culminate in pregnancy, rather than as the majority of sperm entering the vagina, with the result that, in instances of AID, the *rov* is not applicable. The result should be a *safek* with regard to the status of the child according to the authorities who maintain that a child born to a married woman by means of AID is a *mamzer.*

Although, according to the authorities who do not regard a child born of AID to be a *mamzer,* the result should be that, when the husband is a *kohen* and suffers from low or moderate infertility but engages in normal marital intercourse with his wife, a child born pursuant to AID should have the status of a *safek kohen,* or *kohen* doubtful, and consequently be forbidden to marry a divorcée. In such situations, DNA evidence showing that the husband is not the father would result in contradictory *rovs*, *viz.,* the *rov* established by DNA versus a contradictory *rov* in the form of *rov be'ilot.*

37 In cases of fornication a single *rov* is generally not sufficient to establish status

citing *Ḥelkat Meḥokek, Even ha-Ezer* 3:12, the Jerusalem *Bet Din le-Birur ha-Yahadut,* IV, 319–320, ruled that a single *rov* is not sufficient to establish identity as a *kohen.*

---

that flows from paternal identity, particularly as a *kohen.* Accordingly, two parallel *rovs* are required, e.g., a city in which neither intercourse between the woman and one of the male inhabitants nor between her and an itinerant traveler would have a negative effect upon the legitimacy of her offspring. Rabbi Levanon maintains that that the requirement for a double *rov* applies only to a *rubba de-ita kamman, viz.,* a *rov* employed to determine who among a group of people served as the mother's consort because of the possibility that the paramour visited the mother rather than vice versa. If intercourse occurred in a context in which the woman was *kavu'a,* i.e., in an "established" place, meaning that the paramour visits the woman rather than the reverse, *rov* does not apply. That rule, contends Rabbi Levanon, does not apply to a *rubba de-leita kamman, viz.,* an abstract *rov* which serves to establish a general principle, in the present case the reliability of DNA testing.

Chapter Six

The "Jewish" Gene

I. BACKGROUND

In past decades the Israeli government vigorously encouraged *aliyah* on the part of Jews residing in what was then known as the U.S.S.R. Discrimination against Jews, economic deprivation and lack of civil liberties were significant motivating factors spurring emigration. Similar factors also aroused desire for emigration in large numbers of non-Jews as well. But, for reasons of international politics, there was an extended period of time in which Jews enjoyed a unique and probably unprecedented privilege, *viz.*, the Russian government allowed them to leave the country but denied that right to others among its nationals. Probably for the first time since the days of Ahasuerus when "all the populace were becoming Jews" (Esther 8:17) were Jewish identity and proof thereof, authentic or otherwise, assiduously sought by many non-Jews. Concomitantly, the Israeli Law of Return (1950) granted a right of entry, a cornucopia of economic and social benefits as well as citizenship to all immigrants of Jewish extraction and to their spouses and children as well regardless of the halakhic status of the immigrant.

Israeli citizenship is within the province of the State. Identity as a Jew is determined by religious authorities. There is no civil marriage in Israel and virtually all cemeteries are subject to the oversight of religious authorities. Close to one million Russians came to Israel under the Law of Return. The number of immigrants who are presumed to be non-Jews because they have not claimed to be Jews or have not been able to provide satisfactory proof of Jewish identity was conservatively estimated by the Israel Democracy Institute as more than 25%, or 250,000, and by others as approximately 400,000.[1] The vast majority have become fluent in Hebrew, have integrated into Israeli society, served in the Israeli Defense Forces and rightfully consider themselves to be Israeli. The resultant social and political problems were readily predictable. Conversion to Judaism is an obvious expedient to avoid such problems, but an expedient that is fraught with halakhic difficulties when undertaken for material benefit or mere convenience.[2] There are also some who for reasons of conscience or intellectual honesty refuse to profess a faith-commitment they do not harbor but – not unlike many of their secular fellow citizens – are proud of their claimed ethnic heritage as Jews.[3]

Judaism is a religion based upon faith commitment. But as a nomistic religion its rules and regulations recognize identity as a Jew as fundamentally a matter of ethnic origin. Primarily, Halakhah recognizes as a Jew any individual who was born to a Jewish mother and, additionally, any person who has become a convert to Judaism. The first is an accident of birth; the second involves a faith commitment and acceptance of the "yoke of the commandments."

A considerable number of Russian émigrés are indeed Jews by birth but are unable to produce halakhically recognized proof. Many of them had sought to conceal their ethnic origin while yet in their native country in order to avoid rampant persecution. Some lived in

---

1 See Alan Rosenbaum, "Conversion in Israel: The Russian Aliya," *The Jerusalem Post*, Nov. 1, 2017.

2 For comprehensive surveys of the halakhic criteria required to confirm a claim to Jewish identity and their application to Russian immigrants, see R. Moshe Mordecai Farbstein, *Teḥumin*, XII (5751), 17–80; R. Yigal Ariel, *ibid.*, pp. 81–96; and R. Yitzchak Zevi Ushinsky, *Teḥumin*, XXXV (5775), 203–219.

3 Judy Maltz, "Russian Immigrants Leaving Israel, Discouraged by Conversion Woes," *Haaretz*, November 2, 2014.

remote areas in which there were few, if any, Jews who, even if they were available, could vouch for the immigrant's identity as a Jew. Others either did not preserve or lost documentary evidence of their Jewish identity and, for lack of interest, did not identify with Jewish communities in their native land.

A crucial question, then, is whether there exists an empirical criterion that might establish a person's ethnic identity as a Jew comparable to the manner by which, in the days of Shakespeare, a person could establish his identity as a cleric by demonstrating an ability to read and thereby become subject to the jurisdiction of the ecclesiastic courts rather than the courts of the realm.[4] Better still – at least for purposes of establishing ethnic identity: The masses generalized a presumption of Jewish physiognomy from Michelangelo's depiction of Moses. Were that perception correct, a person might establish his identity as a Jew by pointing to keratotic projections emerging from his skull.

In an age of tremendous advances in the science of genetics such a concept is not at all far-fetched. Mitochondrial DNA is presumed to be passed on exclusively from mother to child and thereby from generation to generation. Were it to be shown that Jews, and only Jews, share a particular gene or even a singular unique allele, it might be argued that the presence of that unique fragment of genetic material constitutes a *siman*, or identificatory mark, establishing identity as a Jew.

Absence of such a gene would prove absolutely nothing. It might well be the case that at some time during ancestral history a woman may have undergone conversion to Judaism and hence had no "Jewish" gene to pass on to her progeny. Whether there is a halakhic basis for accepting DNA evidence as proof of Jewishness will be explored presently. But quite baffling is the libertarian hue and cry raised in secular and even quasi-halakhic circles against advocacy of acceptance of the results of mitochondrial DNA testing in support of a determination

4 For a history and description of "clergy privilege" as well as allusions thereto in Shakespeare's plays see B.J. Sokol and Mary Sokol, *Shakespeare's Legal Language: A Dictionary* (London, 2000), p. 42.

of Jewishness.[5] In establishing Jewish identity the burden of proof is upon the claimant. No rabbinic authority seeks to compel any individual to advance such a claim or to compel production of supporting genetic evidence of such a claim. Absence of DNA proof of Jewishness would not negate identity as a Jew and hence is in no way prejudicial; the individual might well be a Jew or a descendant of a Jewish woman by virtue of conversion. If DNA analysis proves to be acceptable proof of Jewish identity it would represent an unmitigated boon to any person claiming to be a Jew with no concomitant negative effect whatsoever.

Examination for the presence of the hypothetical "Jewish" gene herein described is analogous to genetic testing employed to establish personal identification or a blood relationship between two individuals. In each of those situations the proof lies in the presence of a unique genetic sequence that, it is presumed, cannot be random. Such a "Jewish" gene, common to Jews by virtue of birth, would be no different from genes shared, for example, by cousins. In the latter case, the presence of a common gene establishes the existence of a single grandparent. The "Jewish" gene would establish the existence of a Jewish grandmother many, many generations in the distant past who transmitted the gene to her daughter and subsequently the gene was passed on directly from mother to daughter over the span of centuries. Since Judaism recognizes only matrilineal succession, that genetic material must appear in mitochondrial DNA which is passed on from mother to child.[6] The problem is that no one has demonstrated the existence of such a single gene or even claimed that it exists.

The halakhic issues involved in accepting the Jewish gene as probative evidence of Jewish identity are analyzed in *Berurei Yahadut le-Or Meḥkarim Genetiyim* (Sivan, 5777), a monograph authored by R. Israel

5 Marissa Newman, "Rabbinate DNA Tests Seek Jewishness in the Blood, Become a Bone of Contention," *Times of Israel*, October 7, 2019.

6 See Doron M. Behar *et al.*, "MtDNA Evidence for a Genetic Bottleneck in the Early History of the Ashkenazi Jewish Population," *European Journal of Human Genetics*, vol. 12, no. 5 (January, 2004), p. 357.

Barenbaum, a member of the Moscow *bet din,* and an Israeli scholar, R. Ze'ev Litke, and in two more cursory responsa, one by an unidentified author or authors that appears in *Be-Mar'eh ha-Bazak,* vol. IX, no. 30 (5777), published by *Ereẓ Ḥemdah* Institute and the second by R. Asher Weiss, *Oraḥ Mishpat,* I (Jerusalem, Shevat 5778). *Berurei Yahadut* also includes a contribution by R. David Lau, Chief Rabbi of Israel, discussing the level of evidence required to establish identity as a Jew as well as a survey of relevant halakhic issues by Dr. Abraham Steinberg, editor of the *Encyclopedia Hilkhatit Refu'it. Berurei Yahadut* also features two presentations of scientific information, one by Dr. Steinberg and the second by Dr. Shai Tzur and Professor Kalman Skorecki, geneticists renowned for their study of the Jewish gene.

One might be forgiven for assuming that the buzz within the Jewish community in recent years arose because of scientific discovery of a gene or a segment of a gene whose distinctive characteristics are shared by Jews worldwide. After all, if we are all descended from Abraham, his genes should be highly represented in all Abrahamic progeny. It would be reasonable to assume that the descendants of Isaac and Jacob should share aspects of a genotype dissimilar from those of non-Jewish Abrahamic descent. Even more to the point, mitochondrial DNA is passed on only from mother to child and, in theory at least, contains no genetic material of paternal origin.[7] If so, every

---

7 In an extremely small number of instances, mixed haplotypes were found indicating paternal sources. The cause of that phenomenon is not fully understood. Presumably, for halakhic purposes, the rarity of those occurrences render them an inconsequential *mi'uta de-mi'uta.* See M. Schwartz and J. Vissing, "New Patterns of Inheritance in Mitochondrial Disease," *Biochemical Biophysical Research Communications,* vol. 310, no. 2 (October 17, 2003), pp. 247–251; M. Schwartz and J. Vissing, "No Evidence for Paternal Inheritance of mtDNA Mutations," *Journal of Neurological Science,* vol. 218, no. 1–2 (March 15, 2004), pp. 99–101; S. Luo *et al.,* "Biparental Inheritance of Mitochondrial DNA in Humans," *Proceedings National Academy of Science,* vol. 115, no. 51 (December 18, 2018), pp. 13,039–13,044; S. Lutz-Bonengel and W. Parson, "No Further Evidence for Paternal Leakage of Mitochondrial DNA in Humans Yet," *Proceedings National Academy of Science,* vol. 116, no. 61 (February 5, 2019), pp. 1821–1822; and M. Schwartz and J. Vissing, "Paternal Inheritance of

naturally-born Jew should have uniquely identifiable mitochondrial DNA traceable to one or another of the original Four Mothers, i.e., the four wives of Jacob.

But that is not the case. No scientist has claimed to have discovered a single genetic component that is emblematic of all Jews. Geneticists have not even expressed surprise at not being able to do so. It would seem that no such phenomenon exists because of the vast number of genetic mutations that occur regularly. The public is well aware of mutations that are responsible for hereditary diseases. Such mutations are serious but, fortunately, they are few and far between. However, mutations also occur with regularity among the myriad alleles present in the human genome, including the relatively large portions of genes that are forever unexpressed. Every occurrence of mitosis, or cell division, is an opportunity for mutation and since mutations occur regularly, the total number of mutations that take place over the course of millennia is virtually astronomical. The rate of mutation is estimated to be 1.2×10^{-3} per genetic sequence per generation.[8] Little wonder, then, that no allele has survived and been shared in its original form by all collateral relatives from the inception of the Jewish people until the present.

Nevertheless, the so-called Jewish gene or, more accurately, the Jewish genes, are scientifically quite remarkable. The Jewish community has been the subject of much genetic research for a number of reasons, primarily because it is probably the largest identifiable existing ethnic group and because, at least until recent times, endogamy was the normative practice. Scientific interest is concentrated upon the study of genetic diseases and more than twenty recessive disorders have been identified as occurring with elevated frequencies in the Ashkenazic community.[9]

No one has claimed that all, or even a majority of, Ashkenazic

---

Mitochondrial DNA," *New England Journal of Medicine*, vol. 347, no. 8 (May 22, 2002), pp. 576–580.

8 See Behar, "MtDNA Evidence for a Genetic Bottleneck," p. 357.

9 *Loc. cit.*

Jews share a single genetic marker. The evidence does show that some forty percent of Ashkenazic Jews[10] are endowed with mitochondrial DNA that can be traced back to four women.[11] Those genetic components are extremely rare in non-Jewish populations. But, interestingly enough, they do occur in low frequencies in non-Ashkenazic Jews. Similarly, most individual non-Ashkenazic Jewish communities similarly have a high representation of their own unique genetic markers attributable to a small group of female founders ranging in number from one to six.

Present-day Ashkenazic Jews are believed to be descended from a pool of less than 25,000 individuals who began to immigrate from northern Italy to the Rhine Basin in the early part of the 14th century. That population, in turn, was established by a small number of families who arrived in northern Italy during the 7th and 8th centuries.[12] Present-day Ashkenazic Jews are the progeny of those bottleneck immigrations.[13] It would not be at all surprising if, in each of such events, the emigrants were members of extended family groups, a phenomenon that would account for a small number of founding mothers.[14]

---

10 See Doron M. Behar *et al.*, "Counting the Founders: The Matrilineal Genetic Ancestry of the Jewish Diaspora," *PLoSone*, vol. 3, no. 4 (April 30, 2008), e2062, and Doron M. Behar *et al.*, "The Matrimonial Ancestry of Ashkenazi Jewry: Portrait of a Recent Founder Event," *The American Journal of Human Genetics*," vol. 78, no. 3 (March, 2006) 487–497.

11 *Ibid.*, p. 492.

12 Behar, "The Matrilineal Ancestors of Ashkenazi Jewry," p. 492.

13 Such bottleneck immigration has been documented in Italian and Greek populations. There was also a profound bottleneck effect within the Roma (Gypsy) population. See Behar, "Counting the Founders," p. 363.

14 58.6 percent of the mountain Jews of the Caucasus can be traced to one woman; 51.1% of the Georgian to one woman; 39.8% of Libyan Jews to one woman; 41.2% of the B'nai Israel of Mumbai to one woman and 67.6% to four women; 44.4% of the Indians of Cochin to two women; 41.5% of Persian Jews to six women; 43% of Iraqi Jews to five women; 43.2% of Tunisian Jews to one women; and 42% of Yemenite Jews to five women. See Behar *et al.*, "Counting the Founders," e2062.

It is significant that studies of Ashkenazic Jewish genes have established that the genes are by no means found exclusively among members of the Jewish community. Those studies show only that a majority of individuals who possess one of the four "Jewish" genes are independently known to be Jews. That is far different from other forms of genetic analysis designed to show a familial relationship between two individuals. In the latter cases the possibility of a false positive is, statistically speaking, infinitesimal. As has been shown,[15] the halakhic basis for recognizing genetic identity of alleles and familial relationships based upon common genetic sequences is predicated upon principles of *rov*. The known existence of a relatively high incidence of the Jewish gene among some non-Jews means that the argument for accepting the presence of a "Jewish" gene as evidence of Jewish ancestry is quite complex.

Moreover, utilization of the "Jewish" gene to establish identity as a Jew is quite different from other questions of personal identity that might be resolved on the basis of DNA analysis. DNA testing is generally employed to show that two DNA fragments come from the same person or from closely related individuals. Mitochondrial DNA used to establish Jewish identity must show derivation from a female ancestress who flourished many, many generations ago. If all, or the majority of, Jews are endowed with a specific gene, the blood relationship, it is argued, is confirmed. Mitochondrial DNA is transmitted only from mother to child.[16] The fact that a particular group within a populace shares a particular DNA fragment establishes that they are descendants of a single "grandmother." The argument is that, if persons sharing the DNA fragments are independently known to be Jews, the

---

Quite interestingly, 93.3% of the isolated Belmonte Marrano population of 300–400 people possess mitochondrial DNA attributed to a single mother. Not surprisingly, members of the Ethiopian Beta Israel (Falasha) community manifest no similar genetic marker. On the contrary, the most frequent lineages of that ethnic group are of Eastern African origin. See *loc. cit.* Cf., J. David Bleich, *Contemporary Halakhic Problems*, I (New York, 1997), 297–310.

15 See *supra*, p. 52.

16 Cf., *supra*, p. 173, note 7.

"grandmother" must have been a Jewess as well. If it is established that the "grandmother" was Jewish, despite any other presumption to the contrary, it follows that any person who inherits her DNA must *ipso facto* be a Jew as well. Assuming that the science upon which identification of the Jewish gene is correct, the presence of the Jewish gene among non-Jews is readily explained. The reason lies in the fact that, to our sorrow, over the course of millennia countless numbers of Jews were lost to Judaism because of apostasy or intermarriage.

But, although blood relationship speaks for itself and despite the fact that Jewish identity is established by matrilineal descent, it does not follow that all maternal blood relatives are necessarily Jewish – albeit perhaps lapsed Jews. It is quite possible that the "grandmother" whose mitochondrial DNA is manifest in her progeny lived prior to Revelation at Sinai. Jews became Jews as a result of conversion at Sinai.[17] Women who lived prior to the wives of the twelve sons of Jacob may have had other daughters whose progeny never became Jews. If so, those women would have devised the so-called "Jewish" gene to both Jewish and non-Jewish progeny. Present-day non-Jews would have inherited such genes from non-Jewish grandmothers rather than from the latter's female cousins who were present at Sinai. Alternatively, those bearing the gene who profess Judaism and who are known as Jews may be descendants of a later post-Sinaitic female convert to Judaism while those who seek to establish Jewish identity by means of the selfsame gene may be blood relatives of a common ancestress who never converted to Judaism. For the Jewish gene to have any halakhic import it would be necessary for geneticists to present, not only evidence of the existence of a Jewish gene, but also to provide halakhically acceptable evidence that the gene came into existence, presumably by mutation, sometime after the founding of the Jewish people at Sinai.

Ostensibly, the presence of the Jewish gene among non-Jews reflects one of three things: 1) either the carrier of the gene is the descendant of a pre-Sinaitic common grandmother some of whose

17 See *Keritut* 9a.

progeny did not become Jews at Sinai; 2) the carrier is the descendant of a post-Sinaitic non-Jewish grandmother one of whose progeny later became a convert to Judaism; or 3)the carrier is a descendant of a Jewish grandmother whose descendants' identity as Jews was forgotten because of apostasy or intermarriage. Since with regard to any particular bearer of the gene, which of the three occurred cannot readily be ascertained, the presence of the Jewish gene can hardly be accepted as *prima facie* proof of the Jewish identity of any person not otherwise known to be a Jew. Any halakhic grounds that would validate such a finding must be carefully elucidated.

II. THE STANDARD OF EVIDENCE

The issue with regard to acceptance of mitochondrial DNA analysis as evidence of Jewish maternal descent is compound in nature: 1) Is establishment of identity as a Jew subject to a two-witness rule and 2) is manifestation of a Jewish gene sufficiently compelling to qualify as acceptable proof on the basis of some other evidentiary standard? R. Moshe Mordecai Farbstein, *Ein ha-Da'at*, pp. 371–378, Rabbi Ze'ev Litke, *Berurei Yahadut*, chap. 17, and Rabbi David Lau, *Berurei Yahadut*, pp. 117–122, present surveys of halakhic opinions regarding the ambit of the two-witness rule.

It is universally accepted that the testimony of a single witness is sufficient to establish facts pertinent to ordinary matters of Jewish law, e.g., whether a piece of meat is kosher or non-kosher. It is, of course, well-recognized that the two-witness rule is the standard of evidence applicable in judicial proceedings as well as in any matter categorized as a *davar she-be-ervah*, i.e., any matter having an impact upon forbidden conjugal relationships such as adultery and incest. Issues pertaining to marriage and divorce are clearly of that nature.

1. Conversion as a *Davar she-be-Ervah*

There are conflicting views with regard to whether the two-witness rule applies to establishing identity as a Jew by conversion. R. Ezekiel Landau, *Teshuvot Noda bi-Yehudah, Even ha-Ezer, Mahadura Kamma,* no. 55, cites the statement of Rav Sheshet, *Yevamot* 47a, indicating that hearsay evidence is sufficient to establish proof of conversion. Acceptance of hearsay evidence is not compatible with a two-witness rule. *Noda bi-Yehudah,* however, points out that Rav Sheshet's opinion is not accepted as authoritative by Rif or Rambam and is ignored by *Shulḥan Arukh, Yoreh De'ah* 267.[18] Presumably, those rabbinic decisors had reason to categorize conversion as a *davar she-be-ervah,* i.e., a matter pertaining to prohibited sexual relationships, because conversion affects permissibility of marriage between a proselyte and a naturally-born Jew. Accordingly, concludes *Noda bi-Yehudah,* two witnesses would be required. R. Moshe Feinstein, *Iggerot Mosheh, Yoreh De'ah,* II, no. 127, takes issue with *Noda bi-Yehudah* and maintains that, although matters of sexual relationship are consequent upon conversion, the status of a proselyte in and of itself is not of that category.[19] Earlier, R. Shlomoh Kluger, *Teshuvot Tuv Ta'am va-Da'at, Mahadura Telita'a,* nos. 109–110, described conversion as a matter of *issur,* or ordinary religious law, subject to the single-witness rule. The standard of evidence necessary to resolve a question regarding identity as a naturally-born Jew would appear to be similarly contingent upon that controversy.

Nevertheless, as shown earlier,[20] the two-witness rule does not always require eye-witness testimony exclusively. In limited situations testimony of witnesses can be dispensed with because "*anan sahadei* – we are witnesses," i.e., the facts are either known or readily surmised. At times, the facts are so well-known or the presumption is so great that the *bet din* can take "judicial notice" of the facts without benefit of actual testimony. Thus, if a divorced couple seclude themselves there is a presumption that they have reconciled and cohabited for

18 Cf., Rosh, *Yevamot* 4:34.

19 Rabbi Moshe Mordecai Farbstein, *Ein ha-Da'at,* p. 372, cites *Taz, Yoreh De'ah* 157:6 and *Shakh, Yoreh De'ah* 157:12 in explaining *Noda bi-Yehudah* as maintaining that a non-Jewess is considered to be an *ervah.* Consequently, testimony regarding abrogation of her status as a non-Jew is a *davar she-be-ervah.*

20 See *supra,* pp. 59–63.

purposes of marriage. Such cohabitation effects a second marriage that requires a new *get* for dissolution. But, to have that effect, the act of cohabitation requires two witnesses. Nevertheless, seclusion alone in the presence of witnesses is sufficient because "we are witnesses" that, under such circumstances, cohabitation for the purpose of marriage took place. As was earlier shown,[21] the consensus of halakhic opinion is that establishment of personal identity on the basis of DNA analysis does not rise to the level of *anan sahadei*.

For many authorities, deductive evidence comparable to that which was present in the narrative concerning R. Simon ben Shetaḥ recorded by the Gemara, *Shevu'ot* 34a, is acceptable even in capital cases because the result is mandated by reason and is no less compelling than the testimony of two eyewitnesses. Those authorities regard logically compelled deductions based upon empirical evidence to be tantamount to an *anan sahadei*.[22] However, the presence of a Jewish gene cannot establish Jewish identity with deductive certainty, as evidenced by the fact that some non-Jews carry that gene as well.[23]

---

21 See *supra*, pp. 70–71.

22 See *supra*, pp. 16–19.

23 Even were we to assume it to be an invariable rule of genetics that all bearers of the gene in question must be descended from a common ancestress, the presence of the gene would not prove that all bearers of the gene, including those heretofore presumed to be non-Jews, are of Jewish extraction. Were Halakhah to accept such a principle as a matter of certainty, we would be confronted with a factual doubt: Either a) all bearers of the gene are of maternal Jewish lineage with the implication that those considered to be non-Jews are descendants of apostates or progeny of intermarriage; or b) all bearers of the gene are actually of non-Jewish ancestry but at some time in Jewish history one or more carriers of the gene converted to Judaism with the result that carriers of the gene can be divided into two classes, *viz.*, Jewish carriers and non-Jewish carriers.

Furthermore, establishing that the Jewish gene arose by mutation before the establishment of Jewish identity at Mount Sinai would be of no avail. At present, geneticists do not claim to be able to assign a date with any degree of precision to the first appearance of the Jewish gene. But, assuming that such a date could be reliably established and that the date established is prior to Sinai, such a finding would not necessarily entail that all carriers of the gene

Accordingly, treating identification of a person as a Jew as a *davar she-be-ervah* and applying the two-witness rule would serve to exclude reliance upon a Jewish gene to establish identity as a Jew.

2. Status as a Jew as a *Davar she-be-Ervah*

There may, however, be an additional factor that would relegate testimony regarding status as a naturally-born Jew to the category of testimony pertaining to a *davar she-be-ervah.*

Establishing the ambit of a *davar she-be-ervah* involves two issues: 1) Who is an *ervah* and 2) what constitutes a "*davar she-be-ervah,*" i.e., what is the meaning of a matter "pertaining to" an *ervah*? The term *ervah* as used in Leviticus 18:6–19 with regard to forbidden sexual relationships is applied only to sexual relationships punishable by death at the hands of a human court or excision at the hands of heaven.[24] However, Ritva and *Tosafot Rid, Kiddushin* 66b, declare that a single witness lacks capacity to testify that a woman is a divorcée, even though the punishment for cohabitation between a divorcée and a *kohen* is less severe than punishment for incest or adultery. Yet, Rambam, *Hilkhot Sanhedrin* 16:13, rules that if a single witness testifies that a woman is a divorcée and the woman subsequently consorts with a *kohen* she is subject to the statutory punishment, provided that the ensuing sexual act is witnessed by two individuals. That ruling

---

are Jews: Perhaps one or more of the "grandmothers" of women who became Jewesses at Sinai also gave birth to daughters who married men other than those of the seed of Jacob. Such a historical course of events would readily account for the presence of identical mitochondrial DNA both among groups of Jews and among groups of non-Jews.

24 Thus, R. Jacob of Lissa, author of *Netivot ha-Mishpat,* maintains that testimony regarding status as a *mamzer* is not a *davar she-be-ervah.* R. Jacob of Lissa is of the opinion that application of the two-witness rule with regard to *mamzerut* is a rabbinic stringency. See also *Ḥazon Ish, Even ha-Ezer* 11:13. R. Akiva Eger disagrees with R. Jacob of Lissa but acknowledges that such is the position of *Mordekhai.* See *Teshuvot R. Akiva Eger,* no. 124, s.v. *lekhe'orah* and no. 125, s.v. *mah she-katav* as well as *Teshuvot R. Akiva Eger me-Ktav Yad,* ed. R. Nathan Gestetner (Jerusalem, 5728), no. 90, s.v. *ein.* The latter volume, nos. 89–90, includes an exchange of letters between R. Akiva Eger and R. Jacob of Lissa.

seems to contradict the previously stated implication of the Gemara, *Kiddushin* 66b, requiring two witnesses to establish the status of a woman as a divorcée.

Maḥaneh Efrayim, no. 13, presents a number of possible solutions to that contradiction. *Maḥaneh Efrayim* suggests that a divorcée is actually no different from any other unmarried woman and is not an *ervah*. Hence, testimony to her status as a divorcée is not a *davar she-be-ervah*. Nevertheless, the divorcée becomes an *ervah* when she enters into a forbidden relationship with a *kohen*. Therefore, if such an event has already occurred, a single witness cannot be heard to force the couple to separate because at that point the testimony pertains to an *ervah,* i.e., a woman in a forbidden marital relationship. Similarly, testimony that a child was born of a union between a divorcée and a *kohen* is tantamount to testimony to the mother's forbidden liaison with a *kohen* and hence is categorized by the Gemara as a *davar she-be-ervah*. *Avnei Milu'im* 45:6 offers an identical explanation. *Maḥaneh Efrayim,* however, rejects the distinction between a divorcée prior to marriage and a divorcée already married to a *kohen* because the Mishnah, *Yevamot* 53b, in speaking of "*arayot* or [women prohibited] to the priestly class," apparently refers to women who have not yet actually entered into a prohibited relationship with a *kohen*.

Instead, *Maḥaneh Efrayim* proceeds to draw a distinction between testimony designed to establish a prohibition against performing an act, e.g., testimony that meat is non-kosher designed to forbid the act of consuming the meat in question or testimony that a woman is a divorcée designed to prohibit her from cohabiting with a *kohen,* and testimony concerning a person designed to disqualify him from a certain status, e.g., from serving as a *kohen,* or to establish his qualification for such status. The latter type of testimony is directed to a matter of personal status, not to an act. Testimony regarding personal qualification or disqualification, asserts *Maḥaneh Efrayim,* requires two witnesses.[25] Testimony designed to prohibit a woman from

25 See also *Maḥaneh Efrayim, Hilkhot Edut,* no. 19. Rabbi Farbstein cites Re'ah, *Bedek ha-Bayit, bayit* 4, *sha'ar* 2; Ritva, *Avodah Zarah* 39b; *Pri Ḥadash, Yoreh*

cohabiting with a *kohen* is treated as ordinary matters of religious prohibition regarding which a single witness has credibility.

Rambam, *Hilkhot Sanhedrin* 16:13, rules that a single witness may be heard to testify that a woman is a divorcée but he fails to rule that a single witness is qualified to testify that a person is the son of a divorcée. Rambam, unlike Ritva and *Tosafot Rid*, understands the Gemara, *Kiddushin* 66b, as disqualifying a single witness from testimony regarding the son of a divorcée, i.e., testimony regarding the non-priestly status of the son, designed to deny him the privileges of priestly status rather than from testimony designed to forbid an act, i.e., testimony that a woman is a divorcée, the effect of which is only to prevent cohabitation with a *kohen*.

Maḥaneh Efrayim draws a further distinction in asserting that the Gemara declares that the testimony of a single witness to the effect that a person is the son of a divorcée is acceptable only because the subject of the testimony had heretofore identified himself, and was publicly recognized, as a qualified *kohen*. In such cases, testimony that he is the son of a divorcée is designed to negate a previously presumed status. A single witness, asserts *Maḥaneh Efrayim*, cannot be heard to negate a *ḥazakah* of priesthood. Rambam's ruling that a single witness is sufficient, asserts *Maḥaneh Efrayim*, is limited to situations in which nothing was previously known regarding the person's status and hence the testimony of a single witness suffices to establish his status.[26]

Although *Maḥaneh Efrayim* speaks only of priesthood, *Shev Shem'ateta, shem'ata* 6, chap. 15,[27] maintains that some additional categories of personal status require two witnesses and for that reason they are classified as a *davar she-be-ervah*. In a manner similar to that of *Maḥaneh Efrayim*, *Shev Shem'ateta* recognizes that the Gemara,

---

De'ah 119:17; *Rit Algazi, Bekhorot*, chap. 4, no. 32; and *Tosafot R. Akiva Eger, Dem'ai* 4:43, as also espousing this view.

26 See also *Teshuvot Maharik*, no. 72 and *Teshuvot R. Akiva Eger*, no. 107.

27 *Shev Shem'ateta* also formulates the same distinction in *shem'ata* 6, chap. 2. Cf., however, R. Shimon Yehudah ha-Kohen Shkop, *Sha'arei Yosher, sha'ar* 6, chap. 3 and *Ḥazon Ish, Even ha-Ezer*, no. 20, sec. 37, who disagree.

Kiddushin 66b, speaks only of the son of a divorcée in positing a two-witness rule but expresses a somewhat different distinction between testimony regarding a woman as a divorcée and testimony regarding her son as the son of a divorcée. Rambam rules only that a single witness can establish a woman's status as a divorcée; he makes no mention of testimony disqualifying a *kohen* because he is the son of a divorcée. *Shev Shem'ateta* draws a different distinction between testimony with regard to status as a *mamzer* or disqualification from the priesthood as the son of a divorcée and a woman's own status as a divorcée disqualified from marrying a *kohen*. According to *Shev Shem'ateta,* testimony that a woman is a divorcée is testimony with regard to an "accidental" event, i.e., that a bill of divorce was delivered to her. Participation of that act is not "necessary" in the sense that it might or might not have occurred. In contradistinction, testimony that a person is a *mamzer* or the son of a divorcée is not testimony with regard to an "accidental" event; it is testimony to a status acquired at birth arising from a necessary fact of nature.[28] Rabbi Farbstein explains that status that devolves upon an individual upon birth is part of the essential nature of a person whereas a change arising from a later act is an "accident" superimposed upon the essential nature of the individual.[29]

According to *Shev Shem'ateta,* testimony regarding any intrinsic matter of personal status requires two witnesses. Thus, *Shev Shem'ateta* presumes that two witnesses are necessary to declare a person to be a *mamzer*. That rule, asserts *Shev Shem'ateta,* is deduced from the credibility explicitly accorded a father by the Torah to declare his son

---

28 See also *Avnei Nezer, Even ha-Ezer,* no. 21, secs. 22–24. That distinction is peremptorily dismissed by *Sha'arei Yosher, sha'ar* 6, chap. 3 and *Ḥiddushei R. Shimon Yehudah ha-Kohen, Ketubot,* no. 14, as well as by *Ḥazon Ish, Even ha-Ezer* 20:16.

29 The distinction is comparable to the Aristotelian distinction between necessary and accidental attributes. Man is a rational being and is also a featherless biped; the first is a necessary attribute of the human species while the second is simply an accident.

to be a *mamzer*[30] despite the fact that he is but a single witness. The inference, argues *Shev Shem'ateta,* is that other single witnesses have no comparable credibility with regard to matters of personal status that restrict entering into marriage with a person of legitimate birth. Accordingly, such matters are treated as a *davar she-be-ervah.* Thus, disqualifying a person from marriage to a person of legitimate birth by testifying that he is a *mamzer* is a *davar she-be-ervah.* The converse, i.e., qualifying a person for such marriage by testifying that he is not a *mamzer,* asserts *Shev Shem'ateta,* similarly requires two witnesses.[31] By extension, asserts *Shev Shem'ateta,* two witnesses are required to testify that a person is the son of a divorcée and thus disqualified from membership in the "community of priests." That disqualification is an intrinsic disqualification. Hence, status regarding eligibility to marry a *kohen* by reason of birth is treated in the same manner as testimony with regard to status as a *mamzer.* However, asserts *Shev Shem'ateta,* disqualification of a woman from marriage to a person of priestly birth by virtue of the fact that she is a divorcée is an "accidental" disqualification to which the two-witness rule does not apply.[32]

---

30 See *supra,* pp. 29–32.

31 *Sha'arei Yosher, sha'ar* 6, chap. 3, and *Ḥiddushei R. Shimon Yehudah ha-Kohen, Kiddushin,* no. 14, state that two witnesses are necessary to disqualify a person of a heretofore vested status because stripping a person of a privilege, e.g., to disqualify a person from testifying as a witness or from serving as a ritual slaughterer, is tantamount to exacting money from him. Deprivation of privileged status, he asserts, is analogous to relieving a person of property. However, according to *Sha'arei Yosher,* testimony of a single witness is sufficient to establish that a person is endowed with privileged status unless the matter is deemed to be a *davar she-be-ervah.*

Rabbi Farbstein, *Ein ha-Da'at,* pp. 374–375, states that two witnesses are necessary only to qualify a person for a particular status but not to deprive him of such status. Qualification is positive in nature and endows the individual with an otherwise non-existent status. Disqualification, e.g., to testify that a woman is a divorcée, does not endow her with a new quality.

32 *Sha'arei Yosher* observes that Rambam, *Hilkhot Sanhedrin* 16:13, fails to include a *ḥallal, viz.,* a child born to the wife of a disqualified *kohen,* in the category of matters for which a single witness is sufficient. *Shev Shem'ateta* explains that,

Applying the theses developed by *Maḥaneh Efrayim* and *Shev Shem'ateta*, testimony designed either to establish or to negate presumed Jewish or non-Jewish lineage would require testimony of two witnesses regardless of whether or not conversion qualifies as a *davar she-be-ervah.*[33]

3. Status as a Jew Excluded from *Davar she-be-Ervah*

There are additional grounds upon which to conclude that, even if conversion is a *davar she-be-ervah,* testimony of a single witness regarding status as a naturally-born Jew is to be regarded as testimony pertaining to an ordinary matter of Jewish law:

i) In the case of a woman who is known to have committed adultery *Noda bi-Yehudah, Even ha-Ezer, Mahadura Kamma,* no. 11 and no. 69, rules that a single witness is sufficient to testify that the wife was subject to *force majeure* and, consequently, that she is not forbidden to her husband. *Ḥemdat Shlomoh, Even ha-Ezer,* no. 15, sec. 24, explains that testimony that will serve to disturb an existing marital relationship by rendering a woman forbidden to her husband is a *davar she-be-ervah* but testimony that serves to confirm an existing relationship is not a *davar she-be-ervah.*

Similarly, asserts Rabbi Litke, the position of the authorities such as *Shev Shem'ateta* who maintain that testimony of a single witness regarding status as a Jew is not acceptable is limited to situations in which the evidence serves to negate an already presumed status. Thus,

---

since the child is disqualified from birth, the disqualification is necessary rather than accidental and, consequently, the two-witness rule applies.

33 Rabbi Farbstein, *Ein ha-Da'at,* p. 377, finds no reason to distinguish between testimony that a person is a Jew by birth and testimony that he is a Jew by reason of conversion. Establishment of status as a Jew by birth, according to *Shev Shem'ateta,* is a question regarding natural status and requires two witnesses. Conversion, argues Rabbi Farbstein, represents a metamorphosis in the essential nature of a proselyte and therefore, he argues, testimony regarding conversion would require two witnesses even according to *Shev Shem'ateta.* Rabbi Samuel Shapiro, a member of the *bet din* of Jerusalem, is quoted as disagreeing with that distinction.

such testimony would not be accepted regarding a person who is publicly recognized as a non-Jew when the purpose of the evidence is designed to show that the presumption is erroneous. However, in situations in which there is no such *ḥazakah,* the evidence is designed to resolve an unknown status rather than to disturb an existing status. Therefore, even according to *Shev Shem'ateta,* the two-witness rule would not apply.

In developing that argument, Rabbi Litke draws upon a novel concept of his own formulation. Quite independent of the implications for establishing the requisite standard of proof, Rabbi Litke, as will be shown,[34] is of the opinion that, although there certainly is a *ḥazakah* of Jewish identity, there is no parallel *ḥazakah* of non-Jewishness. Rabbi Litke maintains that, although in antiquity ethnic identity was readily established, subsequent to migrations, demographic upheavals, forced apostasy and intermarriage, a *ḥezkat akum,* or presumption of non-Jewishness, no longer exists.[35] In accordance with that position, Rabbi Litke concludes that all authorities would agree that establishing status as a Jew does not require two witnesses.

ii) *Pnei Yehoshu'a, Kiddushin* 63b and 65b, maintains that a single witness has credibility to contradict a *rov* even with regard to a *davar she-be-ervah. Pnei Yehoshu'a* maintains that two witnesses are required only when there are no known exceptions to the *rov*. However, when it is known that two classes exist, i.e., a majority and minority class, and the issue is only clarification with regard to which of the two classes a particular person belongs, *Pnei Yehoshu'a* maintains that there is no two-witness rule. Since Jews and gentiles constitute distinct classes it should follow that a single witness is sufficient to assign a previously unidentified person to one of those classes.[36]

There is significant controversy regarding the question of whether a single witness has credibility regarding a *davar she-be-ervah* when there is no *ḥazakah* establishing the *davar she-be-ervah*. R. Meir Simchah

34 Cf., *infra,* p. 230, note 98 and accompanying text.
35 That position, however, is subject to challenge. See *infra,* pp. 230–231.
36 See also *Sha'arei Yosher, sha'ar* 6, chap. 3.

ha-Kohen of Dvinsk, *Or Sameaḥ, Hilkhot Sanhedrin* 16:6, cites R. Isaac Bekhor David, *Divrei Emet, Kuntres Lavin,* who maintains that, absent a *ḥazakah,* the matter is not regarded as a *davar she-be-ervah* and hence a single witness has credibility. *Shev Shem'ateta, shem'ata* 6, chap. 3, reports that he would have been inclined to assume that a single witness has no credibility with regard to a *davar she-be-ervah* even if the testimony of that witness does not contradict a *ḥazakah.* He acknowledges, however, that *Teshuvot Maimuniyot, Hilkhot Ishut,* no. 3, does make that distinction.

R. Shimon Shkop, *Sha'arei Yosher, sha'ar* 6, chap. 2, and *Ḥiddushei R. Shimon Yehudah ha-Kohen, Ketubot,* no. 14, distinguishes between a single witness whose testimony is designed to disturb a *ḥazakah* and a single witness who testifies that a person is a member of a minoritarian class. Testimony of a single witness contradicting an established *ḥazakah,* he asserts, is not acceptable because it directly contradicts a matter already established by *ḥazakah* whereas testimony that someone is a member of a minoritarian class does not really contradict the *rov.* Such testimony merely serves to establish that the person in question is a member of the minoritarian class. *Rov,* by definition, admits of a minor class. A single witness does not actually contradict a *rov* but clarifies the issue in question by relegating the matter to which he testifies to the minoritarian class whose existence is granted.

That reasoning would serve to provide a basis for accepting the testimony of a single witness when nothing is known regarding the genealogy of a person claiming to be a Jew. However, if the person was previously known as a non-Jew, such testimony would contradict a *ḥazakah* and be of no avail. However, as already stated, Rabbi Litke argues that the testimony of a single witness suffices in all cases because such testimony does not contradict a *ḥazakah.* In arriving at that conclusion, Rabbi Litke again follows his announced opinion that in our day there is no *ḥezkat akum,* i.e., there is no longer an established status as a non-Jew. Consequently, a single witness who testifies to Jewish ethnicity is not contradicting a *ḥazakah.* The witness is countermanding a *rov* that determines that an unknown person must be assigned to an unknown class. But, since the existence of a minor class has been established, that identification is not contradictory to the *rov*.

iii) Applying a similar distinction, *Shev Shem'ateta, shem'ata* 6, chap. 7, cites *Teshuvot Maimuniyot, Hilkhot Ishut*, no. 3, in establishing the principle that even with regard to a *davar she-be-ervah* a single person has standing to testify that the *davar she-be-ervah* never existed, e.g., a presumed act of betrothal was not entered into. That testimony does not constitute a *davar she-be-ervah*; it establishes that there never was a *davar she-be-ervah*. That concept, argues *Shev Shem'ateta*, is similar to the notion that testimony to the effect that a person is a member of a minoritarian class does not contradict the *rov*; rather the testimony establishes that the *rov* is irrelevant and inapplicable.

Such a distinction is also drawn by *Teshuvot R. Akiva Eger*, no. 124, *s.v. gam yesh*. R. Akiva Eger addresses the case of a woman who entered into a second marriage without presenting evidence that her first husband had died. Subsequent to the birth of two children a single witness testified that her husband had died before she contracted the second marriage. Although, as earlier noted,[37] R. Akiva Eger ruled that testimony with regard to *mamzerut* is a *davar she-be-ervah*, he maintained that testimony of the witness was not with regard to the status of the children but to the effect that the first marriage was dissolved by death of the husband for which a single witness has credibility. Consequently, the testimony of the witness was not designed to address a *davar she-be-ervah* but to established *ab initio* that a *davar she-be-ervah* never arose.[38] However, R. Akiva Eger finds that this distinction is contradicted by a number of early-day authorities.

Rabbi Litke finds support for application of that distinction with

---

37 See *supra*, p. 181, note 24.

38 The point is quite akin to Bertrand Russell's Theory of Types: A proposition describing a class of propositions is not a member of the class it describes. See Alasdair Urquhart, "The Theory of Types," *The Cambridge Companion to Bertrand Russell*, ed. Nicholas Griffin (Cambridge, 2003), pp. 286–309. Thus, testimony regarding membership in a class considered to be *ervah* is not itself a matter of *ervah*.

regard to all matters involving a *davar she-be-ervah*. The Gemara, *Gittin* 64a, speaks of a person who designates an agent to betroth a wife on his behalf and gives the agent untrammeled authority with regard to the choice of a bride. In the event that the agent dies without identifying a bride, the principal may not marry any woman. The concern is that in such a situation, even absent the prohibition against polygamy, the principal may enter into a marital relationship with a prohibited female relative of an already existing wife, *viz.*, the unidentified bride betrothed on his behalf by the agent.[39] Ramban, *ad locum*, regards that prohibition as biblical in nature. Ramban adds that, if all female relatives who are members of the class of forbidden relatives testify that they were not betrothed by the deceased agent, the principal is free to marry any one of those relatives.

Ramban recognizes that the majority of all women are not forbidden to the principal. Nevertheless, the principal may not rely upon *rov* in contracting a marriage because the matter constitutes a *davar she-be-ervah* subject to the two-witness rule. Despite that categorization, relying upon her status as a single witness, any woman can establish her own eligibility to marry. That is so because, in asserting eligibility to marry, she is declaring that she is entirely removed from any matter pertaining to *ervah*. Ramban similarly maintains that the single-witness rule suffices to enable any particular woman to identify herself as a member of the majoritarian class even when the testimony is proffered with regard to a matter pertaining to consanguinity. Her testimony is designed, not to resolve a question pertaining to *ervah*, but to establish that she is a member of a class regarding which there can be no issue of *ervah*.[40]

Rabbi Litke argues that given the known existence of two distinct classes, *viz.*, Jews and non-Jews, a single witness is sufficient to establish a person's identity as a member of the class of Jews rather than the

---

39 For obvious reasons the prohibition does not apply in situations in which the woman whom the principal now seeks to marry has no female relatives of a forbidden degree.

40 Cf., however, the conflicting view of Ran, *Gittin* 30a.

class of non-Jews.[41] The claim to be a Jew, argues Rabbi Litke, is not a claim with regard to any particular issue of *ervah*, but an assertion with regard to membership in a class to which various rules of *ervah* pertain.[42]

4. Applicable Standards of Evidence

Demonstrating that the testimony of a single witness is sufficient for confirming identity as a Jew establishes no more than that the two-witness rule does not apply. Establishing that the two-witness rule does not apply allows for the possibility that, apart from testimony of single witness, other forms of proof may suffice to establish identity as a Jew. It does not imply that circumstantial evidence is also sufficient for that purpose.

There is indeed a disagreement with regard to whether circumstantial evidence is acceptable even in matters of financial liability regarding which there is a presumption that a two-witness rule applies. The focus of disagreement with regard to admissibility of circumstantial evidence is the controversy recorded by the Gemara, *Bava Batra* 93a, *Sanhedrin* 37b and *Shevu'ot* 34a, regarding tort liability in the death of a camel. The Gemara records a controversy between Rav Aḥa and the Sages in a situation involving a group of camels. One camel was observed kicking its legs and subsequently another camel was found mauled to death. Rav Aḥa accepts such circumstantial evidence in holding the violent camel's owner liable for damages. *Tosafot, Shevu'ot* 34a, *s.v. de-i,* maintain that Rav Aḥa would recognize the admissibility of comparable evidence in criminal prosecutions as well. Other early-day authorities regard R. Aḥa's view as limited to financial matters.[43]

---

41 Ramban, contrary to *Tosafot, Gittin* 64a, *s.v. assur,* assumes that, even as a matter of biblical law, a *rov* alone would be insufficient. It is unlikely, but perhaps arguable, that Ramban would agree that a *rov* coupled with testimony of a single witness is sufficient for a *davar she-be-ervah.* Of course, with regard to establishing identity as a Jew, *rov* is absent.

42 Cf., *Iggerot Mosheh*'s explanation of why conversion is not a *davar she-be-ervah* as discussed in the introductory comments of this section.

43 See the earlier discussion of these sources, *supra,* pp. 16–17 and 60–61.

In any event, many halakhic authorities rule in accordance with the majoritarian view of the Sages.[44] However, both Rambam, *Hilkhot Sanhedrin* 24:1–2 and *Shulḥan Arukh, Ḥoshen Mishpat* 11:5, rule that the *bet din* is empowered to render judgment in financial matters even on the basis of its subjective contextual assessment of the truth.[45]

Rambam, followed by *Shulḥan Arukh,* apparently maintains that the evidentiary rule "at the mouth of two witnesses ... shall the matter be established" (Deuteronomy 19:15) is limited to matters such as punitive sanctions, *davar she-be-ervah* and the like but that in financial disputes the applicable principle is "with justice shall you judge your fellow" (Leviticus 19:15). Interpersonal justice demands adjudication on the best grounds available. As Rambam emphasizes, failure to render judgment is not an option because judgment withheld is justice denied. Other areas of Halakhah are to be decided on the basis of appropriate standards of evidence. It does not automatically follow that circumstantial evidence, or an *umdena* that is less compelling than *anan sahadei,* is acceptable for other areas of Jewish law.

Rabbi David Lau, *Birurei Yahadut,* p. 226, seeks to establish that *umdena* is sufficient to establish proof of Jewish identity as a conclusion that flows from the accepted rule that a person has standing to declare himself to be a Jew. The credibility of a person to prove his own status as a Jew is based upon one of three halakhic rules: 1) According to *Tosafot, Yevamot* 47a, it is based upon the principle of *rov,* i.e., the majority of those who claim to be Jewish are in fact Jews. 2) According to Rambam, *Hilkhot Issurei Bi'ah* 13:9, it is based upon a *ḥezkat hanhagah,* or a *ḥazakah* to the effect that a person who comports himself in a certain manner is assumed to enjoy the status that would give rise to such comportment, i.e., the person who comports himself as a Jew is presumed to be a Jew. 3) According to Ritva and *Nimmukei Yosef, Yevamot* 37a, a person is believed to declare himself to be a Jew because it is a *milta de-avida le-igluyei,* i.e., a person has credibility with

44 See, *inter alia, Netivot ha-Mishpat* 15:2.

45 See also *Teshuvot Ge'onei Batra'i,* no. 54; *Tumim* 90:14; and R. Elchanan Wasserman, *Kovez̤ Shi'urim,* II, no. 38.

regard to a matter that in the course of time is likely to become publicly known.[46] Each of those principles represents a separate and particular halakhic form of evidence. Neither singly nor in combination do they serve to establish that other forms of *umdena* in the nature of general circumstantial evidence are sufficient for that purpose. Be that as it may, Rabbi Lau himself acknowledges that evidence for the existence of a Jewish gene does not rise to the level of circumstantial evidence sufficiently credible as to constitute an *umdena.*

Whether DNA evidence in the form of the Jewish gene rises to any other appropriate standard of proof will be examined in the following sections.

III. THE "JEWISH" GENE AS A *SIMAN*

1. The Nature of a *Siman*

The more general question of whether, in general, the unique nature of DNA sequences qualifies as a *siman* for purposes of Jewish law has been discussed earlier.[47] It must further be established both that the "Jewish" gene is indeed a *siman* of Jewish identity and that a *siman* is acceptable proof of such identity. Employment of the Jewish gene to prove identity as a Jew presents a number of additional difficulties.

A *siman muvhak* has been defined as a identificatory mark that occurs with a frequency of less than one in a thousand[48] and a *siman*

46 For an elucidation of *milta de-avida le-giluyeih* see *supra,* pp. 147–149.

47 See *supra,* pp. 77–93.

48 Both Rabbi David Lau, *Berurei Yahadut,* p. 219, and Dr. Abraham Steinberg, *ibid,* p. 230, argue that focus upon the ratio of one in a thousand is misplaced. The earliest source for that definition of a *siman muvhak* is *Teshuvot Mas'at Binyamin,* no. 63, who defines a *siman muvhak* as "one in a thousand or one in two thousand." They regard *Mas'at Binyamin*'s lack of precision as an indication that the figure presented is hyperbolic and not to be understood literally. That criticism is misplaced for two reasons: 1) the ratio is cited definitively by *Bet Shmu'el, Even ha-Ezer* 17:72, has been repeated and accepted by countless authorities and has been disputed by none; 2) granted, *arguendo,* that the figure is imprecise, the phrase "one in a thousand or one in two thousand"

beinoni, or an intermediate identificatory mark, as a mark that occurs with a frequency of less than one in two hundred.[49] As has been shown, a *siman muvhak*, or a singular (i.e., highly reliable) identificatory mark, although far from infallible, is accepted for purposes of identifying a corpse. The issue is whether the Jewish gene constitutes a *siman* that is acceptable as proof of identity as a member of the Jewish community.[50]

In halakhic contexts, a *siman* is used to establish ownership of a lost object or identity of a missing person. In both cases, the concern is that the object was lost by another person who is in fact the rightful owner

---

certainly means "extremely rare" and clearly indicates a frequency of *less* than "one in a thousand" and perhaps even a frequency of "less than one in two thousand." See *supra*, pp. 78–79 and p. 79, note 2.

Dr. Steinberg chooses to vocalize *Mas'at Binyamin* as "one in a thousand or one in *alafim*" rather than "one in *alpayim*." If that reading is correct, the connotation would be "one in many thousands" making it even more clear that a frequency of greater than one in a thousand cannot be deemed a *siman*. Rabbi Lau assumes that *Mas'at Binyamin*'s phrase "one in a thousand" is hyperbolic because there is no source for that definition in the Gemara or in early-day authorities. That is not completely accurate. Rabbenu Yeruḥam, *Ḥelek Adam ve-Ḥavvah* 23:3, rules that an acceptable *siman* must be something certain (*barur*) "that cannot be found on another body." It is undoubtedly the case that *Mas'at Binyamin* sought to clarify Rabbenu Yeruḥam's definition because he believed that it should not be taken literally. If Dr. Steinberg's reading of *Mas'at Binyamin* is correct, the connotation of the definition "one in a thousand or thousands" would be identical to that of Rabbenu Yeruḥam. *Mas'at Binyamin* carefully stated "one in a thousand or two thousand" and not "one in *kammah alafim* (many thousands)" because he wished to remedy the literal impression left by Rabbenu Yeruḥam's statement and was quite precise in his employment of the phrase "one in a thousand or two thousand." See *supra*, p. 79.

49 See *supra*, p. 81, note 5.

50 Employment of a *siman* is encountered not only with regard to establishing the identity of an object or of a person but also with regard to membership in a class. The Gemara, *Ḥullin* 79a, permits breeding a male donkey with a female donkey and yoking both together as beasts of burden only if it can be demonstrated that the mother of each of the two animals was either a donkey or a horse. That is established, says the Gemara, by observation of *simanim*, *viz.*, in the comparison of the ears, tails and voices of the two animals.

or that the body is the remains of a man other than the husband of the woman who seeks to prove her widowhood. As earlier explained,[51] in every such instance the *siman* disproves the confluence of two events each having a probability of one in a thousand or one in two hundred, i.e., the probability that some other person manifesting the identical *siman* went missing during the same time period or that a similar object having the identical *siman* was lost by another person. The real probability of the confluence of both events is one in a thousand multiplied by one in a thousand or one in two hundred multiplied by one in two hundred. If that position is accepted, there is no room to entertain the possibility that the Jewish gene might serve as a *siman* because it would probably have to be the case that the frequency of the Jewish gene in the non-Jewish population is far too great for it to be considered even a *siman beinoni*.[52]

In *Berurei Yahadut*, chap. 4, Rabbi Barenbaum adopts a rather different position. He argues that a *siman* is effective as evidence solely because of the statistical probability it brings to bear. The question is what degree of statistical probability constitutes the threshold level of a *siman*. Rabbi Barenbaum points out that description of a *siman muvhak* as an identificatory mark that is known to be present in no more than one in 1,000 people serves to define a *siman muvhak* only when doubt exists with regard to a single individual, i.e., a doubt whether the single corpse that has been discovered is that of a husband whose whereabouts is unknown. Consider the same issue in a situation in which one hundred people have been involved in a common disaster. If one in 1,000 individuals carries a particular identificatory mark and one body is examined and is found to carry that mark, there is only an approximately 90% (90.99%) chance that the body is that of

51 See *supra*, pp. 86–88.

52 Although some occurrences of the Jewish gene among non-Jews have been found, there has been no meaningful attempt to establish the rate of occurrence of such a gene among any non-Jewish population. See Behar, "MtDNA Evidence for a Genetic Bottleneck," p. 361 and *idem*, "The Matrilineal Ancestors of Ashkenazi Jewry," p. 489.

the woman's husband because each of the unexamined bodies might also carry the same mark. In other words, there is an approximately ten percent chance that the examined corpse having the identificatory mark is someone other than the husband. If ten thousand persons are involved in a common disaster it is likely that at least ten of those individuals share a common identificatory mark. It is possible that any one of those ten is the husband. Hence, if one body is examined and is found to bear the mark, the chance that he is the person whose whereabouts is unknown is only approximately one out of ten or 10% (9.09%).[53] The more individuals involved in the common disaster the less likely that the single person bearing the *siman* is the person we seek to identify. The proportion of one in a thousand would be meaningful only if all the bodies are examined and it is established that none of the other bodies carries the mark or that, by other means, those bodies could be excluded from the possibility of being the body of the person whose identity we seek to establish.[54] That leaves us with the problem of defining the minimum statistical probability that must be present for a *siman* to be effective.

Rabbi Barenbaum, *Berurei Yahadut*, chap. 4, regards a statistical probability of 99% or more as sufficient to establish identity as a Jew. He arrives at that conclusion in an interesting manner. There are a host of authorities who maintain that a *siman muvhak* is sufficient to sustain a financial claim against a *muḥzak*, i.e., a person

---

53 These calculations involve application of Bayes' Theorem. See *Berurei Yahadut*, p. 93, and *ibid.*, note 59.

54 Cf., *Teshuvot Galya Masekhet*, no. 8, sec. 9, who writes: "However, when a person who has been killed is found in a distant place such that from the place that [the husband] went missing until [the] place [where the corpse has been found] there are many, many thousands [of men] and among each thousand is possible that one person may be found with a *siman* such as this, how can [the woman] be permitted [to remarry] in this situation?" Cf., R. Ya'akov Kanievsky, *Kehillat Ya'akov*, *Yevamot*, no. 47. Cf., also, *Mishmeret Mosheh*, *Hilkhot Geirushin*, chap. 13 and *Pitḥei Teshuvah*, *Even ha-Ezer* 17:103. See also *Teshuvot Ḥelkat Ya'akov*, *Even ha-Ezer*, no. 15 and *Teshuvot ha-Elef Lekha Shlomoh*, *Even ha-Ezer*, no. 91.

in possession.[55] R. Jonathan Eybeschutz, *Tumim, Kelalei Migu, klal* 46,[56] explains that a *siman* is a "super *rov*" that admits only of a *miu'ta de-miu'ta* – literally, "a minority of a minority." Rabbi Barenbaum then cites Ritva, *Kiddushin* 80a, as well as a latter-day authority, R. Joseph Ber Soloveitchik, *Bet ha-Levi*, II, no. 68, sec. 4, who define a *miu'ta de-miu'ta* as 1%. Accordingly, Rabbi Barenbaum concludes that, since a *siman muvhak* is sufficient to establish personal identity, any statistical probability of 99% is also sufficient for that purpose. Rabbi Barenbaum further proposes that DNA evidence be combined with other forms of circumstantial evidence (which he does not define) so that a resultant 99% statistical probability of Jewish parentage be regarded as sufficient evidence for purposes of Halakhah. In support of the last contention, he cites a number of authorities who maintain that, in some circumstances, a *siman beinoni* and, for some authorities, even a *siman garu'a*, can rise to the level of a *siman muvhak*. A *siman garu'a* is an inferior, i.e., an ordinary or conventional *siman*, that does not qualify as an identificatory mark.[57] One example: "tall" or "short"

55 See *Shakh, Ḥoshen Mishpat* 297:1 and *Netivot ha-Mishpat* 46:8. See also *Teshuvot Divrei Ḥayyim*, I, *Even ha-Ezer*, no. 27; *Teshuvot Ḥelkat Yo'av, Even ha-Ezer*, no. 15; *Teshuvot Be'er Yiẓḥak, Even ha-Ezer*, no. 6, *anafim* 5–8; and *Teshuvot Divrei Malki'el*, V, no. 168. An opposing view is held by *Keẓot ha-Ḥoshen* 46:8 and 159:2. See also *Teshuvot Noda bi-Yehudah, Even ha-Ezer, Mahadura Kamma*, no. 51; *Teshuvot Sho'el u-Meshiv, Even ha-Ezer, Mahadura Kamma*, I, no. 257; and *Pri Megadim, Yoreh De'ah, Klalei Simanim u-Tevi'ut Ayin*, who regard a *siman muvhak* as reliable evidence even in capital cases.

56 Cited also by *Bet Shmu'el* 60: addenda. See also *Bi'ur ha-Gra, Even ha-Ezer* 160:10 as well as *Tumim, Klalei Tefisah*, no. 123.

57 DNA evidence is based upon length and position of gene fragments. Size and position are regarded as *simanim geru'im*. See R. Mendel Senderovic, *Teshuvot Aẓei Besamim*, no. 16. Cf., R. Israel Barenbaum, *Berurei Yahadut le-Or Meḥkarim Genetiyim*, (n.p., 5777), chap. 6, implies that a combination of *simanim geru'im*, or common identificatory marks, may be coincidental but that presence of alleles in each of countless numbers of different cells in which size and sequence of the genetic component is identical cannot be coincidental. That is not quite so because all cells of a human being are reproduced from a single template. Therefore, if the first appearance of a gene sequence is coincidental, that sequence will reproduce itself in all subsequently

is a *siman garu'a*. Nevertheless, *Pitḥei Teshuvah, Even ha-Ezer* 17:103, states that if a corpse can only be that of a particular husband or of but a single other individual in that locale who is "short" or "tall," that identificatory mark is regarded as a *siman muvhak*.

Rabbi Barenbaum's argument does not fully establish his point. The examples of a *siman* are not cast in concrete. The function of a *siman* is to serve as an identificatory mark. If 999 other people must be excluded in order to qualify as a *siman*, an identificatory mark must have a prevalence of less than one in a thousand. Many more than one in a thousand men are tall or short. However, if only two men are confined in a particular area and one is known to be tall and the other short, the identity of one can be established with certainty on the basis of height – an identificatory mark that would otherwise be of no significant meaning. In distinguishing between one of only two men physical stature is highly significant and, in context, becomes a *siman muvhak*.[58] There is significant controversy with regard to whether, in ordinary circumstances, even two *simanim beinonim* can be combined for purposes of identification.[59] If yes, it is because the two together taken in the aggregate become a *siman muvhak*. *Simanim muvhakim* are accepted as a discrete category of evidence. What is or is not a *siman* may be contextual but there is no evidence that a *siman* is nothing more than mere statistical probability or that it can be combined with other entirely different forms of circumstantial evidence in order to reach a threshold level of statistical probability.

Put somewhat differently: A necessary condition of a distinguishing mark that serves as a *siman* is that its frequency of occurrence

---

created cells and, consequently, such reproduction does not at all contribute to establishment of a *siman*. If the size and proximity of the components of an allele constitute a *siman*, it is because of the uniqueness of the pattern formed by those constituents rather than by the myriad repetitions of the sequence. See *supra*, pp. 1–2.

58 Indeed, in this case, the evidence is far stronger than a *siman muvhak* and compelled on the basis of deductive logic: X is either A or B. X is not A and confirmed as not A by *tevi'ut ayin*. Therefore, X must be B.

59 See *Bet Shmu'el, Even ha-Ezer* 17:73.

must be less than one in a thousand. However, a statistical probability other than a *siman* of that or lesser magnitude is not necessarily tantamount to a *siman*. *Simanim* as a halakhic category are not reflective of tautological equivalences any more so than is the two-witness rule entirely reflective of an assessment of the statistical reliability of such evidence.

More significantly, Rabbi Barenbaum's demonstration that the threshold level of a *siman muvhak* is a statistical probability of 99% is not quite compelling. His sources demonstrate only that a minority of more than one percent is no longer a *miu'ta de-miu'ta*. *Simanim* may well be predicated upon the notion of a "super *rov*"[60] but that does not *ipso facto* establish that even a conventional *miu'ta de-miu'ta* does not vitiate the efficacy of a *siman*. Rabbi Barenbaum assumes that one in a thousand is really 99% rather than 99.9% because of the possibility, unknown to us, there may be more than one unidentified corpse and that the discovered corpse may be that of some person other than the husband who is one of the thousand who also bears an identical *siman*. Rabbi Barenbaum fails to take into account the observation of *Shulḥan Arukh ha-Rav* that our concern with regard to correct identification of the husband is cogent only if some other person may have also disappeared without a trace. Thus, the possibility that two people, both having an identical identificatory mark, disappeared without a trace is really one in a thousand times one in a thousand, or one in a million. Allowing for the unquantifiable but extremely low possibility that another undiscovered corpse exists, the statistical probability that the discovered corpse is not that of the husband, the resultant probability is still more than one in a million, but far less than one in a hundred. Why the Sages insisted upon not accepting *simanim* of a category statistically defined as a *miu'ta de-miu'ta* is an open question but it is nevertheless clear that the statistical certainty of a *siman muvhak* is greater than that of a *rov* that admits of a *miu'ta de-miu'ta*. The Sages certainly did not rely upon a conventional *rov* in order to allow a woman to remarry as a widow as evidenced by their refusal to

60 See *supra*, pp. 53–66.

allow such remarriage in instances in which a husband disappears in *mayim she-ein la-hem sof* despite the fact that a majority of people lost at sea have drowned.[61] Abrogation of the principle of *rov* in such cases is a stringency imposed by the Sages because of fear of adultery. That fear might well have prompted the Sages to disregard even a "super *rov*," defined as admitting of a *miu'ta de-miu'ta,* and having insisted upon criteria that reflect an even greater "super *rov*."

2. Bayes' Theorem

The author(s) of the article published in *Be-Mar'eh ha-Bazak*[62] reject(s) the notion that the Jewish gene can be accepted as a *siman* in order to establish identity as a Jew on the basis of *rov*. The fallacy, it is contended, becomes evident upon application of Bayes' Theorem. Bayes' Theorem is a mathematical formula used for calculating conditional probabilities.[63]

Ordinary probabilities are expressed on the basis of raw data. Often, there are other factors present that establish independent probabilities for other cohorts. The probability of including that cohort and the probability of the broader cohort excluding the narrower cohort may be quite different. When a large group is known to include a smaller group, the probability within the larger group must be reconfigured

---

61 See *Tosafot, Yevamot* 36b, s.v. *ha lo, Yevamot* 121a, s.v. *ve-lo* and *Bava Meẓi'a* 20b, s.v. *issura.*

62 See *Berurei Yahadut,* p. 98, note 11. See also *ibid.*, p. 93

63 Bayes' Theorem as it appears in the *Stanford Encyclopedia of Philosophy* is:

> The probability of a hypothesis *H* conditional on a given body of data *E* is the ratio of the unconditional probability of the conjunction of the hypothesis with the data to the unconditional probability of the data alone.
>
> **(1.1) Definition.**
>
> The probability of *H* conditional on *E* is defined as $\mathbf{P}_E(H) = \mathbf{P}(H\&E) / \mathbf{P}(E)$, provided that both terms of this ratio exist and $\mathbf{P}(E) > 0$.

For a full exposition see "Bayes' Theorem," *The Stanford Encyclopedia of Philosophy* (Spring, 2019), https://plato.stanford.edu/archives/spr2019/entries/bayes-theorem/.

to take cognizance of the impact of the quite different probability of the smaller group.

For example, a *siman muvhak* is described as an identificatory sign with a likelihood of random occurrence of no more than one in a thousand. Thus, if one person in a thousand has a sunken nose and a person known to have a sunken nose goes missing and if an otherwise unidentifiable corpse is discovered and found to have a sunken nose, the corpse may be identified on the basis of the identificatory sign as that of the missing person with a 99.9 percent degree of certainty. Such is the classic *agunah* case in which only one person has disappeared.

Suppose, however, that ten men have disappeared or have perished in a common disaster in a town of ten thousand inhabitants. One of those individuals is known to have had a sunken nose. Nothing is known regarding the other men. The corpse of one of the men is found and discovered to possess a sunken nose. Can the sunken nose serve as a *siman* to establish the identity of the corpse so that his wife may remarry?

The issue is: In any group of ten thousand men, the statistical probability is that ten men will each have a sunken nose (instead of only one man, as would be the case in a town of one thousand inhabitants). If only one corpse is discovered having a sunken nose, is the wife permitted to remarry?

In the first case, if all one thousand inhabitants have perished, only one of the thousand is likely to have had a sunken nose. Whether one person, ten people or a thousand people have perished is irrelevant; it is a statistical improbability that the corpse bearing a sunken nose is other than that of the person we seek to identify, i.e., the chance of misidentification is no more than one in one thousand.

In the second case, although the ratios of one in a thousand and ten in ten thousand are the same, the chance of misidentification is far greater. Since, statistically, we may anticipate that, were all corpses to be examined, ten corpses bearing sunken noses would be found, what is the probability that the corpse we have discovered is the one we are seeking rather than one of the other nine? The corpse that has been discovered is one among ten. The probability that the corpse we have found is the one we are seeking to identify is only one in ten. Under those circumstances, since there may be presumed to be nine other corpses bearing the same *siman*, the presence of a sunken nose can serve as positive identification with only a ten percent chance of accuracy. Bayes' Theorem expresses the quandary reflected in the second hypothetical and yields an equation designed to find an accurate degree of probability.

Consider the following hypothetical example: A clinical trial is designed to determine the therapeutic value of an experimental drug. That can be determined by administering the drug to a certain number of patients and determining the number of patients who are cured. The finding will be expressed as a fraction or a percentage determined by the number cured divided by the total number of patients. However, experience has taught that a certain number of patients recover from their illness spontaneously without intervention. The drug certainly cannot be credited with the cure of patients who would have recovered even in the absence of any treatment. For the study to yield meaningful results it is necessary to subtract the number of patients who would have recovered even without treatment from the total number of participants and to divide the number of patients actually cured by the medication by the number of patients enrolled in the study minus the number of those who would have recovered in any event.

The mortality rate of the drug can be determined in a similar manner. Using actuarial tables, it is possible to anticipate how many participants may be expected to die of natural causes during the duration of the study. That number must be excluded from the calculation of the mortality rate of the drug by subtracting that number both from the total number of fatalities and from the original number of participants. The remainder of fatalities is then divided by the total number of participants whose demise can be attributed to the drug.

The implication of Bayes' Theorem is that in order to establish the Jewish gene as a *siman* it would be necessary to exclude the general rate of occurrence of the gene among the general population and then assess the rate of Jewish versus non-Jewish carriers of the gene.

If there are one thousand Jews in the world, each of whom carries the Jewish gene, but only one non-Jew endowed with that gene is in existence, and a stranger appears manifesting the Jewish gene, the statistical probability that the person in question is a Jew would be precisely one in one thousand, or 99.9 percent. But, in point of fact, only 40 percent of Jews are carriers of the Jewish gene and the percentage of non-Jews bearing that gene is not known with any degree of accuracy. The problem is: With what degree of statistical probability can we presume that a person presenting with the Jewish gene is a Jew rather than a randomly appearing non-Jew who happens to bear that gene?

Let us assume that: a) there exist one billion people of European descent and b) one percent are Jews, or ten million of that number are Jews. If so, the non-Jewish population of European descent is 990,000,000.

Let us further assume that: a) 40 percent or four million Jews possess the Jewish gene and b) only .1 percent or 990,000 non-Jews carry the gene.

In order to calculate the probability that a random person bearing the gene is a Jew, we must first calculate the likelihood that the person is a Jew and then calculate the likelihood that a Jew possesses the Jewish gene. The result must then be divided by the overall likelihood that any person, Jew or non-Jew, may bear the gene, i.e., the result must be divided by the addition of the probability of a Jew carrying the gene and of a non-Jew carrying the gene. That process is represented by the following equation:

$$P\,(Jewish \mid gene)$$

$$= \frac{P\,(Jewish) \times P\,(gene \mid Jewish)}{P\,(gene)}$$

$$= \frac{P\,(Jewish) \times P\,(gene \mid Jewish)}{P\,(Jewish) \times P\,(gene \mid Jewish) + P\,(not\ Jewish) \times P\,(gene \mid not\ Jewish)}$$

$$= \frac{0.1 \times .4}{0.1 \times .4 + .99 \times .001}$$

$$= .8016$$

Using the hypothetical figures presented above, the result will be that the likelihood of a random person bearing the Jewish gene is actually Jewish is .8016 or approximately 80 percent. That is far less than 99.9 percent, or even 99 percent, that is the hallmark of a *siman*. That is, if we assume that there are four million Jews who possess a Jewish gene and one million non-Jews who carry the gene, there is an 80% chance that a person selected at random from the total group of five million is Jewish.

It would be necessary to show that the prevalence of the gene among non-Jews is no more than .0004%, i.e., no more than four out of a million, in order to satisfy the 99.9 percent certainty requirement of a *siman* in order to entertain the Jewish gene as emblematic of Jewish identity.

A point closely parallel to the consideration underlying Bayes' Theorem is addressed by *Ḥiddushei R. Akiva Eger, Ketubot* 14b. The hypothetical situation addressed by R. Akiva Eger involves a situation in which a woman cohabited with one person among a group of one hundred and one men. Her paramour cannot be identified. Cohabiting with one or more of fifty-one of those men would not affect the woman's eligibility to marry a *kohen*; fifty of those men are members of a class of males with whom engaging in a sexual act would disqualify a woman from marrying a *kohen*. It might appear that the principle of *rov* would serve to render the woman permissible to a *kohen*. Nevertheless, R. Akiva Eger asserts that, if one of the fifty-one men is a *kohen* who knows full well that he has not consorted with the woman in question, he may not marry her.[64]

R. Akiva Eger's reason is that the *kohen* knows that he did not consort with the woman in question. Consequently, from his perspective, there are only one hundred men with whom she may have cohabited, not a hundred and one. Since, so far as he is concerned, each of the two groups is comprised of exactly fifty persons, there is no major class

64 The same principle is expressed in a different context by *Pnei Yehoshu'a, Bava Meẓi'a* 24a.

of men with whom cohabitation would not disqualify the woman in question from marrying a *kohen*.

R. Akiva Eger's thesis is limited to a situation in which the person seeking resolution of a halakhic doubt has excluded himself from the majoritarian class because he has excluded himself from both classes. Since he knows that he did not cohabit with the woman in question he has excluded himself from the class of persons with whom consortium would serve to disqualify a female partner from marrying a *kohen* as well as from the class of women with whom intercourse would have no effect upon eligibility to marrying a *kohen*. The underlying point is similar to the Fallacy of the Compound Question: "When did you stop beating your wife?" The question is premised upon the presumption that the person addressed has been beating his wife. The only question is whether such beating has or has not ceased. In the manner posed, the question has no meaning and hence no answer. Similarly, if cohabitation did not take place, there can be no logical question regarding determination of the status of the man's non-existent sexual partner.

R. Akiva Eger's point is that *rov* does not operate in a vacuum; it serves to resolve a problem for a person in light of salient facts. Since our chaste *kohen* knows that he did not engage in the sexual act subject to scrutiny, the question of whether that unconsummated act disqualifies the woman in question from marrying a *kohen* is nonsensical.

R. Akiva Eger can be cited for no more than the aforesaid. R. Akiva Eger addresses only a situation in which a person has subjective knowledge of a fact that defeats the *rov* insofar as he is concerned. Nevertheless, Bayes' Theorem is none else then R. Akiva Eger's point writ large. Bayes would argue that if it can be determined that one member of the class of fifty-one men, unknown to himself, was inebriated and temporarily impotent, he must be excluded from the calculus of the majoritarian and minoritarian classes and, moreover, that person must be excluded, even if his identity is forever unknown. That is tantamount to saying that, in assessing statistical mortality of a drug, one must exclude the actuarial probability of death due to other causes or that, in determining the statistical reliability of a gene as an identificatory mark of a Jew one must exclude the probability of its random occurrence in the non-Jewish population.

Reshash, ad locum, disagrees with R. Akiva Eger and maintains that, despite the foregoing, the presence of an objective *rov* renders the woman permissible to the chaste *kohen* who is the subject of R. Akiva Eger's hypothetical. Since *Reshash* rejects R. Akiva Eger's conclusion in instances in which a person is cognizant of the inapplicability of *rov* to himself, *a fortiori,* he would reject application of *rov* in circumstances in which the existence of an anonymous person excluded from the *rov* is known with certainty to all and sundry – a position that entails denial of Bayes' Theorem.

Moreover, it can be shown much more directly that Jewish law does not take halakhic cognizance of Bayes' Theorem. We need but examine the frame of reference used in establishing the *rov* that is applied in determining the status of a foundling discovered in a public area. Only fertile, non-pregnant women between the time of menarche and menopause can bear children. Were *rov* nothing other than statistical probability, identity of a foundling would depend solely upon whether the majority of women of child-bearing age are Jewish or not Jewish. However, that is not the case. The major and minor classes are determined not by the relative numbers of women of childbearing age, or even by the relative number of women inhabitants, but by the relative number of Jews versus non-Jews within the entire populace.[65] Thus, both Rambam, *Hilkhot Issurei Bi'ah* 15:25–26, and

65 See *Berurei Yahadut,* chap. 14, sec. 39. The sole limitation in establishing a *rov* as class-defining rather than idiosyncratic is that of R. Judah, *Makhshirin* 2:7, who declares that only persons "who abandon children," i.e., non-Jews, need be considered in determining parentage of a foundling because the term "who abandons children" is coextensive with the class of non-Jews. Similarly, the Mishnah, *Makhshirin* 2:8, rules that only the identity of bakers is considered with regard to the source of lost bread and *Makhshirin* 2:9, rules that the *kashrut* of meat the majoritarian and minoritarian classes are determined only from among persons "who eat meat" because those activities serve to define a class. Cf., however, *Ḥiddushei R. Akiva Eger,* Johannesburg 5622 edition, *Oraḥ Ḥayyim* 335:5, reprinted in *Shulḥan Arukh* in *Peirush R. Akiva Eger ha-Shalem* (Tel Aviv, 5778), *Ein ha-Gilyon, Oraḥ Ḥayyim* 335:5.

Shulḥan Arukh, Even ha-Ezer 4:33–34, carefully speak of "a city where there are a majority" of Jews and non-Jews.

Bayes' formulation of his theorem represents a determination of statistical probability with regard to which Bayes is certainly correct. But the halakhic principle of *rov* is not always coextensive with application of probability. *Rov* is a halakhic construct with its own rules and definitions and not merely an expression of probability theory.

That the principle of *rov* is not fully consistent with application of probability theory is evident upon examination of a number of applications of *kol de-parish*:

1. R. Shlomoh Zalman Auerbach, in his commentary on *Shev Shem'ateta* (Jerusalem, 5768), *shem'ata* 4, chap. 1, observes that the principle *kol de-parish* is a divine edict rather than simply application of a rational principle. Statistical probability establishes that in the case of ten butcher stores, six kosher and four non-kosher, a single piece of meat found in a public place is probably kosher. But, if by the same token, ten pieces of meat are found one after the other, four of those pieces should be presumed to be non-kosher.[66] It is nevertheless permitted to consume all ten pieces or to cook all of them in the same pot because the rule *kol de-parish* is applicable to each piece.
2. Similarly, in a city whose population is sixty percent Jewish and forty percent non-Jewish a foundling is regarded as Jewish. If ten foundlings are found, they are all deemed to be Jewish. Suppose that, years later, the ten foundlings, now adults, assemble for prayer. The ten constitute a valid quorum for congregational prayer despite the fact that rational application of statistical probability would render it highly improbable that all ten are Jews.[67]
3. In addition, as has been previously noted, in determining whether a foundling is a Jew or a non-Jew, the entire population rather

66 The principle of nullification would not apply if the pieces are large enough to serve as a full portion (*ra'ui le-hitkabed*).

67 See *Sha'arei Yosher, sha'ar* 3, chap. 4. See also *sha'ar* 1, chap. 5 and *sha'ar* 3, chap. 1.

than just women of childbearing age is taken into consideration in determining whether the majority are Jews or non-Jews.[68]

Indeed the very notion of *kavu'a* as an exception to *kol de-parish me-rubba parish* is hardly consistent with probability theory.

Similarly, Rabbi Barenbaum's basic assumption that any form of statistical probability above a certain threshold is tantamount to a *siman* is subject to challenge. The "one in a thousand" criterion of a *siman* is a necessary condition but there is no evidence that it is tautologically definitional of a *siman*.[69]

IV. *ROV*

A number of writers, including R. Asher Weiss, advance an interesting but quite different argument in support of accepting the presence of a "Jewish" gene as a determinative *siman* of Jewish identity. A *siman muvhak* is of sufficient reliability to allow a woman to contract a second marriage even though, as indicated by *Tosafot, Yevamot* 37a, s.v. *rov ha-yoldot, Yevamot* 121a, s.v. *ve-lo-hi, Bava Meẓia* 20b, s.v. *issura* and *Bi'ur ha-Gra, Even ha-Ezer* 16:116, the presence of a *rov* is not sufficient to permit a woman to remarry. Clearly, a *siman muvhak* is more probative than a *rov*. *Ergo*, if *rov* is sufficient to establish identity as a Jew, *a fortiori*, a *siman muvhak* should suffice for that purpose as well.

However, although ostensibly compelling, that argument is a *non sequitur*. The function of a *siman* is identification rather than establishment of independent proof in and of itself. A *siman* found on a lost object only serves to identify that object as the selfsame object that has been lost. Ownership of the object prior to its loss must be established on other grounds. A *siman* found on a corpse serves to establish the identity of the body. Death of the individual who bears that *siman* – upon which license to remarry is contingent – is established by quite different physical criteria. Identification of the

68 See *supra*, p. 187 and *infra*, pp. 230–231.

69 Cf., *supra*, p. 184, note 29.

presence of the Jewish gene serves only to demonstrate that the person belongs to the class of individuals who are endowed with such a gene. The conclusion that people endowed with that particular gene are halakhically presumed to be Jews is based upon the recognition of the fact that persons identified in that manner are presumed to be Jews on the basis of some other halakhic presumption, e.g., *rov* or *ḥazakah*. The Jewish gene can serve as a *siman* only for purposes of identification; conclusions reached on the basis of such identification stand or fall upon attendant principles that are then brought to bear as proof.

Even if the Jewish gene cannot serve as intrinsic evidence of Jewish identity in the form of a *siman*, it is still possible that a person manifesting the Jewish gene can be regarded as a Jew on the basis of *rov*, i.e., that the majority of all known persons endowed with the allele are Jews. As has already been shown,[70] the presence of a *rov* is not dispositive for all halakhic purposes, e.g., it is insufficient to support a financial claim. The question to be addressed is: Is *rov* sufficient to support a claim of Jewish ancestry?

1. One *Rov* or Two *Rovs*?

The Gemara, *Ketubot* 15b, addresses at length the situation of a foundling abandoned in a city having both Jewish and non-Jewish inhabitants. Rambam, *Hilkhot Isurei Bi'ah* 15:25, followed by *Shulḥan Arukh, Even ha-Ezer* 4:53, rules that, for purposes of marriage, the infant's status as a Jew is a matter of doubt regardless of whether the majority of the townspeople are Jews or gentiles. It would appear that, as a matter of rabbinic decree, a person's capacity to enter into marriage as a Jew cannot be determined simply by *rov*.[71] However, *Maggid*

---

70 See *supra*, pp. 42, 55 and p. 94, note 23 and accompanying text.

71 Rashi, *Ketubot* 15a, s.v. *aval le-yuḥasin*, comments that a Jewish majority of townspeople is not sufficient to permit marriage of the child to a *kohen*. Rather, for that purpose the Sages required two majorities, *viz.*, a majority of townspeople and a majority of transient wayfarers. R. Ezekiel Landau, *Noda bi-Yehudah, Even ha-Ezer, Mahadura Kamma*, no. 7, understands Rashi literally and assumes that for the purpose of establishing identity as a Jew, and hence eligibility to marry a non-*kohen*, a single *rov* is sufficient. *Bet Me'ir, Even*

Mishneh, ad locum, cited by *Bet Yosef, Even ha-Ezer* 4:34, asserts that the principle of *rov* does not apply to a foundling. Since the infant has been abandoned, wherever the infant is found it is considered to be *kavu'a,* i.e., in a "permanent" place, because the foundling has not become "separated" from either a major or minor class. Rather, wherever the abandoned neonate is found is regarded as the infant's place of "permanence" and hence the rule of *rov* is not applicable.[72] The Sages did, however, permit marriage to a person of Jewish birth if two separate *rovs* indicating the foundling's Jewish parentage are present. There are two possibilities regarding the child's lineage. The infant may be the child of one of the townspeople or may be the issue of an itinerant wayfarer. Accordingly, the Sages required two *rovs* to establish Jewish lineage, *viz.,* a majority of the townspeople and a majority of the itinerant wayfarers. The purpose of that edict was to make it apparent that the child's status is not that of *kavu'a* and hence is adjudicated on the basis of *kol de-parish.*

Ḥazon Ish, Even ha-Ezer 7:7, notes that, according to some authorities, a single *rov* is sufficient to establish identification as a Jew in at least some situations. *Ḥazon Ish* explains that two *rovs* are necessary only in cases in which, depending upon the circumstances, the rule of *kavu'a* might potentially apply.[73] However, in some circumstances,

---

ha-Ezer 4:26, understands Rashi as agreeing that a single *rov* is never sufficient to establish identity as a Jew for purposes of marriage but that, even though two *rovs* are necessary to sanction any marriage, the Gemara focuses upon the need for two *rovs* in order to establish eligibility for marriage to a *kohen* because, in the presence of but a single *rov,* conversion would be of no avail since a *kohen* may not marry a proselyte.

72 *Bet Me'ir, Even ha-Ezer* 4:33, and *Arukh ha-Shulḥan, Even ha-Ezer* 4:54, aver that this is not an actual *kavu'a* but was treated as such by rabbinic decree.

73 Cf., however, *Bet Shmu'el, Even ha-Ezer* 6:32, who argues that some early-day authorities understand the Gemara as declaring that the Sages required two *rovs* for purposes of marriage as a stringency not at all connected to the possibility of confusion between instances of *kavu'a* and instances of *kol de-parish.* Cf., *Bet Me'ir, Even ha-Ezer* 6:18 and *Ḥazon Ish, Even ha-Ezer,* no. 7, sec. 7.

Rabbi Litke, *Berurei Yahadut,* chap. 11, sec. 5, notes that *Bet Shmu'el, Even ha-Ezer* 4:39 and 6:17, states that two *rovs* are required only when "there are

for example in the situation of an unidentified person who appears before us and claims to be a Jew, the individual has perforce separated himself from all others who retain their earlier state of *kavu'a* and hence there is no reason to promulgate a rule requiring two *rovs*.

R. Moshe Mordecai Farbstein, *Teḥumin*, XII (5751), pp. 17–80, draws a distinction between a *rubba de-ita kamman* and a *rubba de-leita kamman*.[74] A *rubba de-ita kamman* is the formulation of a majoritarian rule in situations in which there is an identifiable major class and an identifiable minor class, e.g., there are ten establishments in the city that sell meat; nine of those establishments sell kosher meat and one of those establishments sells non-kosher meat. A piece of meat found in the surrounding area is presumed to have become "separated" from either the larger class of stores or the smaller class. The principle of *rov* establishes that the meat became separated from the major class. A *rubba de-leita kamman* encapsulates a general empirical principle, e.g., the majority of animals are not *treifot*. There is no class of "animals before us" containing a specific number of kosher animals nor is there a second class before us comprised of a smaller number of animals that are *treifot*. That *rov* is roughly comparable to general statistical probability, i.e., it is more likely than not that the animal in question is emblematic of the larger class. With regard to the second type of *rov*, Rabbi Farbstein cogently points out that, since it is in the nature of an empirical generalization involving both examined and unexamined animals, the notion of *kavu'a* is meaningless and hence inapplicable.[75]

---

a minority of *pesulim* but when there is no minor class of *pesulim* two *rovs* are not required." He expresses doubt whether *Bet Shmu'el* means that it is known that there are no *pesulim* in the city, and hence there is no room for doubt because there is no minor class, or whether a second *rov* is unnecessary because there is doubt whether any *pesulim* are present within the city. In the present case it is not clear that a minor class exists consisting of carriers of the gene who are actually non-Jews because those ostensive non-Jews who carry the gene may actually be Jews.

74 Cf., *supra*, p. 166, note 37.

75 Cf., R. Elchanan Wasserman, *Kovez̤ Shi'urim*, I, *Bava Batra*, secs. 85–86, discussed *infra*, p. 220, note 87.

Consequently, the Sages required a second *rov* only when the first *rov* is a *rubba de-ita kamman* but not when the first *rov* is a *rubba de-leita kamman.*

According to *Ḥazon Ish,* it is certainly arguable that, if the majority of individuals who share a common gene or one of a number of genes are otherwise known to be Jews, a person of unknown parentage who appears and claims to be a Jew might be deemed to be a Jew even in the absence of a second supporting *rov.* In that situation as well, the possibility of *kavu'a* does not exist. Similarly, according to the thesis advanced by Rabbi Farbstein, a finding that the majority of individuals endowed with such genes are Jews establishes a *rubba de-leita kamman*[76] that arguably does not require support of a second *rov.*

2. *Kol de-Parish* versus *Kavu'a*

Talmudic exegesis, *Sanhedrin* 2a, infers from Exodus 23:2 that, although we are commanded not to "follow the majority to make a determination" for "evil," we are affirmatively commanded to follow the majority for "good." On the basis of that verse, the Gemara, *Berakhot* 28a and *Ketubot* 15a, declares, "Go according to the majority." The Gemara, *Ḥullin* 11a, expresses that concept in the form of the maxim "*Kol de-parish me-rubba parish* – All that separates, separates [itself] from the major set." That principle is fundamentally an application of set theory. Assuming that there are two antithetical sets, a major set and a minor set, and one comes upon an item of undetermined provenance that has somehow strayed or separated (*parish*) from one of the two

76 The author(s) of the article published in *Be-Ma'areh ha-Bazak,* vol. IX, no. 30 (5777), p. 97, note 8 (2), cite unnamed sources that maintain that there is no authority to posit a *rubba de-leita kamman* that was not formulated by the Sages. Similarly, R. Menachem Senderovic, *Aẓei Besamim,* no. 16, sec. 3, cites unnamed authorities who assert that only the Sages could establish such a *rov.* When the Sages did so, it is contended that the *rov* was announced on the basis of a received tradition or on the basis of a keen and unique understanding of the natural order. That view is also expressed by Rabbi Samuel Gersten, *Yeshurun,* XII, 525. Cf., however, R. Zalman Nechemiah Goldberg, *ibid.,* pp. 530 and 532, who takes strong issue with that opinion.

sets but its origin remains in doubt, the entity of doubtful status is to be assigned to the major set. A classic example is meat that has been lost and subsequently a passerby chances to find it. Is the meat to be regarded as kosher or non-kosher? Applying the biblical principle "*Kol de-parish me-rubba parish*," the answer depends upon the relative number of known establishments that purvey kosher meat compared to the number of known establishments that sell non-kosher meat. If the majority of butcher stores sell kosher meat, the found meat is deemed to be kosher;[77] if the majority sell non-kosher meat, the found meat is to be deemed non-kosher.[78]

A principle that is the antonym of "*kol de-parish*" is "*Kol kavu'a ke-maḥazah al maḥazah dami* – All that is stationary is considered to be half and half."[79] That principle, derived from Deuteronomy 19:11, is essentially an exception to the rule of *kol de-parish*.[80] *Rov* applies only

---

77 Nevertheless, a rabbinic edict that, in most cases, prohibits all meat that is "*nit'alem min ha-ayin*," i.e., that has been "concealed from the eye" of a Jew, even temporarily, will apply.

78 See *Pesaḥim* 9b, *Ketubot* 15a, *Ḥullin* 95a and *Niddah* 18a.

79 *Ketubot* 15a, *Bava Kamma* 44b and *Sanhedrin* 79a.

80 *Kol kavu'a* is generally regarded as a *gezeirat ha-katuv*, or biblical rule, not necessarily grounded in any particular rational foundation. It may perhaps be suggested that an instance of *kol de-parish*, e.g., the loss of an item of property, is a random occurrence subject only to statistical probability, whereas *kol kavu'a* generally requires an overt act which by its nature, although not necessarily reasoned, is not random in the sense that it might be conditioned by psychological causes. For a strained attempt to predicate the distinction between *kol de-parish* as a distinction between "sets" and "classes," see Eliezer Ehrenpreis, "*Safek* and *Sefek Sefeika*: Their Relation to Scientific Observation," *Gesher*, vol. 8 (5741), 93–97. Ehrenpreis chooses to define a set as a collection of entities not subject to definitive observation in which membership is to be adjudicated on the basis of *rov*, i.e., probability. A class is defined as consisting of entities that have been observed in some way and hence identification is governed by *kol kavu'a* because subsequent to observation any further occurrence cannot be categorized as random. Ehrenpreis considers that distinction to be parallel to the distinction between unobserved events of classical mechanics and observed events of quantum mechanics. The distinction between an observed event and an unobserved event can hardly be halakhically considered as hard

to situations in which a person or an entity has become separated from its set before a question of status arises. The principle of *kavu'a* applies in the case of a question or doubt that arises before any separation has occurred, i.e., in the entity's place of origin or "permanence." A classic example is a situation in which meat was purchased from a butcher store but the purchaser failed to ascertain, or forgot, whether he purchased the meat from a kosher store or from a non-kosher establishment. In such cases, the doubt arises before, or at the time of, "separation" and hence the principle of *kol kavu'a* applies.

Rabbi Barenbaum, *Berurei Yahadut*, chap. 1, raises a fundamental objection with regard to the applicability of the notion of the *rov* that is material in modern-day circumstances. As has been noted, the formulation of the archprinciple is "*Kol de-parish me-rubba parish* – All that become separated become separated from the major class." The *kashrut* of meat found in a public place is determined by the majority of establishments from which the meat might have been removed. However, meat purchased in a butcher store by a customer who has forgotten which establishment he patronized is categorized as *kavu'a* and hence is not subject to the rule of *rov*. The status of lost meat is irrelevant so long as it remains lost and hence no question arises with regard to the *kashrut* of such meat until it is found. At that point the meat has already become "separated" from its original location. In the case of meat purchased from an unknown purveyor the question arises when the meat is yet *kavu'a*, or stationary, i.e., the question is the nature of the establishment from which the meat was removed. Thus, the class of stores to which that establishment belongs arises at the moment of purchase. The question of *kashrut* becomes actual at

---

and fast. Consider an obstetrical ward shared by nine Jewish patients and one gentile patient, all of whom are unconscious and unattended. Presumably, *kol kavu'a* would apply to an unidentified neonate even though the birth has not been observed.

For a quite different explanation of this distinction, see R. Elchanan Wasserman, *Koveẓ Shi'urim*, 1, *Bava Batra*, secs. 86–87.

the time of purchase when the meat is still in its original location and has not yet been separated from its existing place of "permanence."

In days gone by, an immigrant or itinerant traveler appeared without "baggage," i.e., without a history of an already established identity. The question of ethnic or religious identity arose only in the locale in which the traveler presented himself. The question was from which of two groups had he "separated" himself, the larger group or the smaller group. Application of a *rov* based upon genetic criteria would appear to be appropriate. Consider, however, the situation of a census-taker who knocks on a door and makes inquiry regarding religious identity and seeks to apply appropriate principles of supporting substantiation. In that situation invocation of a *rov* would not dispose of the issue because the question arises in the respondent's place of domicile, i.e., a place that is *kavu'a*. The same would be the case even if the census-taker never leaves his office. The question presents itself with regard to a person in his place of "permanence," i.e., in his place of domicile. The same would be true if the individual whose status is in question were to travel to a neighboring village for his wedding with the intention of returning to his original home. That person is regarded as "stationary" because he intends to return to his original place of domicile.[81] The same is also the case in a situation in which an itinerant person's doubtful status travels with him because the doubt originally arose in his place of domicile, e.g., the already established doubtful status can be discovered by means of a phone call or written inquiry. Now that the entire world has become a global village it is often the case that even a cursory investigation would disclose the existence of a known ambiguity regarding religious identity in an individual's original place of domicile. The issue is: Where is the doubt born? If the doubt arose in the place of original domicile the issue involves a matter that is *kavu'a* and hence *rov* does not apply. Of course, if there is no communication with the place of emigration or if that locale is isolated, bereft of a Jewish population or the question of Jewish identity is of no material halakhic concern to anyone in that

81 See *Nazir* 12a. See also *Tosafot, Ketubot* 15a, s.v. *dilma.*

locale, the result is that the question first becomes apropos only after the person has become separated from his original domicile with no likelihood of return. It is only in such circumstances that application of *rov* becomes germane.[82]

3. Establishing the Parameters of a *Rov*

In determining the existence of a *rov* it is perforce necessary to determine the ambit of the class of persons or entities to be separated into a major and minor classes. First, a general class of persons and objects to be divided into major and minor classes must be identified. Then, the characteristics of the major class must be delineated. For example, there exists a broad class of human beings. That class can be divided into major and minor classes, e.g., Mongolians and non-Mongolians. The majority of human beings are not Mongolians; a minority of human beings are Mongolians. It is also possible to describe the inhabitants of China as a distinct class and then to divide that class into two sub-classes, *viz.*, Mongolians and non-Mongolians. Thus, majority of human beings are non-Mongolians, but the same time, a Chinese national is far more likely to be a Mongolian than is a randomly chanced-upon human being. Before determining whether or not evidence of a Jewish gene can be utilized as the basis of establishing a *rov*, it is first necessary to establish that the majority of individuals endowed with the gene in question are indeed Jews. Since it is known that some non-Jews are also endowed with that gene. It is necessary to determine the ambit of the class of human beings that must be divided into sub-classes of Jews and non-Jews. In determining

82 A similar interesting question arises with regard to immersion of utensils possibly manufactured by a non-Jew. The majority of utensils acquired on the open market are of non-Jewish provenance and have become "separated" from their place of origin. However, what is the status of a utensil that is clearly labeled as coming from a particular company but it is unknown whether the proprietor of that company is a Jew or a gentile? The doubt originates at the time of shipping from the seller to the buyer, i.e., at a time at which the utensil is *kavu'a* and hence *rov* would not apply. See *Makhon Hora'ah u-Mishpat*, published by the Belz community in Israel, vol. 2 (Nisan, 5771), pp. 87–90.

statistical probability of the carrier of the gene being a Jew rather than a non-Jew, how large is the total group that must be examined for relevant prevalence of the gene? Must one examine the populace of a city, province, country or of the entire world?

Shulḥan Arukh, Yoreh De'ah 1:4, discusses the case of fowl that are lost or stolen and later found to have been slaughtered in an halakhically proper manner. If the birds are found in a locale frequented by individuals the majority of whom are Jewish, the fowl may be deemed to be kosher. The issue is definition of the area within which a Jewish versus non-Jewish census is to be taken. *Shakh, Yoreh De'ah* 1:17, declares the matter to be contingent solely upon the relevant numbers of people who frequent the "place" in which the fowl are found. The relative number of Jews versus non-Jews who frequent the marketplace or who are found in the city is irrelevant. *Shakh* further declares that, in the event that an equal number of Jews and non-Jews are to be found in that "place," the major and minor classes are established on the basis of their relative proportions in the marketplace; if each group has an equal presence in the marketplace, *rov* is determined on the basis of a census of the city. If it then proves to be the case that there are an equal number of Jews and non-Jews in the city, there is no *rov* and the fowl are forbidden as a matter of doubt. *Tevu'ot Shor* 63:4 explains that the majority of individuals present in the marketplace or in the city is determinative only if a *rov* cannot be ascertained on the basis of the relative numbers present in the more limited immediate area because the majority of persons present in the marketplace or the city is irrelevant if the status of the *rov* present in the "place" in which the question arises can be determined. However, unless more precise information is available, it is presumed that the relative numbers present in the "place" in which the birds are found reflects the proportional division of the populace found in the marketplace or in the city. Hence, determination of the *rov* found in the marketplace or in the city is an indirect mark for determining the *rov* present in the immediate area in which the fowl were found.

Pri Ḥadash, ad locum, objects that the Gemara, *Bava Batra* 23b, followed by Rambam, *Hilkhot Gezelah ve-Avedah,* 15:18, and *Shulḥan*

Arukh, Ḥoshen Mishpat 260:8, establishes that, in cases in which application of the principle of *rov* would lead to one conclusion whereas application of the principle of *karov*, or "closest proximity,"[83] would lead to a contradictory finding, a determination is to be made on the basis of *rov* rather than proximity. If so, questions *Pri Ḥadash*, the determination of the *kashrut* of the fowl should always be made on the basis of a population count of the entire city rather than by adjudicating the matter on the basis of the number of persons of each class at the "place," or "closest" to the "place," at which the birds were found.[84]

---

83 The principle of *karov* is derived from the rule prescribed in Deuteronomy 21:3 regarding determination of the city to be held accountable for an act of homicide when the perpetrator is unknown. See *infra*, note 84.

84 *Shulḥan Arukh ha-Rav, Hilkhot Sheḥitah, siman* 1, *Kuntres Aḥaron*, sec. 10, responds to *Pri Ḥadash*'s objection by asserting that *Shakh* is describing a situation in which the persons in close proximity are Jews who also constitute the majority of individuals within the limited area; hence there is no contradiction between applying the principle of *rov* or applying the principle of proximity (*karov*). *Shulḥan Arukh ha-Rav*, in effect, severely constricts the geographic area to be used in determining major and minor classes as limited to the smallest definable area, *viz.*, the immediate proximity of the fowl.

Shulḥan Arukh ha-Rav limits the rule that *rov* prevails against a contradictory conclusion that would arise from applying the principle of proximity (*karov*) only to situations in which it is impossible to accept proximity as dispositive because of a countervailing *rov* at the place of proximity. The paradigm in establishing that principle is that the rule with regard to the ceremony of breaking the neck of a heifer in a ceremony of expiation in the case of an unknown perpetrator of a homicide victim whose body is found between two cities. The *bet din* of the closest city must make atonement, but only if the city is located in a mountainous area not frequented by non-Jews. However, if it is not in an isolated, untraveled area the assumption is that the murderer was a passing traveler, one of the majority of the inhabitants of the world at large rather than an inhabitant of the closest city. *Shulḥan Arukh ha-Rav* explains that the area used to define the major class cannot be limited to the majority of those in close proximity who happen to be Jews because the majority of Jews are not murderers. The principle of *karov* is applied only because the cities in the mountainous area are "sealed off" from the rest of the world. Otherwise, it is *rov* of "the catchment area" that is determinant.

In order to resolve that problem, *Pri Ḥadash* propounds an interesting thesis. *Pri Ḥadash* regards *Shulḥan Arukh's* codification of the ruling as limited to a ghetto or a neighborhood inhabited exclusively by Jews and not traversed by gentiles. Such areas are regarded as tantamount to autonomous cities and major and minor classes are determined accordingly. However, if a thoroughfare frequented by non-Jews traverses that restricted area it is not to be regarded as a self-contained entity and determination of major and minor classes is made on the basis of the population of the dominant area, i.e., the entire city.

It may be concluded that, in order to invoke the principle of *rov* in establishing that a person of unknown ethnic origin who carries the Jewish gene is indeed of Jewish maternal lineage, it is necessary first to establish that the majority of the inhabitants endowed with the Jewish gene are indeed Jews. According to *Shakh* and *Tevu'ot Shor*, *rov* must be determined on the basis of the population of the narrowest definable area; according to *Pri Ḥadash* the determination must be made upon a census of the smallest quasi-autonomous area.

4. The Nature of *Rubba de-Leita Kamman*

A further problem remains: Allegedly, the majority of persons bearing the Jewish gene are known to be Jews. But that is not known actually to be the case. The entire populace of the world has not been

---

Proximity, or *karov*, serves only to define the narrowest area within which *rov* must be determined and even then *rov* cannot be determined on the basis of that area alone if contradicted by a countervailing *rov*. In such cases the parameter of the area within which the *rov* is to be determined must be extended. According to *Shulḥan Arukh ha-Rav*, it is only because those in close proximity are excluded from the immediate *rov* that another *rov* is constructed. Put somewhat differently: The boundaries of the "catchment area" used are as narrow as can be defined, but only if each of the majority of the individuals within the defined area fits the criteria of the person being sought. When that is not the case, the "catchment area" must be broadened and defined as including the entire city. See also *Ḥiddushei R. Akiva Eger, Oraḥ Ḥayyim* 372:5. Cf., however, *Reshash, Ketubot* 14b.

examined to establish that fact. Examinations have been carried out only upon a small sample of the world's population. Any extrapolation establishing an association between a specific gene and Jewishness is based upon transferring the findings based upon the examination of a representative sample to the global population. The effect is to use a *rubba de-ita kamman* as a representative sample to establish a more general *rubba de-leita kamman.* There is no evidence upon which to conclude that a *rubba de-leita kamman* can be constructed on the basis of a representative sample.[85]

Rabbi Litke, *Berurei Yahadut,* chap. 11, asserts that a *rubba de-ita kamman* can be established on the basis of empirical generalization from a known number of instances. That principle is then turned into a *rubba de-leita kamman* when applied in specific situations in which a *rubba de-ita kamman* is actually present. If so, we can extrapolate from the majority of examined cases in which the carrier of the gene is known to be a Jew to the general population and then apply that *rov* to any unknown case as a *rubba de-leita kamman.*[86] The counter argument is that the same can be said regarding the majority of the world who are non-Jews – a *rubba de-leita kamman* – to a specific individual on the basis of a *rubba de-ita kamman.*

The issue of whether there can be a *rubba de-leita kamman* that is based upon mere "accidents" or whether a *rubba de-leita kamman* can be established only as a reflection of a natural order phenomenon is the subject of disagreement between R. Eliyahu Levin and R. Zalman Nechemiah Goldberg, *Yeshurun,* XII (5763), 506–532. Rabbi Levin agrees that a *rubba de-leita kamman* can be established only as an expression of a natural phenomenon.[87] Rabbi Levin further regards the unique nature of DNA as merely an irrational matter of statistical

---

85 Cf., R. Moshe Mordecai Farbstein, *Even ha-Da'at* (Jerusalem, 5765), p. 323.

86 See also *Berurei Yahadut,* chap. 1. Cf., *supra,* p. 212, note 76.

87 Quite independent of this discussion, it is well established that the position that a *rubba de-leita kamman* is a principle of "reason" while a *rubba de-ita kamman* is a statistical probability at best. See *Shev Shem'ateta, shem'ata* 2, chap. 15, and *Kovez̤ Shi'urim,* I, *Bava Batra,* sec. 86 and II, no. 45, secs. 11–12. See also, *Ḥiddushei R. Akiva Eger,* addenda, *Ketubot* 13b. Cf., however, *Noda*

probability. If so, a *rov* to the effect that the majority of bearers of the Jewish gene are Jews would not be regarded as a *rubba de-leita kamman* and since no one has taken a census of all persons carrying the Jewish gene it cannot serve as a *rubba de-ita kamman*. Hence, the Jewish gene cannot give rise to any halakhically recognized *rov*, neither a *rubba de-leita kamman* nor a *rubba de-ita kamman*.

Rabbi Litke, *Berurei Yahadut*, chap. 11, concedes, perhaps erroneously, that DNA can generate only a statistical *rov* and hence cannot establish a valid *rubba de-leita kamman*. Nevertheless, Rabbi Litke argues that the Jewish gene constitutes a *rubba de-ita kamman*. Rabbi Litke's categorization of the Jewish gene as a *rubba de-ita kamman* is somewhat unclear. Distinct classes comprised of persons endowed with the gene and persons lacking the gene have not been numerically identified; hence, the classes are not "before us." Rabbi Litke may assume that a *rubba de-ita kamman* can be established on the basis of a representative sample.[88]

Rabbi Litke correctly argues that DNA patterns are not a matter of an irrational, accidental statistical probability but reflects a law of nature governing transmission of genetic material. Although Rabbi

---

bi-Yehudah, Even ha-Ezer, Mahadura Tinyana, no. 42; *Pri Yizḥak*, II, no. 90; and R. Chaim Shmuelevitz, *Sha'arei Ḥayyim, Kiddushin*, no. 37.

Cf., R. Elchanan Wasserman, *Kovez̦ Shi'urim*, I, *Bava Batra*, secs. 85–86, who demonstrates that *rubba de-leita kamman* that is not based upon a natural order presumption remains subject to the principle of *kavu'a*. Although they constitute only a minority of the population, *Kovez̦ Shi'urim* points out that the Gemara, *Yevamot* 16b, regards the Ten Tribes as *kavu'a* in their places of habitat. Since no one knows whether he is or is not a member of the Ten Tribes, the fact that the majority of the world's population are not members of that class can only be a *rubba de-leita kamman*. Nevertheless, in their place of origin the Ten Tribes are deemed to be *kavu'a*. It is thus evident that Rosh assumes that the rules of *rov* and *kavu'a* apply even to a *rubba de-leita kamman* that is not based upon a phenomenon of nature. Cf., however, *supra*, p. 211, note 75 and accompanying text.

88 If so, a *rov* comparable to "the majority of animals are not *treifot*" should also serve as a *rubba de-ita kamman*. Rabbi Litke would probably recognize that to be the case.

Litke regards the establishment of a Jewish gene as a *rubba de-leita kamman* he seeks to confirm the basic point that a *rov* based upon mere statistical probability rather than upon a governing rational principle is not to be regarded as a *rubba de-leita kamman*. The Mishnah, *Yevamot* 119a, describes a woman whose husband died without issue. The woman was, of course, subject to levirate marital restrictions. The husband was an only son. In the absence of a surviving brother, the widow would have been eligible to remarry without restriction. However, at a much earlier time, the deceased husband's mother had relocated to a distant land. At the time of her departure the mother-in-law was presumed not to have been pregnant. The Gemara dismisses the consideration that she might subsequently have become pregnant and given birth to a second son. That contingency would have given rise to a requirement that the second son perform *ḥaliẓah* in order to release the childless widow from levirate bonds. The Mishnah disregards that possibility and permits the widow to remarry. The Gemara explains that the dismissal of the possibility of a subsequent pregnancy and birth is based upon a *rov*. Most women do become pregnant and bear children. However, a minority miscarry. Of those that give birth fifty percent of the neonates are female. The net result is that there is less than a fifty percent chance that the woman gave birth to a viable male child whose existence would prohibit the widow from remarrying without *ḥaliẓah*.

The ruling of the Mishnah reflects the application of a *rubba de-leita kamman* and accurately reflects the realities of gestation. But one factor is ignored, *viz.*, the fact that over a period of years a woman may give birth to more than one child. Certainly, over a period of time, the majority of fertile woman do bear multiple children. Hence, the majority of women constituting the class of women described by the Gemara would have given birth to more than one child with the result that there is an actual statistical *rov* leading to the conclusion that, over a period of time, the mother-in-law in question did indeed give birth to a second male child. Rabbi Litke reasons that, since the Gemara does not take cognizance of that concern, it must be concluded that the Gemara fails to take that contingency into consideration because there is no law of nature assuring that women bear multiple children. Hence, there exists no *rubba de-leita kamman.* However, experience does inform us that the majority of women do give birth to multiple children. Nevertheless, since not all women, or even not all members of the class of fertile women of child-bearing age, have been examined or interviewed to determine that women who give birth to multiple children constitute the majoritarian class, a conclusion to that effect is predicated only upon knowledge derived from a representative sample of such women. Since the Gemara does not posit a *rov* to that effect, it must be concluded, argues Rabbi Litke, that the premise that the majority of women bear multiple children does not constitute a *rubba de-ita kamman.*

Rabbi Litke's line of reasoning is subject to challenge. Consequently, the issues of whether an "accidental" *rov* not based upon manifestation of laws of nature is recognized as a *rubba de-leita kamman* and whether a *rubba de-leita kamman* can be established on the basis of a representative sample remain open to question. Although it might appear that the likelihood of multiple births is a statistical probability but does not reflect any law of nature and hence is only an "accidental" statistical *rov,* that is not the case. Natural inclinations and biological principles dictate that the majority of women will become pregnant and give birth to a viable neonate; the same inclinations and principles augur for the likelihood that the majority of women will give birth to multiple children. The reason that a *rubba de-leita kamman* to that effect is not recognized must be that *rov* is not a matter of statistics applied to members of a class in the aggregate but a rule governing individual occurrences used to determine the nature of each discrete event without at all simultaneously considering other occurrences of the same phenomenon.

The fact that a *rubba de-leita kamman* is not simply a matter of statistics is evidenced by our reliance in drinking milk upon the principle "The majority of animals are kosher." The majority of all animals are not *treifot.* Therefore, the milk of any cow is presumed to be the milk of a kosher animal. The problem is that although the majority of animals are kosher, two percent may well be *treifot.* It is the case that one part non-kosher milk becomes nullified in 60 parts kosher milk, but one part in 60 is only 1.6 percent. If two percent of the cows are non-kosher, two percent of their milk in the aggregate must be presumed to be non-kosher as well. Two percent is greater than the 1.6 percent that is subject to nullification. Nevertheless, the milk of fifty cows may be combined even though, statistically, there can be little doubt that there will be a quantity of un-nullified non-kosher milk in the aggregate.[89] That is so because each animal considered separately is kosher and hence its milk is kosher; statistics as applied to the aggregate have no bearing on antecedent halakhic determination of issues pertaining to particular matters or events contributing to the aggregate.[90]

In the case of the childless mother-in-law, the halakhic doubt is attendant upon each pregnancy, i.e., will the pregnancy result in the birth of a viable male child or will it not result in the birth of a viable male child. *Rov* establishes that, in any particular pregnancy, such will not be the result. The probability that, for the majority of women, a series of pregnancies in the aggregate will lead to such a result is ignored because, rather than apply *rov* retroactively in judging the aggregate, Halakhah invokes *rov* to dispose of issues surrounding each event *in seriam*. If so, the rule applied with regard to levirate obligations in the instance of the possible pregnancy of a presumably childless mother-in-law is not relevant.

Rosh, *Ḥullin* 7:37, maintains a similar view with regard to nullification of a foodstuff known to be non-kosher. Rosh's situation involves a dry piece of non-kosher meat mingled with two pieces of kosher meat in which the dry piece of non-kosher meat is nullified by the admixture of a majority of kosher pieces. Rosh rules that the non-kosher meat is not only nullified but that it is transmuted into kosher meat (*nehepakh*

---

89 See R. Menasheh Klein, *Ha-Be'er*, vol. 14, no. 3–4 (Nisan 5763), pp. 125–126 and R. Zalman Nechemiah Goldberg, *ibid.*, pp. 140–143.

90 Thus, R. Elchanan Wasserman, *Kovez̧ Shi'urim, Bava Batra*, sec. 86, that, although some animals are *tereifot*, if all animals in the world but one were slaughtered and consumed the single remaining animal would also be permissible.

ha-issur liheyot hetter). As a result, even if additional pieces of meat are added subsequent to discovery of the original mixture so that together with the original non-kosher piece of meat there is no longer a majority of kosher pieces, the meat is nevertheless permissible. Rema, *Yoreh Deah* 109:1,[91] rules that, in time of need (*be-sha'at ha-deḥak*), Rosh's opinion may be relied upon.

Even the early-day authorities who do not recognize Rosh's principle of transmutation nevertheless acknowledge that, according to biblical law, a single person is permitted to consume all three pieces of meat even at a single sitting despite the fact that the person doing so unquestionably consumes non-kosher meat in the process.[92] Opinions regarding discarding one piece of meat, a need to divide the meat among different people or to consume the meat on different occasions[93] are not expressions of biblical law. It is clear that a person need have no compunction in partaking of non-kosher food rendered permissible by the rule of nullification.[94]

Rabbi Litke further takes note of the earlier-discussed positions of *Shulḥan Arukh ha-Rav*,[95] who maintains that the underlying rationale for accepting identificatory marks as proof of ownership for return of a lost object is the improbability that two persons each owned and lost an object having an identical identificatory mark. That *rov*, he argues, is nothing more than statistical negation of coincidence and contradicts the notion that a *rubba de-leita kamman* cannot be the product of an irrational coincidence.

That proof, enticing as it may seem, also does not stand up under scrutiny. The position that a *rubba de-leita kamman* must rest upon some sort of rational principle is a reflection of a philosophical

---

91 See also *Bi'ur ha-Gra, Yoreh De'ah* 109:11.
92 Cf., however, *Tosafot Rid, Bava Batra* 31b.
93 See *Shulḥan Arukh, Yoreh De'ah* 109:1.
94 For a discussion of possible resultant *timtum ha-lev* (moral corruption) see J. David Bleich, *Bioethical Dilemmas*, II, (Southfield, Michigan, 2006), 160, note 32 and *idem*, *Contemporary Halakhic Problems*, VI, (Jersey City, New Jersey, 2012), 306, note 18.
95 See *supra*, pp. 86–87.

principle to the effect that the universe is governed by causality and, consequently, random occurrences either do not exist or, if they do exist, are few and far between. If so, it is obvious that statistics, in and of themselves, are of no logical significance and certainly of no predictive value. Yesterday's "accidental" statistics create no probability regarding tomorrow's events. It is precisely that negation of coincidence that demands the acceptance of *simanim*. The same rejection of statistics as mere coincidences because of a presumption that random occurrences, regardless of number, are of no predictive value dictates that the presence of identical *simanim*, at least in the majority of cases, is not a mere coincidence. If random coincidental occurrences are rare, it follows that *simanim* are precisely what they are purported to be. In effect, *simanim* reflect a rational meta-*rov* in the form of a *rubba de-leita kamman*, to the effect that in the majority of cases there are no coincidences. That itself is a philosophical formulation of a rational law of nature and rises to the level of a *rubba de-leita kamman*. In effect, *simanim* are predicated upon a rational negative *rubba de-leita kamman*, *viz.*, the vast majority of empirical phenomena are not coincidental. But coincidences do occur. Many people lose objects and, unfortunately, many people die. Their losses and deaths are unrelated. Unless there is reason to conclude otherwise, such discrete phenomena are not unusual and are unrelated in the sense that there is no causal nexus between such phenomena. *Simanim* constitute statistical probability in support of a veridical causal connection between two phenomena. That such a relationship exists is a rational *rubba de-leita kamman*. *Simanim* are dispositive because of the extreme unlikelihood that two people both owned and lost objects bearing the same identificatory mark. That is not a matter of mere statistics but reflects a rational principle similar to the rational basis that must underlie every *rubba de-leita kamman*. *Simanim* constitute a rational *rubba de-leita kamman* that serves to exclude coincidence.

5. Contradictory *Rovs*

Assuming both that the genetic evidence for the existence of a unique allele that might constitute a Jewish gene has been conclusively established and that available data would allow presence of the gene to qualify as an application of the principle of *rov* in instances of otherwise unknown Jewish identity, it is not clear that such evidence would be dispositive. It would appear that in many cases other evidentiary *rovs* must also be considered. Russians seeking to identify themselves as Jews may very well possess identity papers that declare another national identity. The majority of persons in possession of identity documents of that nature that are not stamped "*Ivreska*" are certainly not Jews. Also, many immigrants admitted pursuant to the Law of Return have spouses who are acknowledged to be non-Jews. Decades ago, R. Isaac Herzog, *Teshuvot Heikhal Yiẓḥak, Even ha-Ezer,* I, no. 17, suggested that *Tosafot's* presumption that the majority of individuals who profess to be Jewish are indeed Jews does not apply in instances in which the person in question is married to a non-Jew. Rabbi Herzog noted that the majority of Jews do not intermarry. The result is two contradictory *rovs*.[96] Rabbi Herzog's observation, while certainly correct when it was voiced, may unfortunately no longer be true. Whether the majority of Jewish immigrants to Israel of Russian extraction are also married to Jewish spouses is an empirical matter that must be ascertained.

Recognizing that the Jewish gene might determine identity as a Jew only on the basis of *rov*, Rabbi Ze'ev Litke, *Berurei Yahadut,* chap. 14, sec. 1, points out that the Jewish gene is always accompanied by a contradictory *rov* as well, *viz.,* the majority of the populace in virtually every locale in the Diaspora are non-Jews. If so, the status of the person endowed with the Jewish gene cannot be established on the basis of the fact that the majority of individuals harboring that gene are Jews because that *rov* is contradicted by an opposing *rov*. Rabbi Litke counters that those two *rovs* are fundamentally different in nature. That the majority of inhabitants are non-Jews is a *rubba de-ita kamman,* i.e., a conclusion based upon empirical observation. A *rov*

---

96 That observation is similar to the contention of R. Chaim of Volozhin, *Ḥut ha-Meshulash,* no. 5, that *Tosafot's rov* is not applicable if the individual claiming to be a Jew cannot speak Yiddish.

of that nature is essentially an "accident," i.e., there is no compelling reason that it should or should not be so. On the other hand, the *rov* established on the basis of genetic comparison is based upon scientific considerations born of how the universe is regulated. That the majority of animals are not *treifot* is a biological observation of the nature of animal species rather than simply the product of a head-count. *Rov be'ilot aḥar ha-ba'al* is based, not simply upon frequency of access, but also reflects the nature of human behavior. The presence of a Jewish gene, since it is predicated upon scientific premises, leads to determination of the presence of a *rubba de-leita kamman*. The majoritarian nature of that type of *rov* is inherent in the nature of the universe. A *rubba de-leita kamman* is of greater evidentiary weight than a *rubba de-ita kamman* because it is compelled by nature rather than by mere happenstance. Since *rubba de-leita kamman* is rationally supported, such a *rov* should prevail over a *rov* limited to a series of unconnected occurrences. It then follows that the *rov* arising from the presence of a Jewish gene should prevail over a *rov* based only upon demographic occurrences.

Rabbi Barenbaum, *Berurei Yahadut*, chap. 8, sec. 1, finds an interesting ramification in the balancing of the two *rovs* in a situation in which there are two maternal brothers, one whose identity as a Jew has long been established and accepted in his native community while the non-Jewish status of the second brother has long been presumed and accepted in the latter's community. It is factually certain that one brother cannot be a Jew and the other a non-Jew. Resolution of the status of both brothers will depend upon the superior strength of the evidence bolstering one of the conflicting claims. Rabbi Barenbaum assumes that the presumption of Jewishness of the "Jewish" brother is a *rubba de-leita kamman* and prevails over a presumption of non-Jewishness of the "non-Jewish" brother which is a *rubba de-ita kamman* based upon the fact that the majority of the population are non-Jews.

This writer does not perceive there to be two contradictory *rovs*. *Rov* applies only in situations of otherwise unresolved doubt. Persons known to be Jews on the basis of behavior and comportment retain their status as Jews even if the majority of the populace are non-Jews. There is no contradiction between acceptance of such individuals as Jews and recognition that a *rov* of the population are non-Jews; the persons accepted as Jews are recognized as being members of the known minoritarian class. Otherwise how could a person establish credentials as a Jew when, as is generally the case, the majority of the population in any locale is non-Jewish? There is no contradiction between acceptance of such individuals as Jews and recognition that *rov* of the population are non-Jews; the persons accepted as Jews are recognized as being members of the minoritarian class. *Rov* establishes status as a non-Jew only when less direct evidence is lacking. If carriers of the Jewish gene are presumed to be Jews, they are excluded from the class of unassigned individuals whose status is determined on the basis of *rov*. Since the status of the person carrying the Jewish gene has been determined by the presence of the gene, his status is no longer a matter of doubt to which *rov* need be applied. If Jewishness can be determined solely by the presence of a Jewish gene there is no contradictory *rov* because there is no longer a doubt requiring resolution on the basis of *rov*. Moreover, rather than contradictory *rovs*, there are two distinct *rovs* applied to different cohorts, *viz.*, 1) a cohort of people endowed with the gene; and 2) a cohort lacking the gene. The first cohort, i.e., the majority of those manifesting the Jewish gene, are determined to be Jews on the basis of the fact that the majority of individuals endowed with the gene are known to be Jews. The second cohort, i.e., the majority of inhabitants who are not endowed with the gene, are known to be non-Jews. The latter forms an entirely distinct class of whom the majority are non-Jews.[97]

The situation of two maternal brothers, one presumed to be a Jew

---

97 Rabbi Barenbaum's objection might equally be raised against *Tosafot*'s assertion that the majority of persons who claim to be Jews are indeed Jews. Rabbi Barenbaum might object that a contradictory *rov* exists, *viz.*, the majority of the populace are non-Jews. The reply is: 1) The *rov* establishing that the majority of the populace are non-Jews admits of a minority. Asserting a claim of Jewish lineage establishes a claimant as a member of the minority. 2) There are really two cohorts: a) people who claim to be Jews; and b) people who do not claim

and the second presumed to be a gentile, involves application of an entirely different principle. Neither of the brothers is an unknown person to whom *rov* must be applied for determination. Each of the brothers brings with him an established status, *viz.*, a *ḥazakah* – one as a Jew, the other as a non-Jew. The problem is that application of the principle of *ḥazakah* in the case of the two brothers leads to conclusions that are clearly contradictory. It would be logical to conclude that when there are conflicting *ḥazakot* they cancel one another with the result that, for all intents and purposes, there is no *ḥazakah*.

Rabbi Litke, *Berurei Yahadut*, chap. 13, secs. 5–10, resolves the dilemma by accepting that there is only one *ḥazakah*, not two. Rabbi Litke, of course, accepts the notion that there is a halakhically recognized *ḥazakah* of Jewishness. However, he denies the existence of a *ḥazakah* of non-Jewishness; the individual's comportment may result in the absence of a *ḥazakah* of Jewishness but, maintains Rabbi Litke, that does not establish a *ḥazakah* of non-Jewishness in an affirmative manner. Hence, according to Rabbi Litke the *ḥazakah* of Jewish identity manifested by one brother is not contradicted by the absence of the *ḥazakah* with regard to the second brother. The result, according to Rabbi Litke, is that the *ḥazakah* of the "Jewish" brother prevails with regard to the "non-Jewish" brother as well. Rabbi Barenbaum, *Berurei Yahadut*, chap. 8,[98] does not concur in defining that there is no *ḥazakah* of "non-Jewishness."

It seems to this writer that resolution of the quandary posed by the case of the two brothers depends upon whether the non-Jewish brother is affirmatively known to be a non-Jew or whether he only fails to be known as a Jew. A person who attends a non-Jewish house of worship or otherwise observes the tenets of another faith holds himself out as a non-Jew and is so regarded by members of the community in which he resides; a person whose religious identity is unknown has no established *ḥazakah* whatsoever. In the latter case,

---

to be Jews. The *rov* of the first cohort are Jews; the *rov* of the second cohort are not Jews.

98 See also *Berurei Yahadut*, chap. 2.

religious identity is a *tabula rasa* and established Jewish identity of one brother dictates the ethnic identity of the second brother as well. When each brother has a firmly established *ḥazakah* as belonging to different faith-communities it would seem that the two *ḥazakot* do indeed cancel one another.[99] The case of the two brothers does not present a situation of contradictory *rovs* but it may reflect a case of contradictory *ḥazakot*.

---

99 The Gemara, *Niddah* 2a, describes a situation involving two people who travel along separate paths, one of which is blocked by a corpse, but neither remembers which path he traversed. Each of the parties is known to have previously been in a state of ritual purity. The *ḥezkat taharah* of each of the individuals dictates that both must continue to be regarded as undefiled even though, empirically, one must have become defiled. There is indeed a logical inconsistency when the two conclusions are taken together but the doubts confronting each of the two travelers are not intrinsically connected – nothing compelled either of them to travel the path in question and the fact that both did so is a sheer coincidence.

The case of the two brothers is comparable to the hypothetical presented by *Pri Ḥadash, Yoreh De'ah, Kuntres Aḥaron* 110, involving a quantity of unidentifiable sides of meat, one of which has been found to be non-kosher. Some of the non-kosher meat together with the meat of other kosher animals has already been sold; the balance remains in the slaughterhouse. The principle of *kol de-parish* applies to each piece of meat that has been purchased whereas the meat remaining in the slaughterhouse is *kavu'a*. However, the meat that has been sold cannot be kosher if the balance remaining in the slaughterhouse is non-kosher. The logical entailment between the two questions is intrinsic rather than coincidental. Some authorities rule that the principle of *kavu'a* is a divine edict that does not dovetail with, and even contradicts, the principle of *rov*. Hence, half the side of meat must be regarded as kosher whereas the other half must be regarded as non-kosher. The majority of decisors recognize the logical entailment of the two questions and declare all the meat to be doubtfully non-kosher. See *Shev Shem'ateta, shem'ata* 4, chap. 3 and *Peleti* 110:30. It then follows that the intrinsic logical entailment that exists between the status of the two brothers serves to render *ḥazakah* inapplicable in the case of the brother claiming Jewish identity. *Pri Ḥadash* would presumably concede that, although mutually contradictory conclusions following upon application of *rov* and *kavu'a* can be accommodated, such conclusions cannot coexist in application of other principles in a manner leading to intrinsically connected but contradictory conclusions. Cf., *Berurei Yahadut*, chap. 8.

Rabbi Litke, *Berurei Yahadut,* chap. 14, sec. 3, asserts that, in assessing the relevance of *rov* in establishing the Jewish gene as validation of identity as a Jew, the fact that the majority of the human population are non-Jews is to be ignored. His basic premise is that major and minor classes are established only upon the relevant criteria that serve to define the classes. The full text of the Mishnah, *Makhshirin* 2:7–9, reads:

> If an abandoned child was found there, if the majority were non-Jews, it must be deemed a non-Jew; if the majority were Jews, it must be deemed a Jew; if they were half and half it must be deemed a Jew. R. Judah says: we must consider who form the majority of those who abandon their children.
>
> If one found lost property there, if the majority were non-Jews, he need not announce it; if the majority were Jews, he must announce it; if they were half and half, he must announce it. If one found bread there, we must consider who form the majority of the bakers. If it was bread of pure flour, we must consider who form the majority of those who consume bread of pure flour. R. Judah says: if it was coarse bread, we must consider who form the majority of those who eat coarse bread.
>
> If one found meat there, we must consider who form the majority of the butchers. If it was cooked meat, we must consider who form the majority of those who eat cooked meat.

Indeed, in each case the factors used in establishing the parameters of the major and minor classes depend upon the relevance of those factors to the issue to be determined; other criteria are ignored as irrelevant. Thus, an unknown person newly arrived from a locale in which the population is predominantly non-Jewish would be determined to be Jewish on the basis of evidence that his grandmother was Jewish. If the person's forebears are known to have been Jews, the fact that the majority of populace of that person's city of origin are non-Jews is irrelevant. If it is established that the majority of individuals endowed with the Jewish gene are known to be Jews, the fact that an unknown person bearing the gene resides in an area in which the majority are non-Jews is irrelevant. The non-Jewish majority is irrelevant once it is established that the unknown person is a member of the class known to be endowed with the gene. The presence of the gene establishes the individual as a member of the family possessing a particular genotype. It is only in that group that major and minor classes can be defined. Others are not members of the "catchment group" within which major and minor classes can be defined. The situation is comparable to finding a piece of cooked meat as described in the Mishnah. The meat clearly came from a member of a class of people who eat cooked meat; it is only within the members of that group that majoritarian and minoritarian classes can be meaningful. It is taken as certain that the meat was not lost by a person who does not consume cooked meat; hence such persons are excluded from the census of persons from among whom a *rov* is to be established.

Finally, it is not at all clear that the majority of persons carrying the Jewish gene are Jews. Although only an extremely small percentage of non-Jews carry the Jewish gene, the gross number of non-Jewish carriers may be higher than the total number of Jews carrying the gene. Thus, contrary to Rabbi Litke's assertion, the existence of a *rov* establishing that the majority of carriers of the unique Jewish gene are Jews cannot be confirmed until there is a full tally of the total number of non-Jews carrying the gene. If, as is entirely likely, the majority of the carriers of the "Jewish" gene are non-Jews, the putative Jewish gene is of no evidentiary value.[100]

---

100 The highest estimate of the world-wide Jewish population, including non-Ashkenazi Jews, is fifteen million. If forty percent of that entire population possess the Jewish gene, there are a maximum of roughly six million Jews who are bearers of the gene. (Actually, the highest recorded percentage of carriers of the gene in the various studies is forty-two percent Ashkenazi Jews.) A report released on July 10, 2020 by the Population Reference Bureau, www.prb.org, gives the total world population as 7.8 billion. Subtracting the Jewish population from that figure, the gentile population of the world is approximately 7,785,000,000. If 0.1 percent of the gentile population are bearers of the gene, there are 7,785,000 gentiles who carry the gene. If so, the number of non-Jewish carriers is much larger than six million, the maximum number of Jews who might carry the gene. Thus, a random person presenting with the

V. THE ROLE OF *ḤAZAKAH*

The Jewish gene can serve to establish Jewish identity only if it can be shown that the majority of those endowed with the gene are otherwise known to be Jews. It is possible for those individuals to have become known as Jews on the basis of *ḥazakah,* i.e., their identity as Jews has been independently established and accepted on the basis of conduct and comportment or because they had been known as descendants of ancestors earlier accepted as Jews. Only if it is demonstrated that the majority of those carrying the gene are known to be Jews would it be possible for an unknown person or a person whose status is a matter of doubt to establish Jewish identity solely on the basis of the *rov* upon which the evidentiary nature of the Jewish gene is predicated. That *rov* is effective only because it establishes a relationship with a forebear whose identity as a Jew was established on the basis of *ḥazakah.*

However, Rabbi Litke, *Berurei Yahadut,* chap. 13, points out there are non-Jews who are also endowed with the Jewish gene but who have established identities and been recognized by the public as non-Jews, i.e., their status as non-Jews has been accepted on the basis of *ḥazakah.* If that is so, he argues, presence of the Jewish gene cannot prove membership in either of the established classes because *rov* simply establishes membership of a class of individuals whose status is predicated upon *ḥazakah.* The Jewish gene is basically only a "marker" for a *ḥazakah* but since that gene is also carried by non-Jews it can be a "marker" for either of two antagonistic *ḥazakot.*

Rabbi Litke develops the thesis that the concept of *ḥazakah* can establish imputed identity as a Jew if it is known that an ancestress was a Jewess but that there is no corresponding notion of inherited status as a non-Jew based upon a general assumption that the person's forebears were known to be non-Jews. Rabbi Litke's basic point is that Jews can be known as Jews in an affirmative manner whereas

---

"Jewish" gene is more likely than not to be a gentile. However, note must be taken of the considerations entering into establishing the parameters of a *rov.* See *supra,* pp. 216–219.

non-Jews cannot be affirmatively known as gentiles. That is so because of apostasy and intermarriage. Non-Jews do not comport themselves as Jews and hence will not be mistakenly identified as Jews. On the other hand, assimilation of Jews into non-Jewish society is a well-established socio-religious phenomenon. Assimilated individuals become accepted as non-Jews by the general society without attention being focused upon genealogical lineage or comportment. Hence, he concludes that there is no *ḥazakah* of non-Jewishness in the sense of non-Jewish ancestry.

It seems to this writer that Rabbi Litke's categorization is only partially correct. *Ḥazakah* is a halakhic presumption, not a certainty. A couple living together as man and wife project a general aura of a marital relationship. It is certainly the case that some unmarried partners have falsely held themselves out as husband and wife. It is also the case that there are individuals living in an adulterous relationship who have falsely sought to gain recognition as a lawfully married couple. Jewish apostates gain recognition as members of their newly adopted religion and, if not always at least ofttimes, the public assumption is that they are members of the newly adopted religious faith by virtue of having been born into that faith community rather than as the result of apostasy. The result is indeed a *ḥazakah* of non-Jewish extraction based upon comportment and behavior.

But that is only part of the scenario. There are, at least today, vast numbers of people who profess no religion and even more who are not publicly known as professing any religion. In many circumstances, there are no means to distinguish between a Jewish atheist and a non-Jewish atheist. For such persons there cannot be a *ḥazakah* of non-Jewishness.[101]

In other situations – and certainly in earlier times – a non-Jew could be readily identified as such because he frequented non-Jewish

---

101 Although Rabbi Litke apparently disagrees, Rabbi Barenbaum, *Berurei Yahadut*, chap. 8, assumes that Jews have strong reason to preserve and project an aura of Jewish identity whereas non-Jews have no strong inclination to do so. See also *ibid.*, chap. 2.

houses of worship. Such behavior or a display of similar distinctively non-Jewish practices testify to identity as a non-Jew by means of an affirmative *ḥazakah*. The societal presumption is certainly that adherents of a religious denomination are practitioners of their ancestral religion. The fact that, on occasion, a Jewish apostate may also engage in such conduct does not mar the presumption of inherited non-Jewishness in the eyes of society any more than the occasional ongoing adulterous relationship negates a matrimonial *ḥazakah* or that a foundling cared for by an adoptive mother mitigates the *ḥazakah* of biological maternity established by conduct leading to a presumption of a maternal-child relationship.[102]

However, assuming the Jewish gene to be valid evidence of Jewish identity because of its association with Jews whose status is established

---

102 In support of his argument, Rabbi Litke cites a comment of *Tosafot, Ketubot* 29a, s.v. *ve-al ha-Kutit*. The Mishnah declares that the biblical fine imposed for rape of a virgin is imposed for the rape of a female *Kuti*. One opinion recorded in *Kiddushin* 77a is that the Samaritans are indeed valid converts to Judaism but marriage between a Jew and a Samaritan was nevertheless forbidden because Samaritans allowed a small number of slaves to become assimilated in their communities. *Tosafot* questions, since *rov* is not sufficient to establish proof of a plaintiff's claim in a monetary dispute, why should a man who rapes a *Kuti* virgin be forced to pay the statutory penalty: "Let us tell her, 'Bring proof that you are not a female slave.'" Rabbi Litke's argument is that the *Kutit* maiden in question and her parents are *muḥzak*, i.e. have been accepted as *Kuti*s of legitimate birth. That *ḥazakah* should be sufficient grounds upon which to base a monetary claim and hence *Tosafot*'s query is groundless. Rabbi Litke resolves that quandary by advancing a thesis to the effect that there cannot be a *ḥazakah* when there is positive knowledge of the presence in the group of a person whose existence contradicts the *ḥazakah*, e.g., in the case of the *Kutim*, the presence of a female slave. Similarly, argues Rabbi Litke, the known existence of an assimilated Jew abrogates any *ḥazakah* that would otherwise confirm identity as a Jew. If correct, the logical conclusion of the known existence of an unidentified adoptee would negate the possibility of establishing a maternal-child relationship on the basis of comportment.

However, *Tosafot*'s objection is well taken. There was a positive *ḥazakah* establishing the existence of an identifiable female slave among the *Kutim*. *Tosafot*'s reply is that each individual *Kuti* enjoys a *ḥezkat kashrut* tracing back to a time prior to assimilation.

on the basis of *ḥazakah*, there can be no corresponding *ḥazakah* of non-Jewishness established by non-Jews who carry the gene unless those individuals also engage in distinctive non-Jewish practices. But, if that is the case, the result is that the so-called Jewish gene is associated both with groups that are *muḥzak* as Jews and with other groups *muḥzak* as non-Jews. Genetic investigators have heretofore made no attempt to determine whether or not the relatively rare instances of the Jewish gene found among non-Jews occurred among gentiles who were "asymptomatic" as far as non-Jewishness is concerned or whether some of the examples were found among individuals who, on the basis of conduct and comportment, were assumed by the public to be of gentile lineage. It may be presumed that investigation would confirm the existence of the "Jewish" gene among the latter group as well.

Rabbi Litke argues that, in the absence of a contradictory *ḥezkat akum*, the presence of the Jewish gene becomes a *siman* of Jewishness. If so, the presence of the gene in a person whose lineage is unknown would be tantamount to a *siman* that the person is a Jew. Since there is no contradictory *ḥezkat akum*, any person having the gene would be deemed to be a Jew even in the absence of any known connection with the Jewish community. Nevertheless, it may be countered that the Jewish gene cannot be a *siman* of Jewishness because it is entirely possible that the ancestress who first manifested the gene was a proselyte (or an ancestress of the proselyte whose descendants include both proselytes and gentiles) who gave birth to children both before and after conversion to Judaism. If so, an unidentified person who carries the gene must be presumed to be a non-Jew because, since the gene is of no evidentiary value, the petitioner must be presumed to be a member of a majoritarian class, i.e., a non-Jewish descendant of the Jewish grandmother but a descendant of the daughter of the "grandmother" born prior to the grandmother's conversion.

Rabbi Barenbaum, *Berurei Yahadut*, chap. 7, is not troubled by the fact that the Jewish gene may be shared by both Jews and non-Jews having a common ancestor provided that the majority of those possessing the gene are independently known to be Jews. He offers as a parallel the hypothetical situation in which a non-Jewish Spanish woman converted to Judaism prior to the expulsion of Spanish Jewry in 1492. The hypothetical woman had a physical anomaly caused by a dominant gene. The anomaly was, and continues to be, present in all of her descendants. She had sisters, aunts and cousins who carried the same gene. Every one of those women and each of their descendants carries the same dominant gene and hence manifests the same physical anomaly. The situation in Spain *circa* 1492 was such that the anomaly was certainly not a criterion of Jewishness. If anything, the majority of those suffering from that anomaly were not Jews. Many Jews fled the inquisition and settled in Turkey. Non-Jews had no reason to flee the Iberian peninsula. The anomaly in question did not exist among indigenous Turks. At that time, in Turkey, the only people who manifested that anomaly were Jewish refugees who were independently known to be Jews. In the decades following the expulsion some few of the converted woman's non-Jewish cousins made their way to Turkey. Some generations later, suggests Rabbi Barenbaum, a Turkish national of unknown lineage but possessing that anomaly might seek to establish a claim to identity as a Jew on the contention that, since the majority of persons then residing in Turkey possess that anomaly, that *rov* establishes him as a member of the majoritarian class. The question arises in Turkey and must be resolved in accordance with the relative number of members of the two classes residing in Turkey at that time.

The bottleneck that arose in the northward migration of Jews in the 14th century was quite similar in nature. The majority of those carrying the Jewish gene into the Rhine Basin were otherwise known to be Jews and hence effectively established a population in which the majority of those who carried the "Jewish" gene in that locale were Jews. Consequently, an unknown person bearing that gene and claiming to be a Jew must be recognized as a Jew on the basis of *rov*.

The problem with that analysis is that the hypothetical Turkish petitioner for recognition as a Jew was not an itinerant stranger to whom *kol de-parish* is applicable. Rather, the petitioner and his forebears had resided in Turkey for generations. Was it a Jewish or a non-Jewish female ancestress who fled Spain and relocated in Turkey?

The doubt arose at the time of removal from her native habitat, i.e., a place of "permanence," and, consequently, *rov* should be of no avail. The same is true of the significant number of Russian immigrants to Israel whose status was doubtful even in their place of birth.

Indeed, that is the position of *Teshuvot Maharit, Even ha-Ezer,* no. 18. Maharit refused to recognize North-African descendants of Marranos as Jews on the basis of application of any form of *rov* because the question was really the ethnic identity of the petitioner's "grandmother" as determined before she left Spain. At that time the grandmother was *kavu'a* and therefore Maharit ruled the presence of a *rov* among later generations of Marranos to be of no avail.

There are indeed a host of authorities who apparently disagree with Maharit.[103] Their position is that the status of ancestors is not the question before a latter-day *bet din.* The doubt to be adjudicated arises only with regard to descendants of the original Marranos. Those descendants became separated from their "mothers" who remained in their ancestral homeland. Accordingly, they regard the principle of *kol de-parish* to be applicable.

However, aside from the issue of the time at which the question arises, a problem remains. *Kol de-parish* would arguably apply if the persons in question had suddenly arrived as "foundlings" from an unknown place of origin. *Rov* is applicable when material facts previously known at the place of origin become beclouded at the time of "separation." In those cases the question arises only with regard to doubts that did not exist prior to the time of separation. However, the persons whose plight was addressed by Maharit did not arrive *sua sponte* and petition for the right to marry, or the like, as Jews. Rather, many, if not most, had been living in their communities for decades or longer with a known place of birth. Doubt with regard to ancestral relatives may no longer have been of practical significance and hence the *kavu'a* nature of previous generations may have been

103 See *Teshuvot Maharibal,* 1, *klal* 2, no. 16; *Teshuvot Mahari Beirav,* no. 39; *Teshuvot Maharashdam,* no. 112; *Teshuvot Yakhin u-Bo'az,* no. 31 and no. 3; as well as *Bet Yosef, Even ha-Ezer* 3:3.

immaterial. But the doubt with regard to the status of a petitioner several generations later is a question with regard to the circumstances of that person's birth, or of his grandmother's birth, just as the question with regard to meat stored in a refrigerator whose provenance has been forgotten is a question with regard to relevant contextual facts as they existed at the time of purchase, i.e., whether the meat was obtained from a kosher establishment or a non-kosher establishment. In such situations the question is with regard to facts known at the place of purchase or place of birth, i.e., identifiable places at which the facts were known, as opposed to a quantity of meat or a foundling discovered in the street, cases in which the place of origin or of birth is entirely unknown. A place of origin in which the relevant facts were unknown is tantamount to no origin.

Maharit's refusal to acknowledge the applicability of the principle of *rov* may be regarded as limited to the circumstances of his time. In times gone by, families established residence in a particular locale and remained there for generations. All salient genealogical information was known at the time that domicile was established. With the passage of time memories became hazy and much was forgotten but the status of *kavu'a* did not change. In modern times the situation is often quite different. People know that sometime in the past their progenitors relocated but do not know from where. Since they are ignorant of the family's place of origin they are in the position of *kol de-parish.*[104] Under such conditions Maharit would presumably agree that the "Jewish" gene serves to establish identity as a Jew on the basis of *kol de-parish.*

Accepting those basic principles it would follow that if the *rov* of a particular restricted area, e.g., a ghetto or street, is unknown or

---

104 Indeed, it may be suggested that Maharit and his opponents were really describing what each believed to be a different set of circumstances and hence that there is no substantive halakhic dispute between them. Maharit was describing families that had a continuous presence in a particular locale dating from the time of the Spanish expulsion while those who ruled differently assumed that such was not known to be the case and that any claim to Jewish identity was supported only by oral tradition of descent from Marranos.

unattainable, it is necessary to examine the smallest expanded identifiable area in which a determination of a majority is feasible, i.e., the population of a city or, assuming that a determination of a majority in the city is also unfeasible, the population of the entire country. With regard to genetics, in Western society, the smallest discrete Jewish population for which determination of majoritarian and minoritarian classes can be made on the basis of a restrictive indigenous foundation proves to be Jews of Ashkenazic ancestry. It is then necessary to compare the genomes of that segment of the population with the genomes of the natives of the host countries of origin. The same principle would pertain to determination of majoritarian and minoritarian classes of Jewish communities of mid-East or north-African extraction.

VI. ASCENDING *ḤAZAKAH*

As noted earlier, DNA can, at best, serve only to establish common origin of separate DNA alleles. After a common origin of DNA fragments or a relationship between individuals has been established on the basis of DNA comparison, other issues may be resolved by appeal to other halakhic prescriptions, e.g., *rov* or *ḥazakah*. Thus, if a maternal-filial relationship is established by DNA analysis, paternity can be ascribed to the woman's husband on the basis of the principle *rov be'ilot aḥar ha-ba'al*. Ordinarily, DNA evidence is employed to demonstrate that a person is a Jew because it is used to establish a relationship with a person who is otherwise known to be a Jew on the basis of *ḥazakah* or the like.

Identification of a Jewish gene comes about because it is established that the majority of persons endowed with that particular allele are known to be Jews. However, persons not known to be Jews who possess the same gene cannot *ipso facto* be presumed to be Jews. It is first necessary to show that the heretofore unacknowledged Jew is descended from the same mother as the member of the class of known Jews who are endowed with that particular gene. Ordinarily, once a *ḥazakah* is established, that *ḥazakah* is automatically passed on to subsequent generations by matrilineal succession. The Jewish gene does not establish the person's status but the status of an ancestress: if a person carries the gene, his grandmother must have carried that gene as well. If the majority of grandmothers who carried the gene were Jewesses, it follows that the identical status was transmitted to each grandmother's descendants. That is to say that known identity as a Jew is not, *mutatis mutandis*, transferred by the Jewish gene to that person's progeny but that the reverse, i.e., identification as a Jew by means of possession of the Jewish gene is ascendingly ascribed to progenitors and, only subsequent to doing so, transferred to all persons in the line of descent.[105] The halakhic principle is that status acquired by means of *ḥazakah* is transmitted to progeny. There is no obvious halakhic rule providing for application of a reverse *ḥazakah* of that nature, i.e., a principle that would impute established status to progenitors.

Rabbi Barenbaum, *Berurei Yahadut*, chap. 2, astutely cites a talmudic discussion that would establish transmission of a *ḥazakah* even in the absence of direct halakhic entailment. The Gemara, *Ketubot* 26a and *Bava Batra* 32a, speaks of two witnesses who testify that a person heretofore presumed to be a *kohen* is actually the son of a divorcée while two other witnesses contradict their testimony. The

105 Thus, R. Yoḥanan, *Ketubot* 13b, declares that "a mother's *ḥazakah* is effective for a daughter." E.g., a woman consorts with an unidentified man. The fact that the woman was previously presumed to be permitted to a *kohen* because of a *ḥezkat kashrut* leads to the conclusion that her paramour was not a member of a class that would disqualify her from marrying a *kohen*. Her as yet unborn child has no *ḥazakah*. However, the mother's *ḥazakah* logically entails that the daughter has also not been disqualified. In effect, the mother's *ḥazakah* is transmitted to the daughter. If so, there is recognized logical entailment with regard to consequences of a *ḥazakah*. However, in the case of the Jewish gene there is no logical entailment. The fact that the "granddaughter" possesses the Jewish gene does not necessarily entail that everyone of a long chain of grandmothers was also a naturally-born Jewess. Any one of those ancestresses might have converted to Judaism, but only after already having giving birth to a non-Jewish daughter or daughters. If it cannot be established that the "grandmother" was a naturally born Jewess, any of her descendants endowed with her gene may well be one of her non-Jewish progeny.

Gemara declares that a son of that person is presumed to be a *kohen* because of the earlier established *ḥazakah* of the father as a *kohen*. In that case there is no logical entailment: the father was certainly a recognized *kohen* at one time. The son, if he were the child of a *kohen* who consorted with a divorcée would never have been a qualified *kohen*[106] but, nevertheless, the father's *ḥazakah* is also assigned to the son.[107] Neither the son nor his status is the subject of the testimony of the impeaching witness. However, R. Baruch Ber Lebowitz, *Birkhat Shmu'el, Ketubot*, no. 38, sec. 6, and *Ḥazon Ish, Even ha-Ezer* 2:25, explain that it is the *ḥezkat kashrut* of the father, rather than the heretofore presumption of priesthood, that is the applicable *ḥazakah*. Those authorities maintain that a progenitor's *ḥazakah* is not at all transferred to a child because of logical entailment but that the child enjoys an entirely different *ḥazakah*. They assert that the *ḥezkat kashrut* and the *ḥazakah* as a *kohen* are independent of one another. The father's *ḥazakah* as a *kohen*, when challenged, is of no avail to the son. A *ḥezkat kashrut*, however, is a different matter. The son held and continues to hold his own *ḥezkat kashrut*. That *ḥezkat kashrut* logically entails that the son is a legitimate *kohen* as well.[108] Absent such entailment, there would be no evidence that the *ḥazakah* of one person would be of any relevance to that person's child and certainly not to a progenitor. Thus, it follows that there is no "ascending *ḥazakah*" on the basis of logical entailment. The ancestor had no *ḥezkat kashrut*. Since the Jewish gene cannot establish a *ḥazakah* for earlier generations there is no *ḥazakah* to transmit to later generations.

---

106 The issue of a *kohen* and a divorcée is known as a "*ḥallal*," or a "profaned priest" and is disqualified from serving as a *kohen*.

107 Rashi, *Kiddushin* 66a, s.v. *semokh a-hani*, regards the case under discussion to be limited to a situation in which the eyewitnesses contradict one another with regard to whether a particular woman, i.e., the father's wife and mother of the child was a divorcée. If so, a similar logical entailment does exist.

108 See Ritva, *Ketubot* 26a, *Bava Batra* 32a, and *Kiddushin* 66a.

VII. *SEFEK SEFEIKA*

Rabbi Litke, *Berurei Yahadut*, chap. 13, secs. 26–39, examines another argument for ruling that a person bearing a Jewish gene is to be accorded recognition as a Jew, *viz.*, a *sefek sefeika*, or double doubt: 1) The person in question may be a Jew by birth because each of his or her female forebearers was a Jewess; and 2) even if the "great-grandmother" from whom he or she inherited the gene was not a Jewess by birth, she may have converted to Judaism and given birth to the petitioner's "grandmother" after her conversion to Judaism.

Whether a *sefek sefeika* of that nature is of halakhic import is a matter of significant controversy. A typical *sefek sefeika* arises when two separate and independent doubts are present, either one of which would serve to obviate a given prohibition. For example, a woman who willfully commits adultery is prohibited from continuing to live in a marital relationship with her husband. But consortium is forbidden only if adultery has been established. Having established that the sexual act took place it also necessary to establish that the adultery was consensual. It is further necessary to establish that the wife was not a minor at the time of the act. Accordingly, even if there is evidence of the sexual act, two doubts remain: 1) whether the act was consensual and 2) even if the act was consensual, whether the wife a minor at the time of the adultery. Those are two separate doubts either one of which would obviate the sanction attendant upon an act of adultery.

In a case of an unknown person seeking recognition as a Jew the sole doubt is whether he is of Jewish ancestry. Since it is acknowledged that the petitioner did not himself convert to Judaism, there is only one way that he might be a Jew, *viz.*, that he was born to a mother known to be a Jewess. The mother may be a Jewess for one of two reasons: 1) unbroken matrilineal descent from a known Jewish ancestress; or 2) descent from a female proselyte. But those are "doubts" *mi-shem eḥad*, i.e., two different instrumental ways of establishing a single result, *viz.*, Jewish ancestry. The only pertinent fact is Jewish ancestry. Whether the ancestor's status as a Jew was by virtue of birth or by conversion is of no significance. Many authorities accept the validity of a *sefek sefeika*[109] of that nature and many do not.[110] Assuming that there is a valid *sefek sefeika* there is further controversy with regard to whether *sefek sefeika* prevails against a *rov* or vice versa.[111] In this case the *sefek*

---

109 See Rambam, *Hilkhot Issurei Bi'ah* 3:2 and *Kesef Mishneh, Hilkhot Sotah* 2:4. See also R. Isaac Elchanan Spektor, *Teshuvot Be'er Yiẓḥak, Even ha-Ezer,* no. 9, sec. 7; *idem, Naḥal Yiẓḥak,* no. 38, sec. 4; *Minḥat Ya'akov, Klalei Sefek Sefeika,* sec. 10; R. Jonathan Eybeschutz, *Kereti u-Peleti, Kuntres Bet ha-Safek,* s.v. *amrinan.*

Many authorities accept a *sefek sefeika mi-shem eḥad* only if it involves two separate factual "doubts" rather than two halakhic doubts, each of which, if true, would independently lead to the same result. For example, if a bride is found not to be a virgin, there are two independent doubts: Consensual intercourse may have occurred prior to betrothal or she may have been raped. However, in this case, the petitioner can be a Jew only if his mother is a Jewess. How the mother became a Jewess is irrelevant. The situation is tantamount to a doubt with regard to whether the mother is a Jewess converted by *bet din* A or *bet din* B. The two possibilities that enter into the *sefek sefeika* are not separate procedures through which the person in question might have become a Jew, but two ways of resolving the single doubt of whether the person was born a Jew. Even if a *sefek sefeika mi-shem eḥad* is a valid *sefek sefeika,* that is because the doubts are instrumentally two ways of establishing a single halakhic status rather than two ways of proving that status. *Pri Megadim, Yoreh De'ah, Mishbeẓot Zahav* 17:2, seems to accept even the latter as a valid *sefek sefeika.* However, *Ḥiddushei R. Akiva Eger, Yoreh De'ah* 15:3, takes sharp issue with that position. See also Ritva and *Pnei Yeshoshu'a, Kiddushin* 73a, and *Teshuvot She'erit Yosef,* no. 5; Cf., *Teshuvot Be'er Yiẓḥak, Even ha-Ezer,* no. 7, *anaf* 9; *Teshuvot Maharit,* II, *Yoreh De'ah,* no. 2; *Shev Shem'ateta, shem'ata* 3, chap. 20; *Sha'arei Torah,* I, *klal* 24, *Din Ne'emanut ha-Yuḥasin, Mamzerut ve-Yuḥasin,* sec. 17:7; and *Berurei Yahadut,* chap. 13, secs. 26–32.

110 See primarily *Tosafot, Ketubot* 9a, s.v. *ve-i.*

111 *Kereti, Kuntres Bet ha-Safek,* regards the matter to be a subject of controversy among early-day authorities. *Kereti* cites *Teshuvot ha-Rashba,* I, no. 401 and Ra'avad, *Hilkhot Tum'at Met* 9:2, affirming the decisive weight of *Shev Shem'ateta* and *Tosafot, Ketubot,* s.v., *ve-i,* as disagreeing. *Ḥavvat Da'at, ibid,* sec. 27, disagrees with *Peleti's* understanding of *Tosafot. Ḥavvat Da'at,* in his *Teshuvot R. Ya'akov mi-Lissa,* no. 57, rules that a *sefek sefeika* is decisive over a *rov* only in the presence of a *rubba de-leita kamman* but that a *rubba de-ita kamman* – as is the nature of a *rov* arising from the greater number of non-Jews in the world – prevails over a *sefek sefeika.* Cf., however, the responsum of R. Jacob of Lissa published in *Teshuvot Ḥemdat Shlomoh, Even ha-Ezer,* no. 24,

sefeika is contradicted by the *rov* arising from the fact that the majority of the world's population are non-Jews.

---

sec. 12, as well as *Kuntres ha-Sefekot, klal,* sec. 7. Cf., *Berurei Yahadut,* chap. 13, secs. 33–39.

Chapter Seven

The *Kohen* Gene

I. IMPLICATIONS OF THE *KOHEN* GENE

Identification of a *kohen* gene is an enterprise quite different in nature from identification of a Jewish gene. Jewish identity is transmitted from generation to generation solely by matrilineal succession. Mitochondrial DNA is passed on from mother to daughter without recombination with male genetic material. In contrast, halakhic identity as a *kohen* is the product of patrilineal succession. Hence, any genetic evidence for a common ancestor as the progenitor of modern-day *kohanim* must be found on the Y-chromosome which, fortunately for genetic sleuths, with the exception of a small region of the chromosome, is not recombined.[1] Other than because of mutation, which occurs with great frequency, the Y-chromosome would be uniform among all male descendants of Adam. Such is the nature of the female counterpart of the purported Jewish gene found in mitochondrial DNA. If *kohanim* manifest a distinctive gene one might anticipate that the phenomenon would occur as the result of transmission of a mutant gene by a common ancestor some time in antiquity. That conclusion is bolstered by the similar frequency of

1 See Karl Skorecki *et al.*, "Y Chromosomes of Jewish Priests," *Nature,* vol. 385 (2 January, 1997), p. 32.

occurrence found among *kohanim* of both Ashkenazic and Sephardic ancestry.

Curiously, the *kohen* gene is the relative absence, rather than the relative frequency, of particular haplotypes. In an early study, only 1.5% of *kohanim* were found to carry those distinctive alleles compared to 18.4% of other Jews.[2] Thus, a higher representation of that genetic pattern among non-*kohanim* would suggest that it is among that cohort that the mutation arose while *kohanim* carry earlier unmutated versions of the genetic material. Strangely, however, the frequency of occurrence among Levites[3] is comparable to those haplotypes' frequency of occurrence among Israelites rather than to their frequency among *kohanim*. That phenomenon suggests that the mutation came after the separation of Aaron the Priest and his progeny from the tribe of Levi.

If that assessment is correct, the identification of the *kohen* gene is of limited application. Identification of a *kohen*, even if scientifically sound, would be of scant halakhic consequence. For eligibility to participate in the Temple rites in the absence of established eligibility, the two-witness rule applies.[4] There is significant controversy with regard to whether a single witness is sufficient to permit a *kohen* to partake of *terumah*.[5] There is also considerable controversy among latter-day authorities regarding a person's capacity to declare himself to be a *kohen* for purposes of being permitted to confer the priestly benediction or being accorded the honor of being the first person called to the reading of the Torah.[6] Although it is our practice to grant

---

2 *Loc. cit.*

3 M.G. Thomas *et al.*, "Origins of Old Testament Priests," *Nature*, vol. 394 (1998), p. 139.

4 See Rambam, *Hilkhot Issurei Bi'ah* 20:2 and *Encyclopediah Talmudit* (Jerusalem, 5767), XXVII, 223, note 754. In a case in which the father was a *kohen* and paternity was established on the basis of DNA evidence, the Jerusalem *bet din*, *Piskei Din le-Birur Yahadut*, IV, 319–320, refused to recognize the child as a *kohen* despite a DNA test demonstrating the father's identity. See *supra*, p. 171.

5 See *Encyclopediah Talmudit*, XXVII, 231–233.

6 See *Ketubot* 23b and *Encyclopedia Talmudit*, XXVII, 224–228.

credence to a person's claim to kohanic descent for those purposes,[7] his credibility cannot be greater than the evidence upon which the person asserts his claim. Thus, a claim that information concerning his lineage was conveyed to him by his father is credible whereas a claim of subjective acceptance of conclusions advanced by geneticists is not.

The notion that lack of a gene would rebut any particular *kohen's* claim to priesthood cannot be entertained even if only because the majority of *kohanim* carry no such identificatory mark. In light of the fact that the majority of *kohanim* do not carry such a gene it would be difficult to find grounds for a *kohen* who fails to manifest such a genetic pattern to be permitted to marry a divorcée or to defile himself by coming into contact with a corpse. Thus, the *kohen* gene can be of halakhic import only in the unlikely situation in which discovery of the presence of a *kohen* gene is the sole reason to regard the person as a *kohen*. Such a person may be forbidden to marry a divorcée, come into contact with a corpse, claim the privilege of pronouncing the priestly blessing or receive the first Torah honor. Since financial matters are not adjudicated on the basis of *rov*, an argument might perhaps be made for permitting such an individual to perform the rite of redeeming his own wife's firstborn while retaining the redemption fee for himself.

The principal value of establishing the existence of a unique *kohen* haplotype lies in demonstrating the veracity of the biblical description of *kohanim* as the descendants of Aaron the Priest. Indeed, in 1999, positing an assumed mutation rate and a presumption of 25 to 30 years between generations, some researchers estimated that the *kohen* gene appeared between 2,650 and 3,180 years earlier, i.e., some time between the Exodus and the destruction of the First Temple.[8] A number of later studies established the existence of unique Levite genetic material as well. There is less evidence regarding the dating of the original appearance of those genetic indicators.[9]

---

7 See Rabbenu Nissim, *Ketubot* 23b and *Maggid Mishneh, Hilkhot Issurei Bi'ah* 20:13. Cf., *Hagahot Ramakh* and *Maggid Mishneh, Hilkhot Issurei Bi'ah* 20:13 as well as *Yam shel Shlomoh, Ketubot* 2:44.

8 See Thomas, "Origin of Old Testament Priests," p. 139.

9 See Marta D. Costa *et al.*, "A Substantial Prehistoric European Ancestry

At best, the findings regarding a *kohen* gene do little to confirm the biblical account. The biblical report entails that the genetic mutations described, if they took place, would have occurred either prior to the birth of Aaron the Priest, or less likely, in Aaron himself – but certainly prior to the earliest date postulated by the scientific investigators. Even so, the absence of any higher frequency of occurrence among Levites is not compatible with biblical dating unless, of course, it was Aaron himself who was the first to carry the mutated gene.

A later study including a larger number of participants established that 50% of *kohanim* carry one of a limited number of alleles defined as the "Cohen Modal Haplotype."[10] That study, published in 2009, places the divergence time of *kohanim* as between 3190 and 1090 years earlier.

II. THE LEMBA

Some years ago, an intriguing report in the media concerning DNA analysis as evidence of a *kohen* gene led to widespread fascination with employment of the DNA gene as confirmation of Jewish ancestry.[11] There are many tribes in North Africa, chief among them the Falasha, who practice syncretistic forms of religion incorporating various Judaic practices. One heretofore obscure group numbering some

---

Amongst Ashkenazi Maternal Lineages," *Nature Communications*, vol. 4 (October 8, 2013), p. 2453 and Doron N. Behar *et al.*, "The Genetic Variation in the R1a Clade Among the Ashkenazi Levites' Y Chromosome," *Scientific Reports*, vol. 7, no. 1 (November 2, 2017), pp. 1–11.

10 That study by Michael S. Hammer *et al.*, "Extended Y Chromosome Haplotypes Resolve Multiple and Unique Lineages of the Jewish Priesthood," *Human Genetics*, vol. 126, no. 5 (November, 2009), pp. 707–17, also involved 2099 non-Jewish men of diverse ancestry. The Cohen Modal Haplotype was remarkably absent in that group. Interestingly, that phenomenon would give rise to speculation with regard to whether the *kohen* gene might establish Jewish paternal ancestry. Such lineage would, however, be of no halakhic import since Jewish identity is born of matrilineal succession.

11 See Nicholas Wade, "DNA Backs Tribe's Tradition of Early Descent From the Jews," *New York Times*, May 9, 1999, p. A6.

fifty thousand members living primarily in Venda, one of the Black homelands in the northeast corner of South Africa and an adjacent area in Zimbabwe. The members of that group practice a form of Christianity but profess themselves to be Jews descended from Falasha and, through the Falasha, from white Jewish ancestors. They practice ritual slaughter, circumcise their male children and refuse to eat flesh of the pig as well as of the hippopotamus, which they regard as a species of swine. They are known as Lemba, meaning "people who refuse." Their native tongue is Bantu. The Lemba are divided into ten clans and claim to stem from a city called Sena which they cannot identify but which a contemporary Lemba leader speculates is the Sena'ah of Nehemiah (7:38), a place that he presumed to be north of Jericho. A British scholar who has studied the Lemba, Dr. Tudor Parafitt, director of the Center for Jewish Studies at the School of Oriental and African Studies in London, believes Sena to be a town in Yemen.

Subsequent to publication of Dr. Parafitt's travelogue recounting his search for Sena, *Journey to the Vanished City* (London, 1992), Dr. David Goldstein, a population geneticist and member of the faculty of Oxford University, who had been engaged in research concerning the Jewish gene, analyzed DNA samples collected from the Lemba. Dr. Goldstein reported that nine percent of Lemba males carry the *kohen* gene while among members of one group, the Buda clan, 53 percent had the distinctive kohanic sequences. Quite surprisingly, the latter figure closely approximates the worldwide figures for carriers of the *kohen* gene, *viz.*, 46 percent for Sephardic *kohanim* and 53 percent for Ashkenazic *kohanim*.[12] Presence of the *kohen* gene over a span of millennia as well as a presumed absence of unique mitochondrial DNA is readily attributed to the Lembas' acceptance of female converts, who must undergo a complicated and somewhat bizarre ritual, but concomitant steadfast persistence in refusing to accept any male convert whatsoever.

The Lembas' claim to descent from Falasha is unquestionably incorrect. However, it is entirely probable that they are descended

---

12 *Loc. cit.*

from Jewish traders who, together with many other such traders, made their way to North Africa. That phenomenon also serves to explain elements of Mosaism that crept into the cultic practices of many North African tribes. The Lemba presumably traveled by boat directly from North Africa to their present homeland in South Africa.

The preponderance of *kohanim* among travelers of antiquity might seem odd.[13] Nevertheless, a remarkable parallel does exist in the demographic composition of the Jewish residents of Djerba, an island off the mainland off Tunisia, a community believed to have been established during the days of the First Temple.[14] The overwhelming majority of the Jewish population of Djerba are *kohanim.*[15] They are remarkably different from the Lemba – and indeed from other communities in the Diaspora – in that throughout those millennia they have practiced strict endogamy and have uniformly exhibited consistent fidelity to Jewish law and tradition. The genealogical roots of both communities are probably identical. The difference lies in the Lembas' openness to marrying female natives, possibly because of a dearth of available Jewish women, that, in turn, is perhaps attributable to the vast geographical distance from any center of Jewish population, and to a steadfast resistance to intermarriage on the part of the Jewish settlers in Djerba.

The underlying issue presented in consideration of the *kohen* gene is the halakhic basis upon which evidentiary credence might be

---

13 Perhaps because *kohanim* owned no land and could not subsist on priestly emoluments?

14 See F. Manni *et al.*, "A Y-Chromosome Portrait of the Population of Jerba (Tunisia) to Elucidate its Complex Demographic History," *Bulletins et Memoires de la Societe d'Anthropologie de Paris*, vol. 17, nos. 1–2 (2005).

15 All the *kohanim* of Djerba whose DNA was sampled were found to possess the *kohen* gene. The same is true of *kohanim* residing in Jerusalem's Old City from whom samples were taken. See Yaakov Kleiman, *DNA and Tradition* (New York, 2004), p. 21. Cf., however, Manni *et al.*, "A Y-Chromosome Portrait of the Population of Jerba (Tunisia)," who reports that 13 of 15 natives of Djerba carried the Cohen Modal Haplotype. It is not clear whether each of those 15 claimed to be a *kohen.*

extended to genetic analysis in establishing identity as a *kohen.* Thus far, the sole halakhic issue involving genetic evidence of status as a *kohen* discussed in rabbinic literature does not arise from discovery of the *kohen* gene, but the more general question of whether genetic analysis can serve to establish kohanic paternity. A woman entered into a second marriage and three months thereafter gave birth to a male child. The child was surrendered for adoption. The court papers included an affidavit signed by both the mother and her second husband declaring that the identity of the child's father was unknown. A number of half-brothers were born during the course of each of the two marriages. The second husband was a *kohen.* Years later, the child who had been surrendered for adoption sought to identify his biological father on the basis of DNA analysis and, if the genetic evidence would establish that the second husband was his father, to be recognized as a *kohen.* A petition was submitted to the Jerusalem *Bet Din le-Berur Yahadut* and its brief decision was published in the *Piskei Din shel Bet ha-Din le-Dinei Mamonot u-le-Birur Yahadut,* IV (5756), 319–320.

Rema, *Even ha-Ezer* 3:9, rules that if an unmarried woman cohabits with a *kohen,* marries another man within a three-month period and gives birth to a son some six months thereafter, the child born in that early period of the marriage cannot be recognized as a *kohen. Ḥelkat Meḥokek, Even ha-Ezer* 3:12, questions why Rema does not apply the rule of *rov be'ilot* and concludes that the husband is the father of the child. The principle of *rov be'ilot* establishes that, because of frequency of access, even in an adulterous relationship, presumption of paternity lies with the lawfully married husband. *Ḥelkat Meḥokek* infers from a comment of Rashi, *Yevamot* 100b, s.v. *ela lav,* that such is indeed Rashi's view. *Ḥelkat Meḥokek* explains that Rema's ruling reflects a stringency applicable only to determination of priestly lineage.

Bet Shmu'el 3:16 disagrees with *Ḥelkat Meḥokek* and cogently explains that *rov be'ilot* is applicable only in the case of a married woman who engages in two sexual relationships within a single time frame. As between the two men, she is presumed to cohabit with her husband more frequently than with the adulterer. Rema, however, addresses a situation in which the relationships were not simultaneous. There is no principle establishing that a husband and wife cohabit more frequently than an unmarried couple. Thus, there is no reason to assume that the couple cohabited more frequently subsequent to regularizing the relationship by marriage.

However, as noted, *Ḥelkat Meḥokek* maintains that *rov be'ilot* cannot be invoked to establish priestly descent. The members of the *bet din* found an apparent contradiction to *Ḥelkat Meḥokek*'s view. *Teshuvot ha-Rashba*, I, no. 207, declares that identity as a *kohen*, even for eligibility to participate in the sacrificial service, is established solely on the basis of paternal identity which, in turn, can be predicated only upon *rov be'ilot*. Thus, were the Sages to have excluded reliance upon *rov be'ilot* as proof of identity as *kohen*, there could be no recognized *kohanim*.

In an earlier decision, *Piskei Din shel Bet ha-Din le-Birur Yahadut*, III (5755), the Jerusalem *bet din* established that the principle of *rov be'ilot* is not a mere *rov* but a "super *rov*" regarded as virtual certainty. In the latter decision, the *bet din* declared that *Ḥelkat Meḥokek* fully recognized that to be the case but asserted that *Ḥelkat Meḥokek* regarded the virtual certainty to be factually correct only as between a married woman and a paramour. Thus, the issue of a *kohen* and his wife is regarded as a *kohen* on the basis of a "super *rov*." Frequency of intercourse, between husband and wife during the course of marriage, argued the *bet din*, is indeed greater than frequency of intercourse between unmarried parties, but not inordinately greater than between the same parties in a non-adulterous extra-marital relationship. Thus, the *rov* establishes that the couple cohabit more frequently after marriage than before marriage but not with sufficiently more frequency so as to establish the "super *rov*" necessary to confirm priestly identity. Thus, it is only the ordinary *rov* that Rema rules declares to be rejected as sufficient to establish priestly lineage; the "super-*rov*" reflected in frequency of intercourse between husband and wife, argues the *bet din*, does serve to confirm identity as a *kohen*.

In rejecting the petition for recognition as a *kohen*, the *bet din* cited numerous authorities who regard DNA evidence as constituting no more than a *rov* rather than a matter of scientific certainty[16] and asserted that priestly status can be confirmed only on the basis of absolute proof. That conclusion is certainly equally applicable to evidence based upon the *kohen* gene.

R. Chaim Shmuelevitz, *Sha'arei Ḥayyim, Kiddushin,* no. 37, cites *Sanhedrin* 69a, which quotes the verse "*ve-hitzilu ha-edah* – and the congregation shall rescue" (Numbers 35:25) and interprets the term "the congregation (*ha-edah*)" as denoting the *bet din* and understands the verse as directing an acquittal in some set of circumstances in which application of conventional judicial rules would result in a guilty verdict. The Gemara suggests that "*ve-hitzilu ha-edah*" may be a directive to set aside the rule of *rov* in capital cases.

Ḥiddushei ha-Ran, ad locum, points out that such an inference would be contradicted by the declaration of the Gemara, *Ḥullin* 11b, to the effect that a person sentenced to death for smiting his father can be executed only if the existence of a paternal-filial relationship has been established. It is possible to prove the existence of such a relationship only on the basis of *rov be'ilot. Ḥiddushei ha-Ran* resolves that problem by stating that, since the Torah does provide the death penalty as punishment for that transgression, the Torah clearly demands the death penalty even if *rov* would be insufficient for conviction in other capital cases. Ran's resolution should probably be understood as an observation to the effect that the Gemara postulates that, if *rov* could not be relied upon in capital cases, it would be because the evidence of *rov* is regarded as insufficiently compelling. Consequently, demanding imposition of the death penalty for smiting one's father would indicate that the Torah does not require absolute proof of guilt in instances of smiting a father.

Sha'arei Ḥayyim, however, amplifies Ran's response in explaining that the thrust of Ran's comment is that *rov be'ilot* would suffice for conviction even if other forms of *rov* would not. According to *Sha'arei Ḥayyim,* the distinction is between *rov be'ilot* and other *rovs,* rather than between striking a father and other capital transgressions. The

---

16 See *supra,* pp. 51–53.

reason for the distinction, according to *Sha'arei Ḥayyim,* is that the Torah accepts *rov be'ilot,* unlike other *rovs,* as establishing paternity with virtual certainty. But, since the Gemara concludes that "*ve-hiẓilu ha-edah*" does not exclude other forms of *rov* in capital cases, the implication is that the Torah demands imposition of the death penalty on the basis of any applicable *rov,* regardless of whether or not the *rov* establishes absolute certainty.[17]

This writer's reading of *Ḥiddushei ha-Ran* is as presented above. If so, *Ḥiddushei ha-Ran* represents an early-day authority who contradicts *Sha'arei Ḥayyim*'s distinction between *rov be'ilot* and other *rovs.* Any answer that may be advanced in resolving Ran's perplexity reflects only the Gemara's *hava amina,* i.e., the Gemara's "early thinking" were it forced to accept "*ve- hiẓilu ha-edah*" as negating capital punishment on the basis of *rov* in other cases. There is no evidence that any premise of that nature is retained by the Gemara at the conclusion of its discussion.

Nevertheless, there is other evidence establishing that *rov be'ilot* is a unique *rov.* Rather than predicating paternity upon the principle of *rov be'ilot,* as depicted by the Gemara, *Ḥullin* 11b, the Palestinian Talmud, *Kiddushin* 4:10, posits the Torah's imposition of the death penalty as punishment for striking one's father as the source for the judicial presumption established by *ḥazakah.*[18] That terminology is also employed by Rambam, *Hilkhot Issurei Bi'ah* 1:20.[19] To the Palestinian Talmud, *rov be'ilot* is actually a *ḥazakah* rather than a *rov.*[20]

---

17 See also *Teshuvot R. Akiva Eger,* no. 107.

18 See *Sidrei Taharah* 185:1 and *Teshuvot Ḥatam Sofer, Yoreh De'ah* no. 378 and *Even ha-Ezer,* I, no. 41.

19 R. David Levanon, *Shurat ha-Din,* V, 58–69, similarly regards *rov be'ilot* as different from other *rovs* and categorizes *rov be'ilot* as an *umdena* or *anan sahadi.* See *supra,* pp. 61–62.

20 Cf., however, R. Chaim of Volozhin, *Ḥut ha-Meshulash,* no. 10, who regards the terms "*rov*" and "*ḥazakah*" as used in this context to be synonymous. See *supra,* p. 61, note 59 and accompanying text.

III. A CONCLUDING REMARK

DNA analysis is firmly established as a medical tool and is invaluable in the study of hereditary diseases. DNA analysis has limited halakhic import, particularly in resolving some grievous *agunah* problems. The unique nature of the so-called Jewish gene can, at best, establish a *rov* and be dispositive in situations in which *rov* constitutes acceptable proof. The *kohen* gene, however, remains little more than a curiosity.

Passages Cited

1. BIBLE

2. BABYLONIAN TALMUD

Name and Subject Index

T